CyberJustice

Online Dispute Resolution (ODR) for E-Commerce

CyberJustice

Online Dispute Resolution (ODR) for E-Commerce

Lucille M. Ponte
Bentley College
McCallum Graduate School of Business

Thomas D. Cavenagh
North Central College

PEARSON

Prentice
Hall

Upper Saddle River, New Jersey 07458

Library of Congress Cataloging-in-Publication Data

Ponte, Lucille M.
    CyberJustice: online dispute resolution (ODR) for e-commerce / Lucille M. Ponte,
Thomas D. Cavenagh.
        p. cm.
    Includes bibliographical references and index.
    ISBN 0-13-098636-4 (paperback)
    1. Dispute resolution (Law)—United States—Data processing 2. Electronic
commerce—Law and legislation—United States. 3. Internet—Law and legislation—
United States. I. Cavenagh, Thomas D. II. Title

KF9084.P663 2004
347.73'9'0285—dc22

2004044658

Notice: The information provided in this text and CD-ROM are not intended as legal advice for specific situations, but are meant solely for educational and informational purposes. Readers should retain and seek the advice of their own legal counsel in handling specific dispute resolution matters.

Director of Production and Manufacturing: Bruce Johnson
Executive Editor: Elizabeth Sugg
Managing Editor—Editorial: Judy Casillo
Editorial Assistant: Cyrenne Bolt de Freitas
Consulting Editor: Athena Group, Inc.
Marketing Manager: Leigh Ann Sims
Managing Editor—Production: Mary Carnis
Manufacturing Buyer: Ilene Sanford
Production Liaison: Denise Brown
Production Editor: Trish Finley/Carlisle Publishers Services
Composition: Carlisle Communications, Ltd.
Design Director: Cheryl Asherman
Senior Design Coordinator: Christopher Weigand
Cover Design: Kevin Kall
Cover Printer: Phoenix Color
Printer/Binder: Phoenix Book Tech Park

Pearson Education Ltd.
Pearson Education Australia Pty. Limited
Pearson Education Singapore Pte. Ltd.
Pearson Education North Asia Ltd.

Pearson Education Canada, Ltd.
Pearson Educación de Mexico, S.A. de C.V.
Pearson Education—Japan
Pearson Education Malaysia Pte. Ltd.

10 9 8 7 6 5 4 3 2 1
ISBN 0-13-098636-4

Dedications

To David Riddell, the friendly face of technology.

—*Lucille M. Ponte*

To my splendid writing partner, Lucille, with whom it is a great joy to work.

—*Thomas D. Cavenagh*

Contents

3

Online Negotiation   38

4

Online Mediation   62

5

Online Arbitration   82

6

Online Jury Proceedings   100

7

Online Dispute Resolution System Design   119

8

The Future of ODR   136

A

American Bar Association Task Force on E-Commerce
and ADR-Recommended Best Practices for Online Dispute
Resolution Service Providers   153

Preface

With global online revenues estimated to reach the trillions by 2005, disputes over online transactions are increasing with the lightning speed of the World Wide Web. Because there are no uniform laws or court systems in the global marketplace of the online world, e-businesses and their customers are looking for dispute resolution options that reflect the speed and convenience of the Web. E-commerce professionals are turning to online dispute resolution (ODR) to manage their online conflicts fairly, efficiently, and effectively. Instructors at colleges, universities, law schools and executive education programs will find this text to be an interesting and informative overview of this rapidly emerging field suitable for teaching business students, e-commerce managers and entrepreneurs, and dispute resolution professionals.

This educational text provides a concise, easy-to-understand overview of the cutting edge field of ODR utilizing the familiar FAQ (frequently asked questions) format, found on most e-business web sites. Real-world ODR examples, key court and administrative case excerpts, interactive Web-based assignments, useful charts and tables, and up-to-date web sources are provided. The text can be used on its own or as a supplement to a wide range of law, marketing and e-commerce courses. In addition, this guide will be useful to legal professionals evaluating ODR options for e-business.

To help provide an interactive and informative review of ODR, this text includes the following major features:

Chapter FAQs—At the start of each chapter, readers are guided through the chapter concepts by a list of FAQs that will be answered in text of the chapter. These FAQs provide a good outline of the ODR issues and concepts addressed in each chapter.

Key Chapter Case—Excerpts of important court and administrative decisions are contained in each chapter and help to illuminate major conflict resolution issues. Through the review and class discussion of these case excerpts, instructors can present a legal framework for ODR issues and improve student critical analysis and reasoning skills.

ODR in the Digital Era—These special boxed sections found in every chapter provide real-world examples of ODR use in the resolution of e-commerce conflicts. Each brief segment engages the reader's interest and illustrates how ODR concepts play out in actual online practice.

Quick Clicks—Readers have the opportunity to apply chapter topics by responding to interactive Web-based assignments. These brief assignments can be excellent bases for class discussions or lengthier student research projects.

ODR Bytes—Key ODR issues are summarized at the end of each chapter. This component also provides some practical suggestions on ODR use drawn from chapter materials.

ODR Bookmarks—To facilitate further online exploration and inquiry, this chapter component offers a convenient list of current ODR entities and URLs that were discussed in each chapter. Faculty and students can visit these sites to spur classroom discussions or to aid student and faculty ODR research efforts.

Selected ODR Bibliography—Books, reports, and articles that are major sources for chapter materials and concepts are listed after ODR Bookmarks. This section cites both hard-copy and online sources of ODR information.

The use of ODR will be a key feature of any successful conflict resolution program. As you explore the world of ODR in resolving both domestic and cross-border conflicts, we hope you find this interactive text to be informative and challenging.

—*The Authors*

Supplements

Support for this course, in either a classroom or distance learning environment, can be found by visiting www.prenhall.com/legal_studies. Versus Law access is available for free when packaged with this book for educational accounts.

Acknowledgments

I wish to acknowledge Margrethe H. Olson, Dean of Business and the McCallum Graduate School, and Stephen D. Lichtenstein, Chair and Professor of the Law Department, for previous funding for ODR research through the Summer Research Grant Program at Bentley College.

—*Lucille M. Ponte*

I am indebted to North Central College, from which I received sabbatical time to complete this manuscript. I would also like to thank my colleagues at the college who, as they always do for one another, covered for me in my absence.

—*Thomas D. Cavenagh*

Thanks are also due to the individuals who reviewed this book: Adam Epstein, University of Tennessee; Lucy Katz, Fairfield University; and Judith Stilz Ogden, National Legal Information Systems.

About the Authors

Lucille M. Ponte, J.D., is Associate Professor of Law at Bentley College in Waltham, Massachusetts, where she teaches and writes extensively in the areas of online dispute resolution (ODR), alternative dispute resolution (ADR), cyberlaw, workplace privacy, gender issues in education and employment, and the legal environment of business. She has received eleven Bentley College publication awards and two federal courts have cited her ADR scholarship in their decisions. She currently serves as an arbitrator for National Association of Securities Dealers. She is the editor of the ADR in Business newsletter and serves on the Editorial Board of the Business Law Review (North Atlantic edition). Prof. Ponte, along with Prof. Cavenagh, co-founded and served as co-chairs of the Alternative Dispute Resolution (ADR) in Business section of the National Academy of Legal Studies in Business. She is the recipient of a 1994 Bentley College Innovation in Teaching Award for her course work in the dispute resolution field and was selected as a national finalist in the 2003 Charles M. Hewitt Master Teacher Competition for her use of actors in a live mock arbitration. She has been a licensed attorney in Massachusetts since 1983. She formerly worked as in-house counsel for Apollo Computer, Inc., Codex-Motorola, Massachusetts Bay Transportation Authority, and the U.S. Department of Transportation in Washington, D.C. She holds a Bachelor of Arts in Political Science/Law and Justice from the University of Massachusetts at Boston and a Juris Doctor from the New England School of Law, where she participated as a Case and Note Editor for the *New England Law Review.*

Thomas D. Cavenagh, J.D., is Professor of Business Law and Conflict Resolution and Chair of the Department of Management and Marketing at North Central College in Naperville, Illinois. In addition, he is the founder of and directs the North Central College Dispute Resolution Center. He graduated from Trinity College with a B.A. in religion and philosophy, magna cum laude. His J.D. is from DePaul University College of Law. He is the author of *Business Dispute Resolution: Best Practices, System Design and Case Management,* and the coauthor of *Alternative Dispute Resolution for Business.* He has chaired the Illinois State Bar Association Section Council on Alternative Dispute Resolution and has been widely published in a variety of professional journals, including *Mediation Quarterly.* He is the recipient of the North Central College Dissinger Prize for Faculty Scholarship and the North Central College Clarence F. Dissinger Distinguished Teaching and Service Award as well as the Academy of Legal Studies in Business Charles Hewitt Master Teacher Award.

1

E-Commerce Disputes and the Global Web

CHAPTER FAQS

What is the nature of online business relationships?

Can I be sued for my online business activities?

What are some specific examples of online disputes?

Why not just go to court to resolve online disagreements?

Are there methods for limiting my potential exposure to lawsuits in foreign courts?

You've poured your life savings and endless months of planning and effort into fulfilling your dream of operating your own online business. Your business plan won over some key investors for your e-business. You've developed a sound marketing strategy for your target market. You've nabbed the domain name you wanted and the web site looks great. You think you're ready to go. But with everything on the line, have you thought about how you might protect your investment in money, time, and effort from the risks of lawsuits? Have you considered how you will be handling disputes that may arise online?

Global online revenues are estimated to reach trillions of dollars by 2005, and disputes over online transactions are likely to increase with the continuing expansion of the World Wide Web. There are no uniform laws or court systems in the global marketplace of the online world. With a web site accessible throughout the world, an e-business needs to consider steps to help manage its online disputes fairly, efficiently, and effectively. This chapter considers the nature of online business relationships, the special liability issues facing e-businesses, some methods to help limit online liability, and the limitations of traditional litigation in dealing with online disputes.

What Is the Nature of Online Business Relationships?

Advances in information technology have made it simpler, faster, and more cost-effective for bricks-and-mortar and online businesses as well as consumers to carry out a host of online retail and commercial transactions. The development of the Web has allowed e-businesses to provide product and pricing information, to accelerate and simplify order-entry systems, to distribute products, and to handle account information and customer service inquiries through the online environment. The growth of e-commerce has spawned four basic types of business relationships: business-to-consumer (B2C), business-to-business (B2B), business-to-government (B2G), and consumer-to-consumer (C2C).

The B2C environment brings together traditional retail shopping with the speed and convenience of online technologies. Despite the recent ups and downs of online e-tailers, Web researchers estimate that B2C trade will reach $5 trillion globally by 2005, with the United States grabbing about 35 percent of those online revenues. A well-known example of a typical B2C marketplace is Amazon.com, which provides books, CDs, DVDs, electronics, and other products to consumers in more than 160 countries (http://www.Amazon.com). The barriers to entry into the Web's virtual marketplace, such as advertising goods and services to international markets, can be quite low, so new B2C businesses, both large and small, are springing up on the Internet daily.

B2B transactions may involve a host of online commercial transactions, from the simple submission of electronic purchase orders to a vendor, to participation in market exchange programs with suppliers, to responding to requests for quotes and proposals, to the distribution of software and other products and services to business customers via the Internet. In some instances, a business may deal directly with another individual business through the firm's web site, or it may connect with a variety of other businesses through an online market exchange. It is estimated that B2B trade alone will top $6 trillion by 2005, with over a third of these revenues being generated through online market exchanges. B2B market exchanges provide centralized online marketplaces for businesses to search online for a wide range of products and services, to post requests for quotes and proposals, and to complete commercial agreements either online or offline. For example, auto giants Ford, General Motors, DaimlerChrysler, Renault, Nissan, and PSA Peugeot Citroen, along with their technology partners, Commerce One and Oracle, have allied to create a B2B Internet exchange to support procurement, product development, and supply-chain management services for the global automotive industry (http://www.covisint.com). Covisint's products and services are being offered to all members of the auto industry, and this portal is designed to facilitate a wide range of B2B commercial transactions.

The government also plays a role in e-commerce through B2G activities in an effort to streamline the procurement process for goods and services. Under the auspices of the General Services Administration, FedBizOpps was recently developed as the single point of entry for federal government procurement opportunities over $25,000.00

for nearly thirty government agencies (http://www.fedbizopps.gov). Under GSA's Electronic Posting System (EPS), vendors can browse online for procurement information on the FedBizOpps site and can automatically receive notices of current procurement opportunities once they register with the system. Ultimately, FedBizOpps expects to accept proposals online. Similarly, Onvia.com has become an important portal that allows subscribing suppliers to gain access to state, county, and city procurement information, decreasing the costs of researching bid opportunities and increasing the competition and the diversity of government vendor pools (http://www.onvia.com). Not only can businesses learn about government contracting opportunities, but government agencies can also review a bid library of completed bid awards as models for drafting new government bids. Collectively, state and local governments purchase about $400 billion in goods and services annually.

Consumers have also begun to sell a vast array of goods in virtual auctions and consignment marketplaces. In these C2C relationships, neither party may be a traditional merchant who ordinarily makes and sells goods. Typically, the consumers are casual sellers who may be selling concert tickets or grandma's antique brooch to another consumer. Online businesses such as eBay.com provide a venue for consumers to sell their wares but do not directly participate in the commercial transaction between the buyer and the seller (http://www.ebay.com). Unfortunately, the number of C2C complaints has accelerated rapidly, particularly those involving claims of auction fraud.

Can I Be Sued for My Online Business Activities?

When addressing legal issues, businesspeople often ask the same question: Can I be sued? The answer is that any business can be sued at anytime by anyone for a claim that may or may not have merit. You may end up in disputes with those with whom you have online business relationships or independent third parties who assert that they have been harmed by your online conduct. Defending lawsuits, even frivolous ones, can eat up limited time and resources. It is important to keep in mind that by placing your web site on the information superhighway, you are exposing your e-business and yourself to potential liability throughout the United States and the rest of the world, with its maze of different laws, regulatory requirements, and court procedures.

Recognizing the ever-present potential for liability, a key concern for e-commerce managers revolves around what standards determine where an e-business might be sued. Therefore, an important consideration in any civil lawsuit is determining whether or not a court across the street or across the globe has personal jurisdiction over your e-business. Personal jurisdiction deals with a court's authority to hear and decide a case over a party that may be held liable in a lawsuit. Basically, this concept means that the court must have the legal authority to bring you into court in another state or country before it can render a decision on the merits of the dispute. Although there are many forms of jurisdiction, the arena of personal jurisdiction is one of the main ways that an e-business may find itself summoned into a court in another state or country. In some cases, more than one court may have personal jurisdiction over

Chart 1.1 Comparative Estimates: Worldwide B2C E-Commerce Revenues, 2002–2004 (in billions)					
	2000	2001	2002	2003	2004
eMarketer	$ 60	$101	$167	$ 250	$ 428
Forrester Research	$ 53	$ 96	$169	$ 284	$ 452
Gartner Group	–	–	–	$ 380	–
Goldman Sachs	$238	$494	$870	$1,392	$2,134
IDC	$ 59	–	–	$ 213	–
Merrill Lynch	$218	$398	$734	$1,317	–
Ovum	$ 29	$ 49	$ 81	$ 133	$ 219

the parties, which can lead to multiple legal actions in different courts in different countries concerning the same factual disagreement. An e-business may be able to take proactive steps to better manage personal jurisdiction concerns, helping to reduce exposure to lawsuits in other states and countries.

Gaining personal jurisdiction over a party does not ensure a positive outcome in the case; it merely ensures that the court may listen to the evidence in the case and render a judgment against the parties in the dispute. In the U.S. court system, the plaintiff is the party that initially files the lawsuit. The party that responds to the lawsuit is called the defendant and may bring its own claims against the plaintiff when answering the lawsuit.

In the United States, an e-business may be subject to personal jurisdiction in civil lawsuits through three main avenues: party presence within territorial borders, volunteering jurisdiction, and long-arm statutes. Under party presence, a court normally has personal jurisdiction over a party that is physically present or located within the borders of that state or country. For example, suppose XYZ.com has its headquarters in Massachusetts and sales offices in Illinois, California, and Ontario, Canada. Generally, under the rule of party presence, the state and federal courts in Massachusetts, Illinois, and California as well as the courts in Ontario would likely have personal jurisdiction over XYZ.com because the e-business is physically present within the borders of each state and province.

Looking at the concept of volunteering jurisdiction, an e-business may voluntarily agree to have their dispute resolved in a foreign court once a lawsuit has been filed. More commonly, an e-business may have entered into a contract that contained a forum selection clause. Under such a clause, an e-business can agree prior to a dispute that any conflicts that arise in the business relationship will be resolved in a specific court in a particular state or country. By inserting a forum selection clause into its commercial agreements and under the terms of use of a web site, an e-business may limit its jurisdictional exposure to a particular court and be better able to predict or reduce its legal costs. Traditionally, an e-business will select the state or federal courts in its home state so that it may operate in a familiar legal and business environment using local attorneys.

KEY CHAPTER CASE

Online Contracts and Forum Selection Clauses in Terms of Use

Caspi v The Microsoft Network, L.L.C. and the Microsoft Corporation, 323 N.J. Super. 118; 732 A.2d 528; 1999 N.J. Super. LEXIS 254 (1999)

Fact Summary: Plaintiffs brought a class action to represent a nationwide class of 1.5 million similarly aggrieved MSN members in the state courts of New Jersey against the defendants The Microsoft Network, L.L.C. and the Microsoft Corporation (collectively, Microsoft). The plaintiffs alleged various theories including breach of contract, common law fraud, and consumer fraud against Microsoft for unilaterally rolling over MSN memberships into more expensive plans. Under the alleged practice, Microsoft, without notice to or permission from MSN members, unilaterally charged them increased membership fees attributable to this change in their service plans. Before becoming an MSN member, a potential subscriber is prompted by MSN software to scroll through multiple computer screens of information, including a membership agreement next to blocks providing the choices "I Agree" and "I Don't Agree." Prospective members assent to the terms of the agreement, including MSN's forum selection clause, which indicates that disputes must be resolved in the courts of the state of Washington, by clicking on "I Agree." No registration may proceed nor are any charges incurred until after the potential subscriber has had the opportunity to view and has assented to the membership agreement by clicking on "I Agree." The defendants moved to dismiss the class action lawsuit based on the Washington state forum selection clause. The trial court granted the motion to dismiss and the plaintiffs appealed.

OPINION: The opinion of the court was delivered by KESTIN, J.A.D.

We are here called upon to determine the validity and enforceability of a forum selection clause contained in an on-line subscriber agreement of the Microsoft Network (MSN), an on-line computer service. . . .

Generally, forum selection clauses are prima facie valid and enforceable . . . [unless] . . . (1) the clause is a result of fraud or "overweening" bargaining power; (2) enforcement would violate the strong public policy. . . . or (3) enforcement would seriously inconvenience trial. . . . The burden falls on the party objecting to enforcement to show that the clause in question fits within one of these exceptions. . . . Plaintiffs have failed to meet that burden here. . . .

We reject as meritless plaintiffs' arguments on appeal that the terms of the forum selection clause do not prevent plaintiffs from suing Microsoft outside of Washington or, alternatively, that the forum selection clause lacks adequate clarity. The meaning of the clause is plain and its effect as a limiting provision is clear. Furthermore, New Jersey's interest in assuring consumer fraud protection will not be frustrated by requiring plaintiffs to proceed with a lawsuit in Washington as prescribed by the plain language of the forum selection clause. As a general matter, none of the inherent characteristics of forum selection clauses implicate consumer fraud concepts in any special way. If a forum selection clause is clear in its purport and has been presented to the party to be bound in a fair and forthright fashion, no consumer fraud policies or principles have been violated. . . .

Also, it seems clear that there was nothing extraordinary about the size or placement of the forum selection clause text. By every indication we have, the clause was presented in exactly the same format as most other provisions of the contract. It was the first item in the last paragraph of the electronic document. We note that a few paragraphs in the contract were presented in upper case typeface, presumably for emphasis, but most provisions, including the forum selection clause, were presented in lower case typeface. We discern nothing about the style or mode of presentation, or the placement of the provision, that can be taken as a basis for concluding that the forum selection clause was proferred unfairly, or with a design to conceal or de-emphasize its provisions. To conclude that plaintiffs are not bound by that clause would be equivalent to holding that they were bound by no other clause either, since all provisions were identically presented. Plaintiffs must be taken to have known that they were entering into a contract; and no good purpose, consonant with the dictates of reasonable reliability in commerce, would be served by permitting them to disavow particular provisions or the contracts as a whole. . . .

. . . We agree with the trial court that, in the absence of a better showing than has been made, plaintiffs must be seen to have had adequate notice of the forum selection clause. . . . Affirmed.

Lastly, in the United States, a court may have personal jurisdiction over parties outside their borders who have not expressly volunteered to enter their courts under long-arm statutes. Under these laws, an e-business may be brought into a foreign court if it can be shown that it had sufficient minimum contacts within those territorial borders and if an e-business has purposefully availed itself of a particular forum's market, even if the e-business is not physically present. Typically if an e-business has conducted business or committed a tort (causing personal injury or property damage to another party) within that state or country, it may be found to have sufficient contacts to justify personal jurisdiction. An e-business may have purposefully availed itself of a forum market by inserting a pull-down menu on its website listing the names of different states or countries as part of an online ordering process. Therefore, your e-business may be subject to personal jurisdiction in the locations listed in the pull-down menu because your e-firm is seeking business in those markets.

The U.S. courts are still trying to determine what is meant by doing business or committing a tort as related to e-businesses operating in the online world. In one case, the courts determined that an individual in Texas who had entered into a contract with an Ohio firm in which he intentionally uploaded and downloaded software for sale and distribution by that Ohio firm could be brought into the Ohio courts for an intellectual property dispute. Conversely, a Missouri web site that provided information solely about local music events could not be brought into New York court for a trademark dispute by virtue of its mere presence on the Web. Yet another court determined that a Mississippi Internet service provider could bring a legal action against a Texas resident who allegedly caused harm to their business by sending unsolicited e-mails (spam) over their system. The court decided that the purposeful act of sending even one e-mail message would give the Mississippi courts personal jurisdiction over the Texas party. No simple formula exists, and each situation must be judged on its given facts. Generally speaking, a mere electronic presence on the Web may not be sufficient to provide personal jurisdiction in the United States. However, based on current precedent, the more interactive a web site is, the more likely that a court may find that the online firm has done business within the territory and therefore is subject to personal jurisdiction. If a web site allows parties to order products online or to download software from a site, then that e-business may find itself more likely to be exposed to liability in the various states and countries of its customers.

In the global marketplace, other countries follow different approaches to personal jurisdiction. Some nations may accept notions of territoriality, volunteering presence, and sufficient minimum contacts. The European Union generally follows the effects doctrine and will look to see if the online firm's conduct had a substantial impact or harm on parties or commercial activity within its national borders. In order to protect consumer rights, the EU is moving toward allowing its consumers to choose to bring an action against an e-commerce firm in the consumer's home country or in the domicile of the business. However, the French courts unsuccessfully sought to enforce French law against Yahoo! in the United States, claiming personal jurisdiction based solely on the accessibility of the Yahoo! web site in France. In a recent decision, Australia's highest court determined that a citizen in Victoria, Australia, could sue an online publisher located principally in New Jersey in his local Victorian court for the tort of defamation. Even though the online publisher lacked sufficient contacts in and did not purposefully avail itself of the Australian market, the Australian high court found personal jurisdiction solely because the alleged defamatory article could be viewed online and downloaded in Australia (*Dow Jones & Co. Inc. v Gutnick*, [2002] HCA 56 (10 December 2002), *available at* http://www.austlii.edu.au). It is apparent that this area of law is still evolving both domestically and internationally and is very unsettled.

What Are Some Specific Examples of Online Disputes?

The Web provides a new virtual marketplace in which parties can enter into a broad range of commercial activities. As online transactions continue to increase, so will the number and types of disputes resulting from online transactions. Clearly, many online disputes will likely mirror the business conflicts that arise in the offline world, such as customer complaints about product quality or e-business complaints about disputed delivery dates or pricing with vendors or suppliers. However, there are some unique twists on standard business disagreements when online business relationships are involved. Some special conflict issues in online transactions include disputes arising from online contracting, privacy, and intellectual property.

Starting with online contracting, it is important to recognize that entering into online contracts can be dramatically different than the offline world. There are major differences in the formation and execution of online contracts. Typically, the parties do

Chart 1.2 Active Adult Internet Users Aged 14+ Worldwide, 2002–2004 (in millions)					
	2000	2001	2002	2003	2004
North America	97.6	114.4	130.8	147.7	160.6
Europe	70.1	107.8	152.7	206.5	254.9
Asia/Pacific Firm	48.7	63.8	85.4	118.8	173.0
Latin America	9.9	15.3	22.1	31.0	40.8
Africa and the Middle East	3.5	5.3	7.2	9.0	10.9
Worldwide Total	229.8	306.6	398.2	513.0	640.2

not hold face-to-face meetings or negotiations over online contract terms. Parties are often strangers to each other and may not have an ongoing business relationship after the transaction is completed. In addition, there may not be any manual signature to verify party agreement; for instance, one person may merely click on "I Agree," as in the *Caspi* case.

Whenever you browse a web site or order products or services online, you are normally entering into a contract by agreeing to use the site in accordance with the web site owner's terms of use. You may be giving up the laws of your home state or country, surrendering personal information that may be traded with third parties without your consent, limiting your warranties, or giving up your right to pursue legal remedies in a court. Typically, online businesses offer contract terms on a take-it-or-leave-it basis without the opportunity for parties to negotiate the terms; such agreements are called adhesion contracts. Courts usually uphold these agreements unless it can be shown that they are unfairly oppressive, unconscionable, or not within the reasonable expectations of the weaker party. Because parties do not enter into a traditional contract formation and execution process, disputes may crop up when a business transaction goes sour and one of the parties decides to contest provisions that they feel are unfair to them or harmful to their commercial interests. To help make it clear that a contract is being formed, some e-commerce firms include "I Agree" icons on their web pages to make certain that parties have reviewed their terms and conditions before ordering goods and services online.

Federal and state digital signature laws allow parties to enter into binding agreements without the requirement of manual signatures on paper. To avoid later conflicts, the Center for Public Resources (CPR) Institute for Dispute Resolution has adopted online contracting policies under its CPR Business-to-Business E-Commerce Initiative, in which companies can agree in advance to recognize electronic signatures in B2B transactions (http://www.cpradr.org). Despite the recognition of digital signatures, online contracting conflicts may develop when a party challenges the validity and authenticity of an online contract or order. At times, it may be difficult in online activities to determine with whom you are doing business, which e-firm or individual actually sent the order to your e-business, and whether or not the original communication has been tampered with or otherwise altered during transmission. Someone may be improperly using the identification name and password of another party to gain access to private account information, to change data, or to order products online without authorization. Conflicts may arise when parties refuse to accept the delivery of or to pay for goods they claim they never ordered. Some e-businesses try to avoid this problem by sending confirming e-mails to those who have placed orders online.

Privacy has become a very important matter for all e-commerce participants. Consumers are typically concerned about whether an e-business is collecting personal data from them based on their online activities, how the data are being used and distributed, and whether the data are being kept secure from improper review by unauthorized persons or intentional attacks by computer hackers. When a consumer visits a web site, an e-business may deposit cookies, computer files that track online visits and deposit information on consumer hard drives. Cookies are intended to personalize the shopping experience for consumers and to streamline the ordering process, but they may be viewed as intrusive by some consumers. Special concerns are raised regarding the protection of the personal data of children under the age of thirteen, who are specifically protected under the federal Children's Online Privacy Protection Act of 1998 (COPPA). The language of COPPA and other information about protecting online privacy for children and adults can be found at the web site for the Federal Trade Commission (http://www.ftc.gov). Consumers seeking to safeguard their personal information may bring actions such as invasion of privacy or misappropriation under common law tort or the current patchwork of state and federal privacy laws.

Self-regulatory organizations such as TRUSTe (http://www.truste.org) and BBBOnline Privacy (http://www.bbbonline.org) have established policies to help guide e-businesses regarding online customer privacy. Privacy standards generally require an e-business to post its privacy policy on their website, to disclose what data it collects, and to identify how it uses and protects that consumer data. In addition, consumers may be given the choice of whether to allow the e-firm to share or sell their personal information and the opportunity to correct inaccuracies in personal data. Stricter standards limiting the collection, use, distribution, and storage of consumer personal data are found in the EU, Australia, and other nations of the world.

E-businesses also need to deal with a host of both external and internal privacy issues. Online companies are normally focused on whether or not trade secrets, customer data, and other proprietary information are adequately protected from improper use or unauthorized access. A recent survey indicated that online firms are about 57 percent more likely to face the loss of proprietary data than traditional offline businesses. Cryptography, firewalls, passwords and other online technologies may help to protect data, but firms must continually monitor and update their online security systems to fend off intrusions.

Internally, online firms must also be concerned about proper employee use of company e-mail and Internet systems to avoid both civil and criminal liability for employee online conduct. For example, an employee who downloads pornographic materials at the office or sends this material to others in the workplace may provide grounds for sexual harassment lawsuits from coworkers. Wise e-businesses need to develop, post, and implement clear external and internal policies about privacy, the protection of sensitive information, and proper e-mail and Internet usage. Appropriate employee training about these policies will help to avoid legal liability later on.

The unprecedented reach of the World Wide Web has yielded a fresh crop of intellectual property disputes. The protection of intellectual property presents special challenges in the online world because of global access to a site, the proliferation of online businesses, and the lack of uniform international laws regarding intellectual property rights. A person who downloads software from a web site may illegally sell and transmit it to others around the world in a few minutes. Another e-business may seek to steal your firm's goodwill by placing your trademark or service mark on its web site or including it in its URL or the underlying code used to create web sites (metatags) to divert your customers. A web site designer may decide to borrow the original art on a web page to enhance a client's lackluster web site, or a competitor may borrow a novel business method to speed up its online purchasing process. In recent years, numerous lawsuits have been filed by parties seeking to protect their intellectual property from online pirates with varying results.

Any online business spends substantial time and money on the development and marketing of its products and services. Your copyrights, patents, trademarks, and service marks identify important business assets that you must vigilantly protect. In the online world, copyrights often come into play in the original and creative development of a web page, with its unique arrangement of databases and informational articles or its use of electronic clip art or special design effects. Or perhaps your online business allows parties to license and download copyrighted software from your web site. Patents protect the invention of a novel product, design, or process. This issue has been litigated in the much-publicized dispute between Amazon.com and barnesandnoble.com over the use of Amazon.com's patented one-click ordering system. Trademarks and service marks are used mainly to protect items such as your online company name, slogan, logo as well as designs, sounds or symbols that identify your products and services, respectively.

Within the United States, you may try to protect your intellectual property by registering with the U.S. Patent and Trademark Office (http://www.uspto.gov) or the U.S. Copyright Office (http://www.loc.gov/copyright). In the United States use of your intellectual property without your permission provides grounds for either civil or criminal actions for infringement. Your copyrights, trademarks, and service marks are important business assets that you must protect vigilantly, particularly in the fast-paced arena of cyberspace. If third parties borrow your copyright, trademark, or service mark, their actions may lead to confusion about your business identity, the quality of your goods and services, and your e-firm's affiliation with less reputable online firms. Ultimately, the improper use of your business marks by others may result in the loss of legal protections for these valuable business assets. But the global reach of the Web makes it far more difficult to police and enforce your intellectual property rights around the world in a fast, efficient, and cost-effective manner.

ODR IN THE DIGITAL ERA World Intellectual Property Organization (WIPO)

Dr. Kamil Idris, Director General

Protecting Intellectual Property and Resolving Disputes in Cyberspace

One of the main business concerns of the global Web is the protection of intellectual property rights from domain names to trademarks, patents, and copyrights. The World Intellectual Property Organization (WIPO), located In Geneva, Switzerland, has the task of administering twenty-three treaties aimed at the protection of a wide range of intellectual property rights on the international stage. About 179 countries, nearly 90 percent of the nations of the world, are members of WIPO. The organization expressly states that its main goals are to

- harmonize national intellectual property legislation and procedures;
- provide services for international applications for industrial property rights;
- exchange intellectual property information;
- provide legal and technical assistance to developing and other countries;
- facilitate the resolution of private intellectual property disputes;
- marshal information technology as a tool for storing, accessing, and using valuable intellectual property information (http://www.wipo.org).

As part of its mission, WIPO's Arbitration and Mediation Center, with 1,000 mediators and arbitrators from more than 70 countries, aids parties in resolving their international domain name and other intellectual property disputes using arbitration and mediation rather than traditional litigation. The Center offers four forms of alternative dispute resolution: arbitration, expedited arbitration, mediation, and mediation-arbitration (med-arb) for parties hoping to resolve intellectual property conflicts.

In response to the growth of the World Wide Web, WIPO launched its Digital Agenda in 1999. This project seeks to aid the development of new norms in the distribution and protection of intellectual property, such as music, films, and other proprietary information, over the Internet. The Digital Agenda project also seeks to promote greater access to and understanding of the Internet in developing nations. WIPO considers online conflict resolution as one of the key aspects of its Digital Agenda. The organization has developed a guide of best practices to avoid dispute and resolve conflict for industry.

WIPO has taken a leading role in resolving domain name disputes as a recognized dispute resolution service provider for the Internet Corporation for Assigned Names and Numbers (ICANN). In 2003 alone, parties filed 1,063 domain name cases under ICANN's Uniform Dispute Resolution Policy. Claimants may file complaints and respondents may file their answers to complaints regarding domain name disagreements online with WIPO. Using primarily e-mail communica-

(continued)

tions, WIPO panels have reviewed party information and resolved cases drawn from parties representing more than hundred countries since WIPO's inception in December 1999. WIPO expects to continue to be a leader in resolving international intellectual property disputes both in the offline and online worlds.

Data originally provided by World Intellectual Property Organization (WIPO), the owner of the copyright. The Secretariat of WIPO assumes no liability or responsibility with regard to the transformation or translation of this data. Use of WIPO information and photo courtesy of World Intellectual Property Organization (WIPO). All rights reserved.

Why Not Just Go to Court to Resolve Online Disagreements?

Your e-business and you, individually, may be involved in commercial transactions with parties from other states or countries. Third parties, as in the *Dow Jones* case in Australia, may claim online harm even though you have no direct commercial contacts with them. From a practical perspective, going to court is a time-consuming, expensive, and complicated method of conflict resolution in the global environment of the Internet. If a business dispute arises between you and any of those business partners or customers, they may file civil lawsuits against you in a foreign court located in their home state or country. Defending against these civil lawsuits may involve tremendous costs, including traveling to the other state or country for court matters and losing valuable time away from your e-business. In some instances, you may find yourself dealing with the same civil case in different courts in different states or countries, depending upon the parties involved in the conflict.

Many online disputes, particularly those involving B2C and C2C transactions, involve very low dollar amounts, ranging on average from $300 to $3,000. In one reported case, the parties were disputing a shipping charge of $2.00. It is unrealistic to expect that parties will spend the time and money to travel to foreign small-claims courts to prosecute or defend against such small amounts. Even if larger sums are in dispute, parties may not want to use significant resources paying legal and travel expenses to deal with a foreign court in another state or country, perhaps with untested local counsel, unfamiliar procedures, uncertain cultural differences, and language barriers. Aside from these practical concerns and the jurisdiction issues discussed earlier, the global legal environment involves complex issues of choice of law, enforceability of judicial awards, and due process of judicial proceedings not normally found in domestic litigation.

By choice of law, we mean that a court that has personal jurisdiction over your e-business must decide which laws apply to your dispute. Different courts in different nations apply distinct rules in determining which set of laws will be used to interpret the parties' rights and responsibilities in a particular disagreement. National courts may find that they must interpret and apply the laws of a foreign nation to a dispute. E-businesses may find themselves dealing with different courts that are applying different laws to the same dispute, resulting in enormous costs and lost time and productivity. For example, suppose a Texas manufacturing company entered into an online agreement with a firm in Costa Rica. The online contract did not state which laws would be applied in case of a disagreement. The contract called for the U.S. company to provide parts for the Costa Rican company's manufacture of airplanes in its manufacturing facility in Chile. The parts were supposed to be delivered to the Costa Rican company's distribution center in Brazil. The U.S. company sent only half of the order for the requested parts to Brazil. The smaller order was received in Brazil, but the Costa Rican company was upset that not all the ordered parts were delivered in a timely fashion, causing the firm to lose valuable production time. The firm also claimed that the parts delivered were defective and damaged the Costa Rican company's equipment at its manufacturing facility and shut down that facility in Chile for two weeks.

In a subsequent breach of contract lawsuit, a court might consider a number of important questions before determining the proper choice of law to be used in handling the disagreement. Where was the contract negotiated? Where was the contract executed? Where was the contract to be performed? Where did the circumstances arise that resulted in the lawsuit? The answers to these questions may result in either inconclusive or inconsistent answers. If the contract was negotiated and executed online, it is even less clear where these early contract stages actually occurred. Costa Rica? The United States? Cyberspace? The delivery portion of the contract was not fully performed in Brazil, but the damage to the Costa Rican company's equipment occurred in Chile. Yet the claimed defects occurred at the U.S. firm's manufacturing facility in Texas, whereas the alleged damages were suffered by a firm in Costa Rica. A U.S. court may have personal jurisdiction over the parties and then may decide that it must use the laws of Costa Rica to resolve the complaint, and a Costa Rican court may determine that the laws of Brazil must be interpreted and applied. In this short fact pattern, it may be very difficult to determine with any certainty what laws will be applied to this online contracting dispute. Parties could spend a great deal of time and money trying to sort out the legal no-person's land of choice of law in cross-border conflicts.

Even if a party is successful in court, that judgment does not end the process. The losing party does not automatically pay out the damage award or follow any other nonmonetary instructions of a court. This aspect is true in both domestic and international litigation but is greatly exacerbated in the global context. The winning side must be able to enforce the judgment against the noncomplying party. At times, enforcement may be delayed if one of the parties decides to appeal the decision. In other instances, enforcement may be difficult to obtain because national courts are not bound by the decisions of courts in other countries. In still other cases, parties may refuse to pay because they are so geographically distant that actually enforcing the award may be impractical or virtually impossible.

If the Costa Rican firm just described wins a judgment against the U.S. company in the Costa Rican courts in the amount of $100,000, the U.S. defendant may simply refuse to comply with that court's judgment. The Costa Rican firm must then find a way to enforce the judicial award. It may seek out property or assets of the U.S. party located in Costa Rica to satisfy the judgment. If the U.S. firm has no assets in Costa Rica, then the company must travel to the courts in Texas, where the defendant may have assets, to try to enforce the court judgment. Yet national courts are not required to enforce the judgments of foreign courts. The Texas courts may legally refuse to enforce the Costa Rican judgment unless expressly required to enforce it by law or by treaty. It is actually much more difficult to enforce a foreign court award than a foreign arbitration award because existing international treaties favor arbitration over the national courts.

It may seem strange that arbitration awards are easier to enforce than court judgments, but our last global issue of due process plays a role here. Due process means that parties in a legal proceeding are entitled to a fundamentally fair and impartial process. A fair procedure usually requires at minimum that parties be provided with notice of the claims being made against them, an opportunity to fully present their side of the dispute, and an objective decision based on the evidence in the record. Many national courts refuse to enforce foreign judgments because of concerns that these courts may not uphold basic standards of fairness. There are also concerns that some tribunals may lack impartiality based on a desire to favor the party from the home country or due to inherent fraud or corruption in the legal proceedings. Unlike arbitration, parties may be forced by a lawsuit to appear before a foreign court, follow unfamiliar procedures, and have an outcome imposed upon them without having an opportunity to select an impartial and experienced decision-maker. In addition, the desire to uphold a nation's sovereignty, its laws, and its court system may result in a reluctance to enforce the awards of foreign courts, particularly if the award violates a country's laws or public policy.

Are There Methods for Limiting Potential Exposure to Lawsuits in Foreign Courts?

There are a number of steps that e-businesses can take to limit their potential liability exposure outside of their state or national borders. The most important step is to avoid legal liability from the outset by engaging counsel to perform a legal audit that will help your e-firm to address important legal issues in structuring and operating your e-business, to undertake the legal work needed to protect important business assets, and to identify areas of future potential liability for the purposes of obtaining appropriate insurance and taking other needed protective steps. Waiting until you are embroiled in legal trouble to contact an attorney is much more costly and time-consuming than proactively addressing legal issues in advance. It is important from the outset to retain an attorney well versed in Internet law to undertake an effective e-business legal audit.

Also consider legal and business concerns in the development of your e-business web site. Although it is a vital tool for your e-company, consider the issues of interactivity and geographic scope when creating a web site and its terms of use. If it is important for your customers to order online, then recognize that this approach will likely broaden your potential liability. If you wish to do business only within your state or region, then limit the locations identified in pull-down menus in your ordering process or include language in your terms of use limiting your business activities to a specific geographic territory. You may even wish to indicate explicitly in your terms of use that your web site is not intended for access by or to do business with parties outside of your own state or nation and then abide by those disclaimers. You may use technological filters that block access from other states or countries. If your site is intended to be primarily informational, then consider designing it to be more passive and therefore less likely to expand personal jurisdiction over your company.

In formalizing your terms of use, you may also wish to discuss with your attorney the insertion of a choice-of-forum and a choice-of-law clause in your paper and online contracts as well as your web site's terms of use. Under these clauses, parties agree to bring legal actions against you in the courts of your choosing, applying the laws of the state or nation you have selected. As long as the selected forum and laws are reasonably related to your business activities, many courts will uphold these clauses. Outside of the United States, some courts will not uphold such clauses in consumer transactions that have been agreed to before the dispute arises. However, the ability to determine the forum and the applicable laws in many online business transactions as well as some consumer dealings, where valid, will help your e-business to better control and predict potential legal costs while providing your e-business with the advantages of a more local and familiar court system and applicable laws.

Quick Clicks: Online Forum Selection and Choice of Law Clauses   Go to a popular web site. Click on the link for its terms of use. Read them and determine whether or not these terms of use contain forum selection and/or choice-of-law clauses. Be aware that such clauses are often found in the last few paragraphs of a site's terms and conditions. Print out the relevant clauses and attach them to a separate piece of paper in which you identify the site and summarize the applicable clauses for instructor review and/or class discussion.

Most importantly, your e-business should consider the development of a fair and effective online conflict resolution program to help quickly and efficiently resolve disputes with customers, vendors, suppliers, and other third parties. These methods emphasize the importance of resolving conflicts outside of traditional litigation and have the aim of protecting important business relationships. We discuss alternative dispute resolution and online dispute resolution methods in greater depth in Chapter 2.

ODR Bytes

The World Wide Web has spawned numerous online business relationships, including business-to-consumer (B2C), business-to-business (B2B), business-to-government (B2G), and consumer-to-consumer (C2C).

Any business can be sued at any time by anyone for a claim that may or may not have merit. By placing your web site on the information superhighway, you are exposing your e-business and yourself to potential liability throughout the United States and the rest of the world with its maze of different laws, regulatory requirements, and court procedures.

In the United States, an e-business may be subject to personal jurisdiction in civil lawsuits through three main avenues: party presence within territorial borders, volunteering jurisdiction, and long-arm statutes. Yet others, such as the European Union, follow the effects doctrine and look to see if an online firm's conduct had a substantial impact or harm on parties or commercial activity within its national borders. No uniform or simple formula exists in this unclear area of law.

In general, a mere electronic presence on the Web may not be sufficient to provide personal jurisdiction in the United States. But the more interactive your web site is and the more your e-business purposefully avails itself of the market in a particular state or country, the more likely that it will be subject to personal jurisdiction in another state or country.

Some conflict issues unique to online transactions include disputes arising from online contracting, privacy, and intellectual property.

Within the United States, you may try to protect your intellectual property by registering it with the U.S. Patent and Trademark Office or the U.S. Copyright Office.

International civil litigation may involve tremendous costs and the loss of valuable time away from your e-business, particularly if the same dispute is being considered in different courts in different states or countries.

The global legal environment involves complex issues of choice of law, enforceability of judicial awards and due process of judicial proceedings not found in domestic litigation.

The most important step is to lessen potential legal liability from the outset by engaging counsel to help your e-firm to address important legal issues in structuring and operating your e-business, to undertake the legal work needed to protect important business assets, and to identify areas of future potential liability.

It is important to discuss with your attorney limits on the interactivity and geographic reach of your web site and the use of choice-of-forum and choice-of-law clauses in your terms of use.

Fair and effective dispute resolution programs can be developed to resolve conflicts outside of traditional litigation.

ODR Bookmarks

Amazon.com (B2C)
http://www.Amazon.com

Australasian Legal Information Institute
http://www.austlii.edu.au

BBB*Online* Privacy
http://www.bbbonline.org

CPR Institute for Dispute Resolution
http://www.cpradr.org/e-commerce.htm

Covisint (B2B)
http://www.covisint.com

eBay.com (C2C)
http://www.ebay.com

Federal Trade Commission
http://www.ftc.gov

FedBizOpps (B2G)
http://www.fedbizopps.gov

Onvia.com (B2G)
http://www.onvia.com

TRUSTe
http://www.truste.org

U.S. Copyright Office
http://www.loc.gov/copyright

U.S. Patent and Trademark Office
http://www.uspto.gov

World Intellectual Property Organization (WIPO)
http://www.wipo.org

Selected ODR Bibliography

Almaguer, Alejandro E., and Roland W. Baggott III. "Note & Comment: Shaping New Legal Frontiers: Dispute Resolution for the Internet." *Ohio St. J. On Disp. Resol.* 13 (1998): 711.

August, Ray. *International Cyber-Jurisdiction* (2000). Unpublished manuscript on file with author.

Bernstein, Matthew. One Click... Two Click: The Litigation of Internet Business Method Patents: Amazon, Inc. v Barnesandnoble.com, Inc. Gray Cary Ware & Freidenrich LLP. (2000–2001): *Findlaw.com.*

Bordone, Robert C. "Notes: Electronic Online Dispute Resolution: A Systems Approach—Potential, Problems, and a Proposal." *Harv. Negotiation L. Rev.* 3 (Spring, 1998): 175.

Campanelli, Melissa. "Trading Places—Whether You Start One or Just Use One, B2B Exchange Will Be Part of Your Business." (November 2000): *Entrepreneur.com.*

Cona, Frank A. "Focus on Cyberlaw: Application of Online Systems in Alternative Dispute Resolution." *Buff. L. Rev.* 45 (Fall, 1997): 975.

Enos, Lori. "Auto Giants Unveil Net Parts Exchange." *E-Commerce Times* (December 8, 2000).

Ferrera, Gerald R., Stephen D. Lichtenstein, Margo E. K. Reder, Robert C. Bird, and William T. Schiano, *Cyberlaw: Text and Cases.* St. Paul, MN: Thomson/West Legal Studies in Business, 2000.

"Jurisdiction—Sending a Single E-Mail Message Sufficient to Support Exercise of Personal Jurisdiction." *Electronic Commerce & Law,* 6 (April 25, 2001): 446.

Lide, E. Casey. "Note & Comment, ADR and Cyberspace: The Role of Alternative Dispute Resolution in Online Commerce, Intellectual Property and Defamation." *Ohio St. J. On Disp. Resol.* 12 (1996): 193.

Mosquera, Mary. "Global E-Commerce to Hit $5 Trillion in 2005." *E-Business-PlanetIT* (May 24, 2001).

Ponte, Lucille M. "Boosting Consumer Confidence in E-Business: Recommendations For Establishing Fair And Effective Dispute Resolution Programs For B2C Online Transactions." *Albany L. J. of Sci. & Tech.* 12 (2002): 441.

Ponte, Lucille M. "Throwing Bad Money after Bad: Can Online Dispute Resolution (ODR) Really Deliver the Goods for the Unhappy Internet Shopper?" *Tulane J. of Tech. & Intell. Prop.* 3 (Spring 2001): 55.

2

Understanding Online Dispute Resolution

What is online dispute resolution (ODR)?

Is ODR different from alternative dispute resolution (ADR)?

What types of ODR processes can e-businesses utilize?

What are some of the advantages of ODR?

What are some of the disadvantages of ODR?

Do e-commerce groups support the use of ODR?

What Is Online Dispute Resolution (ODR)?

With the rapid emergence of e-commerce, online businesses and their customers soon recognized the need to develop dispute resolution options that reflect the speed and convenience of the Web. The emerging field of online dispute resolution (ODR) refers to a collection of conflict resolution methods that utilize online technologies to help resolve disputes. Parties might decide to negotiate a conflict through an exchange of e-mails or by posting messages to each other in a secure chat room. A mediator may work with two disputants in real-time online conversations over the Web or use information distributed through a listserv. Disputants may agree to have the outcome of their dispute determined through a virtual jury. Others might present information to an arbitral panel via streaming video over the Web or other videoconferencing devices. In some instances, parties may blend together traditional offline forms of communication, such as fax, telephone, and standard mail, to augment their use of online technologies.

Although ODR was originally intended to handle disagreements that arose online, ODR can also be applied to ODR service providers who handle offline disputes using online technologies. Many ODR providers hope that in the future more parties with offline disputes will look to ODR for its projected lower costs, speed, and convenience.

Chart 2.1	Top Products/Services for Internet-Related Fraud Complaints, January 1–December 31, 2002[a]
Internet auctions	50%
Shop-at-home/catalog sales	13%
Internet access services	11%
Foreign money offers	5%
Internet information and adult services	5%
Business opportunities	3%
Computers	2%
Internet Web site design	2%
Others	9%

[a]Percentages are based on the total number of Internet-related complaints (102,517) received between January 1 and December 31, 2002.

Data from Bureau of Consumer Protection, U.S. Federal Trade Commission (http://www.consumer.gov/sentinel/; http://www.ftc.gov). Used with permission.

Is ODR Different from Alternative Dispute Resolution (ADR)?

Most conflicts are currently resolved in our society without completing the full litigation process. About 90 percent to 95 percent of all lawsuits are settled without a trial. This high settlement rate means that most disputes already are being handled outside of the courts. The concept of ADR encompasses all forms of dispute resolution that seek to resolve conflicts outside of traditional litigation.

ADR involves a collection of practices and techniques that retain certain common, or core, attributes. Some traditional characteristics of ADR emphasize the importance of opening up the lines of communication between the parties, improving the speed and cost-efficiency of the conflict resolution process, providing confidentiality during and after the proceedings, and allowing for greater control by the parties over the process and its outcomes.

In the past, ADR normally was used as conflict resolution techniques in the offline world for offline disputes. With the growth of online technologies and online disputes, ADR mechanisms are being hailed as constructive ways to handle these disagreements in a fast and efficient manner. The field of ADR embraces the evolving arena of ODR.

The concept of ODR involves the practice of ADR methods that use online technologies to facilitate the resolution of conflicts. ADR principles and practices are the foundation for ODR practice. ODR presents new challenges in that parties are more likely to be strangers to each other, so it may be more difficult to create an environment of trust and open communication. In addition, unlike ADR, ODR processes usually anticipate that disputants will try to resolve conflicts without any face-to-face contact. Skilled ODR neutrals and interactive technologies may help to bridge the gaps resulting from these important differences.

What Types of ODR Processes Can E-Businesses Utilize?

Most ODR experts recognize that no one form of ODR will work in every dispute for every kind of e-business on the Web. E-businesses must determine what kind of ODR program and methods will work best for them and their customer base in their given industry. Some e-firms may decide to create their own in-house conflict resolution program. Others may contract out these services to third-party ODR service providers, which may be either nonprofit or for-profit entities. Still others may be members of professional organizations or a trustmark or seal program, which may provide dispute resolution services for their member businesses. For example, the National Association of Manufacturers (http://www.nam.org) has teamed with the Center for Public Resources (CPR) Institute for Dispute Resolution (http://www.cpradr.org) to establish the Mediation Center for Business Disputes, providing non-binding mediation services for its 14,000 member firms dealing with business and employment disputes. The development of an ODR program is discussed extensively in Chapter 7.

Today, many different forms of ODR are already available to e-businesses and their customers. ODR methods are drawn primarily from the offline world of ADR. On the Web, the main forms of ODR practice are negotiation, mediation, arbitration, virtual juries, and hybrid processes such as med-arb. Negotiation and mediation are referred to as *settlement mechanisms* because they focus on the efforts of the competing parties to determine their needs and the outcomes of their dispute. Arbitration and virtual juries are considered *adjudicatory processes* because third-party neutrals, and not the opposing sides involved in the conflict, decide the results. Med-arb is a blend of both settlement-driven and adjudicatory methods.

Typically, parties that wish to maintain an existing business relationship or to promote good customer satisfaction will opt for settlement-driven approaches that emphasize party collaboration and decision-making. These types of processes tend to stress the importance of solving a conflict in a manner that allows the parties to continue to do business with each other. Also, the settlement-driven process may help the parties to recognize how to better communicate and deal with conflicts between themselves in the future.

The selection of adjudicatory mechanisms may indicate that the parties are strangers to each other and are involved in a one-time transaction, with little interest in preserving a business relationship. Using adjudicatory methods suggests that the disputants want a clear determination of their rights and responsibilities in a rapid, cost-effective manner.

Let's briefly review each main type of ODR process. Each of these ODR mechanisms is discussed in greater depth in the forthcoming chapters of this book.

Negotiation

The negotiation process involves two or more disputants who meet to discuss and resolve their conflict in a mutually agreeable fashion. Typically, only the disputants are in the talks, and third parties do not play a role in resolving the conflict. The parties work on their own to identify their conflict issues and to find common ground. In order to effectively negotiate an outcome with which both parties can comply, the disputants must strive to achieve a result that is satisfactory to both of them, often referred to as the "win-win" result. A willingness to compromise can be key to a successful negotiation process. If no settlement is reached, the parties are free to continue the litigation process.

In online negotiation, the parties may try to resolve their conflict through a simple exchange of case information and online negotiations, as can be done with Square Trade's Direct Negotiation Tool (http://www.squaretrade.com) or Online Resolution Inc.'s Confidential Information Form (http://www.onlineresolution.com). In other cases, parties may be disagreeing only on the dollar amount of the settlement and may use automated software programs that select a dollar amount from several confidential offers or blind bids based upon an agreed-upon settlement range. Some representatives of automated negotiation programs that compare blind bids can be found at http://www.cybersettle.com and http://www.clicknsettle.com. Blind bidding and other forms of online negotiation and process tools are discussed in Chapter 3.

Mediation

This process is often referred to as a form of *facilitated*, or *assisted*, *negotiation*. In mediation, a third party, called a "mediator," aids the parties throughout the settlement talks. The mediator often possesses expertise that is relevant to the nature of the dispute to aid the competing parties. For example, a mediator with a background in software development and licensing may be asked to help two e-businesses settle a conflict over their respective rights under a software-licensing agreement.

The mediator is normally not a decision-maker but helps the parties to define and discuss their conflict issues and guides them toward a mutually acceptable, or "win-win," set of results. As with negotiation, the mediation is binding only if the parties have agreed to a settlement. At times, some issues may be successfully resolved in a mediation, with outstanding issues either sent to the courts or shepherded through another form of conflict resolution, such as arbitration, based on party consent.

The online mediator and the parties to the disagreement may communicate in asynchronous formats using e-mail, list servs, chat rooms, and other conferencing software. With online technologies, the mediator may send confidential individual or group e-mail messages seeking party input. Parties may respond by e-mail, be directed to a listserv that will automatically distribute responses to all participants, or post e-mail exchanges on a confidential bulletin board for party review. In some cases, the mediator and the disputants may also use Internet Relay Chat (IRC), sometimes referred to as instant messaging, to converse online in real time in a private chat room. Examples of online mediation services include the Online Ombuds Office (OOO) at http://www.ombuds.org/center/ombuds.html and SquareTrade at http://www.squaretrade.com. Online mediation is discussed in greater detail in Chapter 4.

Quick Clicks: Exploring Procedures and Offerings of ODR Service Providers   Visit one of the ODR service providers mentioned in this chapter. Explore the site and summarize their ODR procedures, and outline the synchronous and/or asynchronous forms of online communication that the ODR service provider offers to parties. Consider the types of online disputes you think would benefit from the ODR services at this site. What do you think are some of the benefits and limitations of the processes of the selected ODR service provider? Draft a brief report of your findings for instructor review and/or class discussion.

Arbitration is a method derived from standard litigation practice. Arbitration allows parties to present their views in an abbreviated trial-like process before one or more decision-makers. These decision-makers are referred to as "arbitrators" and, like mediators, they normally have expertise relevant to the dispute. In the offline world, some arbitration proceedings are relatively similar to the adversarial litigation process, with mounting costs and expanded time demands.

Some online arbitration services are trying to streamline the process using an array of online technologies. Some ODR providers may use only e-mail, whereas others might offer more sophisticated groupware, videoconferencing, or streaming video over the Web to help bridge the distance between parties in arbitration proceedings. Evidence may be sent by e-mail attachment or by standard mail, if desired. The arbitrator's award may be e-mailed to the disputants or posted in a private or public chat room for review.

Unlike mediation or negotiation, the determination of the arbitrator(s) is normally binding with only limited grounds for appeal, such as fraud or bias. Based on party agreement or the selected procedures, the arbitration award may be nonbinding. A nonbinding decision allows parties the opportunity to bring the matter to an appropriate court or serves as a guide to the parties in resolving their disagreement in further settlement discussions. Check out the following online arbitration sites for more information: http://www.icann.org/udrp/, http:///www.resolutionforum.org, and http://www.webdispute.com. The role and processes of online arbitration or private judging are reviewed in Chapter 5.

Virtual Juries

Borrowing from the notion of peer review, ODR providers can offer parties simulated jury decisions for either online and offline disagreements. The online community becomes a potential pool of jurors for the competing sides. An interesting example of online or virtual jury sessions is iCourthouse (http://www.i-courthouse.com).

Under iCourthouse's procedures, an unhappy party may file or register a complaint online with iCourthouse. The registering party fills out the complaint outlining the

TABLE 2–1

Summary of Main Characteristics of ODR Methods

Main ODR Methods	Negotiation	Mediation	Arbitration	Med-Arb
Type of process	Settlement	Settlement	Adjudicatory	Settlement and adjudicatory
Main online technologies	E-mail; blind bid software; secure bulletin boards and real-time chat rooms	E-mail; list servs; secure bulletin boards, and real-time chat rooms	E-mail; video conferencing; streaming video over Web	E-mail; list servs; secure bulletin boards and real-time chat rooms; video conferencing; streaming video over Web
Role of third-party neutral	None	Mediator aids party communication/ settlement	Arbitrator supervises hearing; renders decision	Initially mediator aids party communication/ settlement; unresolved issues determined by mediator acting as arbitrator
Nature of party participation	Voluntary, normally by oral agreement	Voluntary, by written mediation agreement	Voluntary, by written arbitration agreement	Voluntary, by written med-arb agreement
Use of witnesses/ documentary evidence	Not generally utilized	Not generally utilized	Allowed, but may be limited	Allowed, but may be limited
Privacy of proceedings	Confidential	Confidential, unless otherwise agreed to by parties	Confidential, unless otherwise agreed to by parties	Confidential, unless otherwise agreed to by parties
Nature of outcomes	Nonbinding, unless parties enter into settlement contract	Nonbinding, unless parties enter into settlement contract	May be nonbinding or binding with limited grounds for appeal, depending on party agreement	May be nonbinding or binding with limited grounds for appeal, depending on party agreement
Enforcement of outcomes	By contract	By contract	Valid arbitration awards enforceable in court	By contract for mediation; valid arbitration awards enforceable in court

main facts in the disagreement. Notified by e-mail, the responding party may choose to participate and may then supply their view of the disagreement. Within a limited time period, the opposing sides fill out a trial book that contains their respective opening statements, spelling out their main contentions, augmented by relevant evidence and supportive legal authorities. The parties may also request proposed jury instructions that summarize how the law applies to their dispute.

At the outset, the registering party can request either a peer jury or a panel jury to review and decide the conflict using iCourthouse. A request for a peer jury invites anyone in the online community to review the case, to ask the parties for more information, and to render a verdict in the matter by a certain deadline. A party seeking a panel jury is asking for a limited number of jurors to be selected based on certain specific demographic criteria. The disputants can agree in advance that the virtual jury's verdict is binding or nonbinding. The disputants can review the verdicts rendered by accessing their password-protected trial book. Already, iCourthouse has handed down verdicts in more than 250 cases. Online jury proceedings are dealt with in Chapter 6.

Hybrid Processes

Some ODR processes are a combination of separate ODR processes. Med-arb is a common example of a hybrid process. Utilizing this mechanism, parties in conflict agree to use a blend of mediation and arbitration to handle their conflict. First, a mediator will work with the parties to mediate any areas of disagreement between the feuding parties. If the disputants cannot agree on solutions for all their concerns, the mediator then acts as an arbitrator and decides the results of the remaining issues. Therefore, the final resolution of the conflict is a combination of both settlement and adjudicatory processes. Under this hybrid mechanism, the parties work together to determine the outcome of certain matters and then can rely on the expertise of the arbitrator(s) to iron out any remaining issues. This two-step approach helps avoid throwing the conflict into the more cumbersome and time-consuming litigation process. NovaForum provides med-arb services through its Electronic Courthouse at http://www.novaforum.com.

What Are Some of the Advantages of ODR?

Drawing on ADR principles, ODR provides a number of advantages in dealing with either online or offline disagreements. Some of these advantages directly benefit the disputing parties, whereas others yield positive contributions to society as a whole. The typical advantages of ODR for disputants include opening lines of communication and trust between the parties, saving the parties both time and money in resolving the conflict, and improving the parties' control over the process and its outcomes. The main advantages of ODR to the public involve helping to increase conflict resolution options, to reduce court caseloads, and to prompt reforms in existing court systems. Let's first take a look at the main benefits to the parties.

Opening the Lines of Communication

In a typical lawsuit situation, both parties are likely to be instructed by counsel not to discuss the matter with the other side to protect the case, which seriously hampers or completely stops the parties from being able to do business with each other. Derived from ADR practice, ODR mechanisms seek to open the lines of communication, encourage parties to talk about the dispute, and develop constructive ways to solve it. ODR processes tend to be less confrontational and try to remove the counterproductive hostility and suspicion that underlies our adversarial system. Because parties generally are communicating online and not face-to-face, the parties may be more open and communicative than if they were in the same room and fearful or uncomfortable about directly communicating negative feelings or critical concerns. The less adversarial the process, the more likely the parties will be able to preserve the business relationship, allowing for future commercial dealings between the disputants.

In addition, court documents and proceedings are normally open to public review. The glare of public exposure may make it difficult for responsible parties to admit any blame or innocent parties to avoid fraudulent or frivolous claims that may unfairly harm their reputation. Unlike traditional litigation, ODR is normally a confidential process, which allows parties to feel greater ease and openness in communicating with the other side. A private setting helps foster a more trusting environment geared toward settlement. Through confidential proceedings, parties may be better able to recognize their best interests in resolving the conflict and in going forward with productive business relationships. ODR proceedings and outcomes are normally not made publicly available unless otherwise agreed to by the parties.

For example, under ICANN's Uniform Dispute Resolution Policy (UDRP), domain-name decisions are posted on their web site to keep the community informed about developments in this conflict area. (See special boxed section.) The authority to post these decisions comes from UDRP, and parties agree to the terms of UDRP when they register domain names. Also, the Online Ombuds Office (OOO), the clinical arm of the Center for Information Technology and Dispute Resolution at the University of Massachusetts, has a link to posted transcripts of five online mediation cases for educational purposes. These online mediation cases were part of the OOO's pilot project with eBay to help mediate the resolution of online auction disputes between buyers and sellers. Any party identifiers have been removed from the transcript to protect party privacy. The transcripts of the disputes provide interesting insight into the use of e-mails to mediate conflicts (http://www.disputes.net/cyberweek2000/ebay/ebayintro.htm).

ODR IN THE DIGITAL ERA
ICANN's Uniform Dispute-Resolution Policy (UDRP)

ICANN

What's in a Name? Using ODR to Resolve Domain Name Disputes

What do GE, Abercrombie & Fitch, and Madonna all have in common? They have all used ODR to help resolve domain name disputes in their favor. The names of successful businesses and famous celebrities are valuable business assets that may rake in millions of dollars in revenues. But what happens if someone else has registered your name or trademark as a domain name in order to profit from years of your marketing efforts and the goodwill you have established? Perhaps it is a competitor trying to block your establishment of an online presence, or maybe the registering party will demand money from you in order to facilitate the transfer of the

(continued)

name, commonly referred to as "cybersquatting." ICANN may be able to help you under its Uniform Dispute Resolution Policy (UDRP).

Established in 1998, ICANN is a nonprofit, private-sector corporation responsible for managing the domain name system, among other duties. Any person or company that registers a domain name with one of ICANN's accredited registrars agrees to UDRP. The policy requires registrants to participate in a mandatory administrative proceeding to resolve a domain name dispute. Aggrieved parties may file complaints by e-mail with one of ICANN's approved ODR providers, which includes the Center for Public Resources, eResolution, the National Arbitration Forum, and WIPO. The other party may respond with its own view of the facts and its contentions for domain name ownership. All complaints, responses, and evidentiary materials may be filed by e-mail, fax, telecopy, or standard mail. There are no in-person hearings, videoconferencing sessions, or streaming video over the Web. If parties wish, they may also seek court intervention in the dispute, because litigation may run on a parallel track to the UDRP proceedings.

In order to win, the complainant must show that (1) the domain name is identical or confusingly similar to their trademark or service mark; (2) the registering party has no legitimate rights or interest to the name; and (3) the domain name has been registered and used in bad faith. If the complainant can prove each element, then the panel is limited to either canceling or transferring the domain name. If a party disagrees with the outcome or is seeking additional damages or equitable remedies, that party must go to national courts for further assistance. But in many instances, the transfer or cancellation of the name provides an important benefit to an injured party.

As of January 2004, nearly 9,200 domain name proceedings had been initiated under ICANN's UDRP with ODR providers resolving some 7,671 disputes by decision. You can visit the ICANN site, http://www.icann.org/udrp/udrpdec.htm, and search its decision database either by case name or key words. The decision database is updated on a weekly basis to help keep you in step with the latest ODR determinations in the domain name game.

Time and Costs Savings

It is clear to most people that the U.S. courts are inundated with a host of criminal and civil matters. Due to heavy court backlogs in the United States, parties filing lawsuits must recognize that it may take years before their cases are heard and decided. In addition, as discussed in Chapter 1, legal actions in the global environment can be very costly and time-consuming if brought in the courts of foreign nations. In many instances, particularly in B2C transactions, the time and costs involved in resolving a conflict may actually dwarf the claimed losses in the initial commercial dispute.

ODR mechanisms offer parties the opportunity to reduce the time and the costs of resolving conflicts in several ways. First, parties need not spend the time or money needed to travel to another country to enter into settlement talks or to arbitrate a dispute. Using ODR, parties can reduce the loss of productivity involved in traveling to other nations to resolve conflicts. Online options are available that will allow disputants to handle conflicts from the relative ease of their office or home computer 24 hours a day, 7 days per week, 365 days per year. Second, in the offline environment, opposing parties must passively await action in overloaded courts, sometimes for many years, before any decision is rendered. Unlike standard litigation, parties can proactively schedule their ODR sessions to accommodate their own schedules and may garner outcomes within days or months, rather than years. Third, ODR methods normally involve a more limited information exchange or discovery process between the parties, which accounts for about 80 percent of all legal fees in standard litigation. Fourth, in some instances, the parties may not require the use of an attorney or may require only limited attorney assistance to resolve a claim, which saves both time and money. Also, because mediators and arbitrators are normally experienced professionals, a parade of expert witnesses for each party is unlikely to play a significant role in ODR processes, reaping additional cost and timesavings.

Greater Party Control over Processes and Outcomes

In standard litigation, courts must follow a specific set of procedures. The disputants do not have any input in determining the process that will be utilized or the solutions and remedies that will most benefit both parties in resolving the conflict and continuing in their commercial dealings. Furthermore, the opposing parties do not have the chance to select the judge or to make certain that the judge has the requisite expertise in their industry or in their type of dispute. Also, bound by precedent and existing laws, judges are limited to primarily determining who has won the case and what outcomes must be imposed on the losing side. Most outcomes are reduced to monetary awards and may not resolve underlying issues or preserve the business relationship between the parties.

It is important to note that even though a party may prevail in a court case, the winning side may still end up empty-handed. The losing side may refuse or be unable to pay the award or may delay payment for years while appealing the court's decision. As indicated in Chapter 1, enforcing awards, particularly in the global environment of the Web, is one of the biggest challenges facing businesses and their customers in cross-border transactions.

ODR procedures and decisions are not imposed on unwilling parties, as in our adversarial system. First of all, parties must agree to use ODR and normally cannot be forced to use these processes. By agreeing to use ODR, the disputants retain much greater control over the process and the outcomes in dealing with their conflict. The parties have the flexibility to decide what ODR process will be used, what ODR procedures will be followed, and who the third party neutral will be in the proceedings, if desired.

In negotiation, mediation, and med-arb, the parties may also be much more creative in determining a set of solutions that best meets their needs. Unlike lawyers and judges, the parties may decide to put aside strict legal arguments in favor of creating solutions that work for them in the real world of business. In some instances, the best outcome may involve extending warranties on a product, providing credits toward future purchases, or renegotiating selected terms in an existing contract, rather than solely awarding money damages. In resolving the conflict, the parties may also learn about problems that need to be addressed to improve customer satisfaction, to promote a favorable environment for upcoming business transactions, and to avoid unnecessary conflicts in the future. Through the use of ODR, the parties may have significantly greater input in crafting results that will most effectively benefit both parties and help preserve any long-standing business ties.

In addition, it is more likely that the opposing sides will comply with the agreed-upon settlement or arbitral award, because the parties play a major role throughout the process. Parties are less likely to balk at compliance when they have been active in arriving at the agreed-upon solutions or in selecting the appropriate decision-maker, who determined the resolution of the disagreement. Also, for online parties choosing arbitration or med-arb, a number of existing treaties make it easier to enforce a valid arbitration award than a court judgment primarily because the parties have had greater control over the procedures and the selection of the decision-maker.

Outside of the disputing parties, ODR also provides some benefits to the society as a whole.

Increases Conflict Resolution Options

In the world of the Internet, parties must contend with the fact that there is no uniform court system and no uniform set of laws. Disputants may look to the courts for help but may find that jurisdictional concerns, legal mandates, and enforcement issues may hamper their ability to resolve conflicts effectively. The online community is looking for conflict resolution options that mirror the speed and efficiency of the Web. ODR mechanisms may respond more quickly to the needs of the online community through its use of the tools of online technology and its 24-hours-per-day, 7-days-per-week, 365-days-per-year access. ODR processes may provide online parties with the flexibility and responsiveness to conflicts that are often difficult to find when using cumbersome judicial systems.

KEY CHAPTER CASE

Resolving International Domain Name Disputes Using ODR

Madonna Ciccone, p/k/a Madonna v Dan Parisi and "Madonna.com," Case No. D2000-0847 (WIPO Arbitration and Mediation Center, October 12, 2000)

Fact Summary: The complainant, Madonna, is a well-known professional entertainer and holds a registered U.S. trademark in the name Madonna for entertainment services and related goods. She has used her name and mark MADONNA professionally for entertainment services since 1979. Respondent purchased the registration for the disputed domain name for $20,000 and registered MADONNA as a trademark in Tunisia in 1998. On or about June 8, 1998, Respondent began operating an "adult entertainment portal web site" which contained a notice stating "Madonna.com is not affiliated or endorsed by the Catholic Church, Madonna College, Madonna Hospital or Madonna the singer." By May 31, 1999, it appeared that the site merely contained the above notice, the disputed domain name and the statement "Coming soon Madonna Gaming and Sportsbook." On June 9, 1999, Complainant, through her attorneys, objected to Respondent's use of the Madonna.com domain name. Complainant contends that the disputed domain name is identical to her registered and common law trademark MADONNA, the Respondent has no legitimate interest or rights in the domain name, and the Respondent merely used the domain name to attract Internet users to a pornographic web site for commercial gain based on confusion with her name and mark. Respondent does not dispute that the disputed domain name is identical or confusingly similar to Complainant's trademark. Respondent argues that Complainant cannot show a lack of legitimate interest in the domain name because Respondent (a) made demonstrable preparation to use the domain name for a bona fide business purpose; (b) holds a bona fide trademark in the word MADONNA; and (c) has attempted to make bona fide noncommercial use of the name by donating it to the Madonna Rehabilitation Hospital.

ADMINISTRATIVE PANEL DECISION: MARK V. B. PARTRIDGE, Presiding Panelist, with JAMES W. DABNEY and DAVID E. SORKIN, Panelists.

. . .

The Evidentiary Standard For Decision

Paragraph 4(a) of the Policy directs that the complainant must prove each of the following:

(i) that the domain name registered by the respondent is identical or confusingly similar to a trademark or service mark in which the complainant has rights; and,

(ii) that the respondent has no legitimate interests in respect of the domain name; and,

(iii) that the domain name has been registered and used in bad faith.

. . . In this case, there are factual disputes over Respondent's intent in obtaining and using the disputed domain name. For the reasons just stated, these disputes do not preclude a decision. Instead, we reach a decision based on the preponderance of the evidence submitted by the parties on the basic issues under the Policy.

Similarity of the Disputed Domain Name and Complainant's Mark

As noted above, Respondent does not dispute that its domain name is identical or confusingly similar to a trademark in which the Complainant has rights. Accordingly, we find that Complainant has satisfied the requirements of Paragraph 4(c)(i) of the Policy.

Lack of Rights or Legitimate Interests In Domain Name

Complainant has presented evidence tending to show that Respondent lacks any rights or legitimate interest in the domain name. Respondent's claim of rights or legitimate interests is not persuasive. First, Respondent contends that its use of the domain name for an adult entertainment web site involved prior use of the domain name in connection with a bona fide offering of goods or services. . . . However, Respondent has failed to provide a reasonable explanation for the selection of Madonna as a domain name. . . . [N]othing in the record supports a conclusion that Respondent adopted and used the term "Madonna" in good faith based on its ordinary dictionary meaning. We find instead that name was selected and used by Respondent with the intent to attract for commercial gain Internet users to Respondent's web site by trading on the fame of Complainant's mark. We see no other plausible explanation for Respondent's conduct and conclude that use which intentionally trades on the fame of another cannot constitute a "bona fide" offering of goods or services. . . .

Second, Respondent contends that it has rights in the domain name because it registered MADONNA as a trademark in Tunisia prior to notice of this dispute. Certainly, it is possible for a Respondent to rely on a valid trademark registration to show prior rights under the Policy. However, it would be a mistake to conclude that mere registration of a trademark creates a legitimate interest under the Policy. . . . Here, Respondent admits that the Tunisia registration was obtained merely to protect his interests in the domain name. Respondent is not located in Tunisia and the registration was not obtained for the purpose of making bona fide use of the mark in commerce in Tunisia. A Tunisian trademark registration is issued upon application without any substantive examination. . . .

Third, Respondent claims that its offer to transfer the domain name to the Madonna Hospital in Lincoln, Nebraska, is a legitimate noncommercial use under Paragraph 4(c)(iii) of the Policy. We disagree. The record is incomplete on these negotiations. Respondent has failed to disclose the specifics of its proposed arrangement with Madonna Hospital. Complainant asserts that the terms of the transfer include a condition that Madonna Hospital not transfer the domain name registration to Complainant. It also appears that the negotiations started after Complainant objected to Respondent's registration and use of the domain name. These circumstances do not demonstrate a legitimate interest or right in the domain name, and instead suggest that Respondent lacks any real interest in the domain name apart from its association with Complainant. . . .

Bad Faith Registration and Use

Under Paragraph 4(b)(iv) of the Policy, evidence of bad faith registration and use of a domain name includes the following circumstances:

> (iv) by using the domain name, you have intentionally attempted to attract, for commercial gain, Internet users to your web site or other on-line location, by creating a likelihood of confusion with the complainant's mark as to the source, sponsorship, affiliation, or endorsement of your web site or location or of a product or service on your web site or location.

The pleadings in this case are consistent with Respondent's having adopted <madonna.com> for the specific purpose of trading off the name and reputation of the Complainant, and Respondent has offered no alternative explanation for his adoption of the name despite his otherwise detailed and complete submissions. Respondent has not explained why <madonna.com> was worth $20,000 to him or why that name was thought to be valuable as an attraction for a sexually explicit web site. . . . Respondent's use of a disclaimer on its web site is insufficient to avoid a finding of bad faith. First, the disclaimer may be ignored or misunderstood by Internet users. Second, a disclaimer does nothing to dispel initial interest confusion that is inevitable from Respondent's actions. Such confusion is a basis for finding a violation of Complainant's rights. . . . Because the evidence shows a deliberate attempt by Respondent to trade on Complainant's fame for commercial purposes, we find that Complainant has satisfied the requirements of Paragraph 4(a)(iii) of the Policy.

Decision

Under Paragraph 4(i) of the Policy, we find in favor of the Complainant. The disputed domain name is identical or confusingly similar to a trademark in which Complainant has rights; Respondent lacks rights or legitimate interests in the domain name; and the domain name has been registered and used in bad faith. Therefore, we decide that the disputed domain name <madonna.com> should be transferred to the Complainant.

Reduces Court Backlogs

The ODR option allows disputing parties to elect to resolve their conflicts without bringing an action in the courts, which helps to reduce court backlogs. Cutting down on court caseloads frees up the time of judges and court officials and allows other cases, not suitable for ODR, to move more quickly through the system. In addition, court resources are limited, and reductions in court dockets helps save on the public resources needed to operate the court system.

Prompts Court Reform

Many in society are clamoring for significant reforms of the judicial system in an effort to speed up court processes, improve public access to the courts, and increase public confidence in the judiciary. Yet it is often difficult to find broad consensus on the changes that should be made in court processes. The successful development of ADR methods and techniques have led the courts to learn from and borrow ADR methods to help streamline or augment court processes. In many states, the use of court-supervised ADR programs is required before a matter can be litigated or ADR processes may run a parallel track with court procedures. Over time, the use of ODR and the associated development of faster and more efficient interactive technologies may help provide important technological models for courts to aid in the streamlining of court proceedings and to improve the overall speed and effectiveness of the courts in meeting the needs of an ever-changing society.

What Are Some of the Disadvantages of ODR?

It is interesting to note that many of the advantages of ODR hide a double-edged sword. The main disadvantages of ODR flow from some of its essential benefits. These concerns include the need for party consent, the lack of face-to-face meetings, the problems with limited discovery, the loss of public access to ODR proceedings and public pressure on ODR participants, the difficulties related to the enforcement of ODR outcomes against noncomplying parties, and the absence of ODR standards and regulation. It is important to weigh both the advantages and disadvantages of ODR before developing or using these processes.

Need for Party Consent

Unlike traditional litigation, parties may prefer ODR because they must agree to participate in the process. Parties also enjoy greater control over the process and its outcomes. Unfortunately, although ODR gives parties the freedom to choose their method of conflict resolution, both parties must be willing to cooperate. Because ODR options are new, disputants may not use them because they are unfamiliar with these processes. Also, if one of the parties does not wish to use ODR or views settlement of the dispute as not in its best interest, then ODR proceedings cannot commence. Unlike the courts, which possess warrant and subpoena powers, no party or witness can be required to appear and resolve a dispute using ODR. If a disputant is uncooperative, then the parties may need to turn to the courts to process their disagreement.

Lack of Face-to-Face Contact

One of the benefits of ODR is that it allows parties who may be great distances from one another to work on resolving their difficulties. If the parties do not have to be in the same place at the same time, they can save time and money associated with travel to distant lands. Also, without ODR, the parties may be completely unable to find any forum in which to address their conflict issues.

Clearly, however, communication is more than the written word. Facial expressions, tone of voice and other body language are important components in human interaction. When using online technologies, such as instant messaging, chat rooms, list servs, and e-mail, the parties do not have a chance to face each other and to express themselves fully using body language or other nonverbal cues. Personal contact may help some parties to better understand the other side's concerns and recognize the importance of acting quickly to resolve the dispute. Also, some disputants may hide behind online technologies, flaming their opponent with one-sided e-mails or postings, thereby increasing the hostility and unfairly blurring the facts in a conflict. In addition, some online experts have indicated that a party may abuse online technologies to purposefully avoid face-to-face meetings, drag out the process, or ignore vital issues.

In such cases, the presence of a skilled online mediator or arbitrator may help to reduce such concerns if they arise. Also, the continued development of videoconferencing or streaming video over the Web may help to deal with the lack of traditional face-to-face contact. Further experimentation with new interactive technologies may also work to alleviate the gap between online and personal contact. But these potential problems should be considered when deciding whether or not to use ODR, because some online disputes may best be settled through direct personal contact, either in face-to-face meetings or over the telephone.

For example, internal employee disputes that arise online might be better handled in person or over the telephone. In a hypothetical example, let's say that a software development manager in Boston is very upset about remarks that a marketing manager in London made in an e-mail to a customer, blaming a product problem on the Boston development team. This manager believes that the marketing manager has made his department the scapegoat and insulted him and his software development unit. The software development manager fires back an e-mail to the marketing manager indicating that his unit refuses to work with her and is demanding an immediate retraction and an apology. In that instance, it may be best to have a conference call between the disputing employees rather than have them exchange possibly more inflammatory e-mail messages. By speaking directly to one another, with the help of their supervisors, their differences may be more quickly aired and resolved. If an apology is necessary, a spoken one over the telephone will carry much more weight than a written one sent online. Conversely, a consumer's installation problems with a particular product may be able to be ironed out in a few e-mails rather than requiring any face-to-face meetings.

Problems with Limited Discovery

In most nations of the world, discovery is already very limited, if it is allowed at all. However, in the United States, the discovery process is viewed as vital to due process or fundamental fairness in conflict resolution proceedings. By exchanging relevant documents, each side is putting a fuller picture of the case on the table, including documents that may be damaging to their position. Many times critical documents that support a claimant's assertions are found in the responding party's files or e-mail logs. Records in the claimant's control may also help a responding party to mount a worthy defense of its actions. With each side fully informed about the strengths and weaknesses of their contentions, the parties can sit down to meaningful settlement talks or present a complete view of a dispute for adjudication. Using ODR, discovery is more limited, which can save time and money, but which may also make it difficult to bring or defend against online claims. In simple cases, in which both parties are dealing primarily from the same documents, this restriction may not cause a problem. But in other more complex matters, limited discovery may not be beneficial to some parties.

Loss of Public Access and Pressure

Often parties wish to use ODR to allow the resolution of their conflicts in a confidential setting. In a private forum, disputants are more likely to be willing to exchange information, knowing that it will not be discussed outside of the conference room or appear in the newspapers. Courts have typically upheld the confidentiality of ADR proceedings. Yet critics of confidentiality express concerns that without the threat of public exposure or the risk of bad publicity, many parties, particularly corporations, may be able to hide information or wrongdoing from the general public. Under the cloak of ODR confidentiality, vital information about defective products, poor customer service, discriminatory hiring practices, or other unethical business conduct that may impact business, government, and consumer purchasing choices will remain largely unknown. Although confidentiality is the norm, some online experts are calling for greater openness in ODR cases to protect the public and to provide information to government agencies concerned about rooting out fraudulent Web-based conduct. There is still great debate about the broader policy issues of whether or not to limit confidentiality in ODR proceedings to protect the online community at large.

Enforcement of ODR Outcomes

As indicated in Chapter 1, it is often very difficult to obtain and enforce a foreign court judgment. It may be easier to enforce ODR arbitration awards than court decisions because of existing treaties on the enforcement of such awards. However, besides ODR arbitral proceedings, parties using negotiation and mediation must rely on their settlement agreement or contract as the enforcement tool. Similarly, those parties opting for virtual juries may need to enforce any verdicts under the contract terms of the simulated jury service. Good faith compliance with the agreed-upon set of solutions is expected but is not always assured. If a party decides not to comply with the settlement agreement, that party may be in breach of contract. The other party will have to turn to national courts to seek enforcement of the settlement contract, with all of its attendant complexities. Therefore, the time, effort, and money spent on the ODR proceeding will be lost, and a party may find itself right back in its initial position.

Even if parties look to national courts for enforcement help, it is unclear whether the courts will enforce such online settlement agreements or the settlement provisions of the ODR service provider's terms of use. There is no clear case law that indicates that courts view such agreements or provisions as valid or enforceable. Until ODR case law develops further, there is no certainty that courts will be able to play a role in the enforcement of online settlements.

Absence of Clear Standards for ODR Practice

At the present time, there are no clear standards for regulating the practices of ODR professionals and ODR services. Any person or business could claim to be an expert in ODR, even without the necessary educational, professional, and technological skills to provide quality ODR services. If a party feels that an ODR service provider has acted improperly or fraudulently, there is no regulatory body to turn to for help. Until appropriate standards are developed, parties must act very cautiously in their selection of ODR providers. The issues of ODR standards and regulation are discussed in greater length in Chapter 8.

Do E-Commerce Groups Support the Use of ODR?

Efforts to determine appropriate polices for the Web are the daily subject of great, and often acrimonious, debate. Although consumers worry about privacy, e-businesses decry attempts to curb their trade in customer information as hurting their marketing efforts. Government efforts to crack down on Internet pornography and hate speech are challenged as censorship and violations of free speech. State governors demand the right to tax e-commerce in an effort to recoup lost sales taxes, whereas dot.coms fight to remain profitable and to survive in a global marketplace. There seem to be no easy answers to the numerous business, legal, and ethical dilemmas facing the use of the Internet.

Yet, remarkably, virtually every major e-commerce stakeholder—governments, consumer groups, e-businesses, regulatory agencies, and academics—agree that national courts are not suitable for the resolution of most online disputes, because most disputes arise from cross-border transactions. Nearly all recognize that ODR holds great promise for fast, fair, and effective processing of online disputes in the global marketplace. In March 2000 and June 2000, respectively, a European Commission workshop in Brussels and an international conference hosted by the FTC and the Department of Commerce illustrated nearly across-the-board support for the use of ODR to help deal with online disagreements. Several key organizations, such as the Organisation for Economic Cooperation and Development (OECD), the BBBOnline, Electronic Commerce and Consumer Protections Group (ECCPG), and the Global Business Dialogue on Electronic Commerce (GBDe), have also stepped forward with codes of online business conduct that recommend the use of fair and transparent out-of-court mechanisms to handle online conflicts. You can review these various codes by visiting these sites: http://www.bbbonline.org/code/ code.asp, http://www.ecommercegroup.org/guidelines.htm, and http://consumerconfidence. gbde.org/trust_rec.html.

The American Bar Association (ABA) formed the Task Force on E-Commerce and Alternative Dispute Resolution that has studied the ODR field and the need to handle online disputes quickly, fairly, and effectively. The task force considered such ODR concerns as provider disclosure duties, security measures, record retention, process and document confidentiality, and conflicts of interest. The task force drafted its final report on dealing with disputes in e-commerce and proposed best practices, with an emphasis on disclosure obligations, for ODR service providers. To review the final report and proposed recommendations, visit http://www.law. washington.edu/ABA-eADR/home.html.

Although much work still needs to be done to address appropriate standards for ODR use, there is clear and comprehensive support for using these methods. Without ODR, many parties will be left with little or no recourse for dealing with their online disagreements.

ODR Bytes

The concept of ODR involves the practice of ADR methods that use online technologies to facilitate the resolution of conflicts. ADR principles and practices are the foundation for ODR practice.

E-businesses must determine what kind of ODR program and methods will work best for them and their customer base in their given industry. E-firms may decide to create their own in-house conflict resolution program, contract out these services to third party ODR providers, or rely on ODR services provided to them as members of professional organizations.

On the Web, the main forms of ODR practice are negotiation, mediation, arbitration, virtual juries, and hybrid processes, such as med-arb.

Negotiation and mediation are referred to as settlement mechanisms because they focus on the efforts of the competing parties to determine their needs and the outcomes of their dispute.

Arbitration and virtual juries are considered adjudicatory processes because third parties, and not the disputing sides involved in the disagreement, decide the result of the conflict.

Med-arb is a hybrid process blending both settlement-driven and adjudicatory methods.

The typical advantages of ODR for disputants include opening lines of communication and trust between the parties, saving the parties both time and money in resolving the conflict, and improving the parties' control over the process and its outcomes.

The main advantages of ODR to the public relate to helping to increase conflict resolution options, to reduce court caseloads, and to prompt reforms in existing court systems.

The major disadvantages of ODR include the need for party consent, the lack of face-to-face meetings, the problems with limited discovery, the loss of public access and pressure on ODR participants, and the difficulties related to the enforcement of ODR outcomes against noncomplying parties.

Virtually every major e-commerce stakeholder—governments, consumer groups, e-businesses, regulatory agencies, and academics—agree that national courts are not suitable for the resolution of most online cross-border disputes. Nearly all recognize that ODR holds great promise in dealing with the fast, fair, and effective processing of online disagreements.

ICANN's accredited ODR providers can help parties to protect their legitimate rights in trademarks and service marks from bad faith registrations of identical or confusingly similar domain names.

ODR Bookmarks

American Bar Association (ABA) Task Force on E-Commerce and Alternative Dispute Resolution
http://www.law.washington.edu/ABA-eADR/home.html

Better Business Bureau/BBBOnLine, Code of Online Business Practices
http://www.bbbonline.org/code/code.asp

Center for Public Resources (CPR) Institute for Dispute Resolution
http://www.cpradr.org

clickNsettle
http://www.clicknsettle.com

Cybersettle
http://www.cybersettle.com

ECCPG Guidelines for Merchant-to-Consumer Transactions and Commentary
http://www.ecommercegroup.org/guidelines.htm

GBDe Consumer Protection Guidelines
http://consumerconfidence.gbde.org/trust_rec.html

ICANN
http://www.icann.org

iCourthouse
http://www.i-courthouse.com

National Arbitration Forum
http://www.arb-forum.com

National Association of Manufacturers
http://www.nam.org

NovaForum
http://www.novaforum.com

OECD Consumer Protection Guidelines for E-Commerce
http://www.oecd.org/document/51/0,2340,en_2649_201185_1824435_1_1_1_1,00.html

Online Ombuds Office (OOO)
http://www.ombuds.org/center/ombuds.html

Online Resolution, Inc.
http://www.onlineresolution.com

Resolution Forum, Inc.
http:///www.resolutionforum.org

SquareTrade
http://www.squaretrade.com

WEBdispute
http://www.webdispute.com

Selected ODR Bibliography

Center for Law, Commerce and Technology, University of Washington School of Law. *Online Alternative Dispute Resolution: An Issues Primer* (2000). http://law.washington.edu/lct.

Council of Better Business Bureaus, Inc. *Protecting Consumers in Cross-Border Transactions: A Comprehensive Model for Alternative Dispute Resolution*. Arlington, VA: Council of Better Business Bureaus, Inc., 2000.

Ponte, Lucille M. "The Brave New World of ODR." *ADR in Business Newsletter* (Spring/Summer 2001). http://www.alsb.org.ADRNEWSLETTER.pdf.

Ponte, Lucille M. "Throwing Bad Money After Bad: Can Online Dispute Resolution (ODR) Really Deliver the Goods for the Unhappy Internet Shopper?" *Tulane J. of Tech. & Intell. Prop.* 3 (Spring 2001): 55.

Ponte, Lucille M., and Thomas D. Cavenagh. *Alternative Dispute Resolution in Business*. St. Paul, MN: West Educational Publishing, 1999.

Withrow, Kris. "Online Alternative Dispute Resolution: The 'Write' Forum for the Right Parties." *Mich. Tele. & Tech. L. Rev.* 6 (1999–2000). http://www.mttlr.org/forum/withrow.html.

3

Online Negotiation

CHAPTER FAQS

What is online negotiation?

How does a typical automated blind-bid negotiation site work?

What are some examples of software-enhanced negotiation sites?

Do asynchronous discussion negotiation sites provide another useful online negotiation option?

Are there other innovative approaches or features online negotiators should seek?

How does one prepare to negotiate online?

What advantages can be obtained through online negotiation?

What disadvantages may be entailed in online negotiation?

Process Introduction and Overview

Where will online buyers and sellers, both individual and corporate, go when they have a dispute that is not settled over the telephone with a customer service representative or the other party to an online transaction? As discussed in Chapter 1, traditional litigation is one option, but it is often more costly than the amount at stake in the dispute. Online negotiation is an attractive alternative to litigation for the resolution of a wide variety of disputes that arise in the course of online purchase transactions, other e-business matters, and disputes arising offline.

Negotiation is simply the process of refining and agreeing to the issues requiring resolution, establishing a range of compromise options from which to choose and selecting the appropriate options for settlement. Negotiation requires a balancing of one's own needs against the competing needs of another with a view toward arriving at an agreement that satisfies both sets of requirements. Negotiation is the most private of all dispute-resolution processes, because it normally does not require the introduction of third parties into the case and it can be faster and cheaper than litigation and other more formal dispute-resolution processes. Particularly effective negotiators endeavor to create a range of settlement options that address all the needs of the parties, with a view toward reaching a mutually satisfactory agreement.

For many though, negotiation is a challenging and daunting process because it is normally done face-to-face, often for significant stakes, and because many people fear and avoid conflict. Disputants rarely look forward to meeting with an opponent to consider negotiated outcomes, so they may leave a dispute unresolved or retain a lawyer to assist in negotiations, which can lead to a more formal, acrimonious negotiation process. In addition, many parties think that negotiation is risky, because there are usually no procedural rules or protection for the parties, such as those that protect them from unwise choices. Online negotiation processes can minimize many of these negotiation obstacles.

What Is Online Negotiation?

Negotiation in the context of an ongoing dispute is often a game of brinkmanship; both sides posture and make excessive demands and offers to settle. The result can be a protracted period of negotiation, one that is rarely cost- or time-effective and that is likely to do irreparable harm to a long-term business relationship. It is, in short, a game of legal 'chicken,' in which the party that blinks first and concedes gets the short end of the bargain.

Online negotiation eliminates from the bargaining process many of the aspects of negotiation that deter people from using negotiation more often. It is conducted electronically, without personal contact between the disputants; a computer functions as an intermediary, a conduit through which communication takes place. Parties thus have no need to feel apprehensive about live interaction with the other side or about having to respond instantly to new factual or legal issues or settlement proposals. Moreover, online negotiation is sometimes automated, so parties do not need to learn a complicated set of tactics or behaviors to conclude a dispute successfully. Finally, it is not subject to the normal time and space boundaries from which ordinary negotiation suffers; it can be done day or night and, generally, from any computer with Internet access. In short, online negotiation offers a large group of 'negotiation-phobic' people, particularly those who are comfortable with technology, a comfortable process for dispute resolution in a wide range of cases.

There are three types of online negotiation. In "automated blind-bid" models, parties use an online ADR service provider to enter dollar offers of settlement, all at once or in rounds of traded offers and counteroffers. One's opponent is made aware that an offer or series of offers has been entered, usually by means of an automated e-mail message, although the amount of the offer is typically not revealed without a visit to the web site. The responding party then enters a counteroffer or series of counteroffers. The case is declared settled when the numbers entered by each party are within a specified distance or within a preset dollar range; the case is declared closed without settlement if this does not occur. This form of online negotiation is popular with the insurance industry. Examples of each approach appear later in the chapter.

Parties with cases that present multiple issues, nonmonetary issues, or disputed facts may prefer a second online negotiation model called "software-enhanced negotiation." In this approach, parties enter information into 'groupware' applications that assist them in identifying and refining issues, seeing points of agreement, and generating mutually acceptable settlement options. In some instances, optimization software may be used to improve on the parties' proposed solutions.

Other parties may benefit from the use of a third online negotiation approach called "asynchronous communication"; this is useful in cases involving factual or legal disputes over multiple issues or noneconomic remedies, but in which consistent, direct contact with the other party is desirable. In this model, parties use a web site to communicate with one another through means that look very much like a chatroom. Instead of simply entering dollar figures, parties can electronically discuss the case and consider a range of settlement options.

Chart 3.1 offers a summary of the major characteristics of each online negotiation process as well as face-to-face negotiation.

How Does a Typical Automated Blind-Bid Negotiation Site Work?

What does an automated blind-bid negotiation process look like? Let's consider Cybersettle (http://www.cybersettle.com) as an example. The company first offered its approach to online dispute resolution in 1998 and has since then been named the "official and exclusive online settlement tool" of the *Association of Trial Lawyers of America*. The site employs a patented "double-blind bidding" process created by Cybersettle. Indeed, the company believes it has the first multiround online dispute resolution

Chart 3.1 Comparison of Negotiation Processes				
	Blind Bid	Asynchronous	Software Enhanced	Face-to-Face
Interactive	No	Yes	Yes	Yes
Duration	Limited	Indefinite	Indefinite	Indefinite
Binding	Yes	Yes	Yes	Yes
Noneconomic options	No	Yes	Yes	Yes
Multiple parties	No	Limited	Yes	Yes
Simultaneous multiple offers	No	Limited	Yes	Yes
Complex offers	No	Limited	Yes	Yes
Evidence to support offers	No	Limited	Limited	Yes

patent issued. To date, Cybersettle has processed more than 75,000 claims, representing more than $500 million in settlement dollars. There are in excess of 110,000 registered users currently on the Cybersettle system, including at least 100,000 attorneys, 10,000 claims adjusters, 180 major insurance companies, and 1,900 claims offices in the United States and Canada.

The Cybersettle site allows any party, plaintiff or defendant, to initiate a settlement negotiation, whether a formal lawsuit has been filed or not. Individuals represented by attorneys may use the site, consulting with their attorneys before making or responding to offers or allowing their attorneys to bid for them. No additional software (beyond an Internet browser) or special hardware is required of users of the blind-bid process because all the actual processing of the offers and counteroffers is conducted on the Cybersettle server. In addition, parties do not need to be technologically savvy to use the site because the site is user-friendly.

The process is entirely voluntary and, if successful, binding, although parties are expected to prepare settlement documents themselves. Costs associated with the process are relatively modest when compared to traditional methods of dispute resolution or conventional litigation. Cybersettle suggests that early use of the blind-bid process has maximum savings benefit, because litigation costs accelerate later in the life of a lawsuit as discovery and trial preparation intensify. Cybersettle charges an initial filing fee that depends on case size and the number of cases a client submits to the site; no additional fees are assessed if the case is not resolved. However, if the case is settled, an additional "success fee" is added; the amount of the fee depends upon the size of the settlement, but is never greater than $200.00 for attorneys or $250.00 for claims professionals. Users may apply for discounted rates based on a larger volume of claims.

A dispute is made available to parties for settlement through Cybersettle when a party to the dispute initiates the claim on the Cybersettle system. The opposing party is immediately notified, via e-mail, that the dispute is available for settlement online. The Cybersettle process allows parties to make a series of three rounds of maximum offers and minimum demands. These maximum offers of settlement represent the most a claim can settle for during any respective round. Cybersettle adds 20 percent to each minimum demand to create a "settlement range." If the maximum offer is greater than or equal to the minimum demand, the claim will settle for the average of the two amounts up to the maximum settlement offer made in that round. The service utilizes a system of offer and response that allows instantaneous comparison of the most recent bids from the parties.

Neither party has access to the other party's proposed settlement figures at any time during the process, so all offers are made based on a party's beliefs regarding their own case strengths and weaknesses. Claims are password-protected to further ensure privacy and cannot be accessed by anyone other than authorized users participating in a particular case. To protect information from hackers, data submitted to Cybersettle's secure web site is protected by a proprietary 128-bit SSL encryption system. In fact, Cybersettle itself never actually monitors the settlement offers and demands made by users. When a claim settles successfully, only the amount of the settlement is disclosed. Unsuccessful offers and demands expire and are erased from the system without further action by the parties.

A typical case negotiated on the Cybersettle site follows these steps: ordinarily, an insurance carrier/defendant begins by submitting three rounds of maximum offers, the greatest amount for which the party is willing to settle at each round, into the Cybersettle system (Screen 3.1).

The opposing party is notified that offers have been made and, after logging in, submits up to three rounds of minimum demands, the lowest number for which that party is willing to settle during any given round (Screen 3.2).

Cybersettle compares initiator round 1 with respondent round 1, and so forth. When the offer and demand reach the prescribed parameters, the case is declared settled; a case only settles when the offer exceeds the demand (Screen 3.3).

If the bid is not in that range, another bid may be entered (Screen 3.4).

Insurance carriers or other high-volume users may opt for a daily "batch upload" process. Using Cybersettle's customized software, an insurance company may automatically submit claims into Cybersettle after an adjuster has completed his or her case evaluation and assigned claim-settlement offers on each case. The system no

Screen 3.1

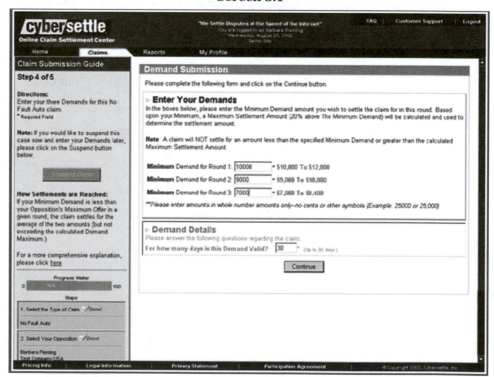

http://www.cybersettle.com/demo/walkpop.asp?wid=26

Screen 3.2

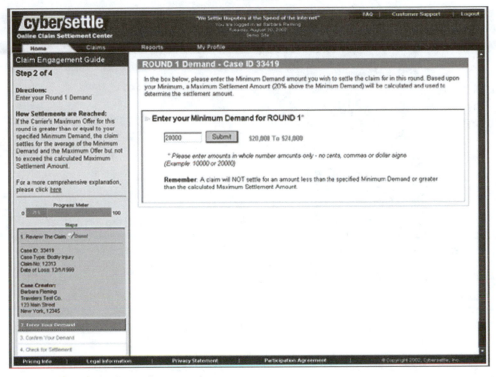

http://www.cybersettle.com/demo/walkpop.asp?wid = 18

longer requires that individual adjustors log on to a transactional Web site to submit claim information manually on a case-by-case basis.

The following brief, hypothetical situation illustrates the automated blind-bid process: Assume that Bill is involved in an auto accident with Melinda and suffers property damage and minor physical injuries. Following Bill's claim, Melinda's insurer submits the claim to Bill for negotiation on Cybersettle by making three rounds of offers in the amounts of $16,000, $20,000, and $24,000; Bill's attorney responds to Cybersettle's invitation to negotiation with demands of $32,000, $26,000, and $22,000. The result of each round and of the case would look like the following:

	Melinda: Maximum Offer	Bill: Minimum Demand	Maximum Settlement	Result
Round 1	$16,000	$32,000	$38,400	No settlement
Round 2	$20,000	$26,000	$31,200	No settlement
Round 3	$24,000	$22,000	$26,400	Settled: $23,000

(The case settled for the average of $22,000 and $24,000.)

Screen 3.3

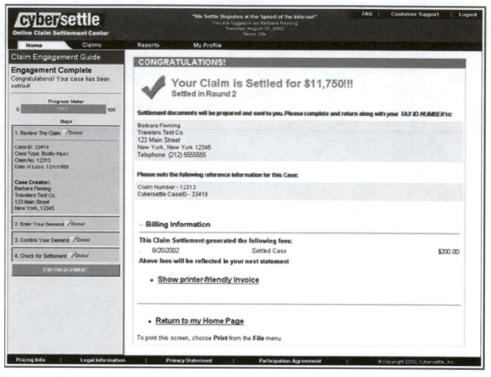

http://www.cybersettle.com/demo/walkpop.asp?wid=21

Although the overall advantages and disadvantages of online negotiation are considered later in this chapter, a number of benefits accruing to users of the automated blind-bid process are worth noting now. It is a process that allows parties to settle cases quickly and in a cost-effective manner relative to both litigation and traditional ADR, with or without attorneys. In addition, it eliminates personality conflicts and the communication difficulties that often arise between parties, because they do not interact directly with one another during the process. The process also allows participants the unique opportunity to make offers and demands confidentially—even as to the other party—without compromising future negotiations either online or offline and without hiring a live mediator.

Moreover, the process is almost always described as contractually binding on the web sites offering it, so consider the following cases, which offer guidance on when a party is bound by an online agreement. The first, involving a software-licensing question, confirms that users of Internet sites must specifically and affirmatively assent to any agreement that they expect courts to enforce. The second, somewhat more surprising, decision holds that in court-ordered proceedings, attorneys have the authority to settle on behalf of a client, even if they have not specifically discussed the terms of the agreement with the party. So, you may be sure that agreements are binding only

Screen 3.4

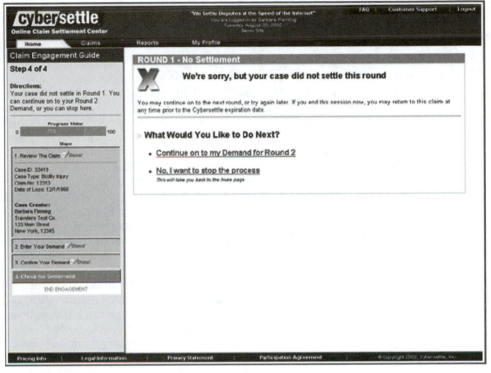

http://www.cybersettle.com/demo/walkpop.asp?wid=19

if someone, you or your attorney, explicitly and positively agree. However, you might find yourself bound to a settlement you don't like if you don't manage your attorney properly.

KEY CHAPTER CASES

When Is a Settlement Final?

Specht v Netscape Communications, **150 F.Supp.2d 585 (United States District Court for the Southern District of New York, 2001)**

Fact Summary: In these actions, Plaintiffs allege that usage of SmartDownLoad software transmits to Defendants private information about the user's file-transfer activity on the Internet, thereby effecting an electronic surveillance of the user's activity, in violation of two federal statutes. Defendants move to compel arbitration, arguing that the disputes reflected in the Complaint, like all others relating to use of the software, are subject to a binding arbitration clause in the End User License Agreement, the contract allegedly made by the person offering the software and the party effecting the download. Thus, I am asked to decide if an offer of a license agreement, made independently of freely offered software and not expressly accepted by a user of that software binds the user to an arbitration clause contained in the license.

OPINION: The opinion of the court was delivered by HELLERSTEIN, J.

I must determine whether the parties entered into a binding contract. More specifically, I must consider whether the web site gave Plaintiffs sufficient notice of the existence and terms of the License Agreement, and whether the act of downloading the software sufficiently manifested Plaintiffs' assent to be bound by the License Agreement.

Promises become binding when there is a meeting of the minds and consideration is exchanged. So it was at King's Bench in common law England; so it was under the common law in the American colonies; so it was through more than two centuries of jurisprudence in this country; and so it is today. Assent may be registered by a signature, a handshake, or a click of a computer mouse transmitted across the invisible ether of the Internet. Formality is not a requisite; any sign, symbol or action, or even willful inaction, as long as it is unequivocally referable to the promise, may create a contract. The case before me involves this timeless issue of assent, but in the context of free software offered on the Internet. If an offeree downloads free software, and the offeror seeks a contractual understanding limiting its uses and applications, under what circumstances does the act of downloading create a contract? On the facts presented here, is there the requisite assent and consideration?

The sale of software, in stores, by mail, and over the Internet, has resulted in several specialized forms of license agreements. For example, software commonly is packaged in a container or wrapper that advises the purchaser that the use of the software is subject to the terms of a license agreement contained inside the package. The license agreement generally explains that, if the purchaser does not wish to enter into a contract, he or she must return the product for a refund, and that failure to return it within a certain period will constitute assent to the license terms. These so-called "shrink-wrap licenses" have been the subject of considerable litigation [and courts have consistently held that] a vendor, as master of the offer, may invite acceptance by conduct, and may propose limitations on the kind of conduct that constitutes acceptance. A buyer may accept by performing the acts the vendor proposes to treat as acceptance [even if] he had no choice, because [for example] the software splashed the license on the screen and would not let him proceed without indicating acceptance.

A "click-wrap license" presents the user with a message on his or her computer screen, requiring that the user manifest his or her assent to the terms of the license agreement by clicking on an icon. The product cannot be obtained or used unless and until the icon is clicked. The few courts that have had occasion to consider click-wrap contracts have held them to be valid and enforceable. A third type of software license, a "browse-wrap" license presents notice of a license agreement on the plaintiff's web site. Clicking on the notice links the user to a separate web page containing the full text of the license agreement, which allegedly binds any user of the information on the site. However, the user is not required to click on an icon expressing assent to the license, or even view its terms, before proceeding to use the information on the site.

The SmartDownload License Agreement resembles the browse-wrap license. Smart-Download allows a user to download and use the software without taking any action that plainly manifests assent to the terms of the associated license or indicates an understanding that a contract is being formed. An offeree, regardless of apparent manifestation of his consent, is not bound by inconspicuous contractual provisions of which he was unaware, contained in a document whose contractual nature is not obvious.

Netscape argues that the mere act of downloading indicates assent. However, downloading is hardly an unambiguous indication of assent. The primary purpose of downloading is to obtain a product, not to assent to an agreement. In contrast, clicking on an icon stating "I assent" has no meaning or purpose other than to indicate such assent. Netscape's failure to require users of SmartDownload to indicate assent to its license as a precondition to downloading and using its software is fatal to its argument that a contract has been formed.

Furthermore, unlike the user of Netscape Navigator or other click-wrap or shrink-wrap licensees, the individual obtaining SmartDownload is not made aware that he is entering into a contract. SmartDownload is available from Netscape's web site free of charge. Before downloading the software, the user need not view any license agreement terms or even any reference to a license agreement, and need not do anything to manifest assent to such a license agreement other than actually taking possession of the product. From the user's vantage point, SmartDownload could be analogized to a free neighborhood newspaper, readily obtained from a sidewalk box or supermarket counter without any exchange with a seller or vender. It is there for the taking. The only hint that a contract is being formed is one small box of text referring to the license agreement, text that appears below the screen used for downloading and that a user need not even see before obtaining the product.

The case law on software licensing has not eroded the importance of assent in contract formation. Mutual assent is the bedrock of any agreement to which the law will give force. Defendants' position, if accepted, would so expand the definition of assent as to render it meaningless. Because the user did not assent to the license agreement, they are not subject to the arbitration clause contained therein and cannot be compelled to arbitrate their claims against the Defendants.

Koval v Simon Telelect, 693 N.E.2d 1299; 1998 Ind. LEXIS 34 (Supreme Court of Indiana, 1998)

Fact Summary: The issues arise out of a product liability suit in federal court by Michael and Jean Koval against both the manufacturer and distributer of a device that allegedly caused injuries to Michael in the course of his employment. Michael's employer, Henkels & McCoy, and its insurance carrier, Liberty Mutual, paid Michael's medical and disability benefits. The certified questions result from a settlement agreement reached at a mediation attended by persons who seemingly believed they represented all interested parties. One of those was an attorney apparently representing both H&M and Liberty Mutual, who agreed to a settlement that compromised the interests of both the employer and the insurer. H&M had not authorized Liberty Mutual or the attorney to settle and later refused to honor the settlement.

OPINION: The opinion of the court was delivered by BOEHM, J.

If an attorney settles a claim as to which the attorney has been retained, but does so without the client's consent, is the settlement binding between third parties and the client? The answer to this question is the same as to many others: it depends. An attorney's authority may be derived from the conduct of the client, either with respect to the third parties who deal with the attorney or with respect to the attorney. It may also derive from the nature of the proceedings in which the attorney represents the client and enters into a settlement agreement. In order to bind the client the attorney must have either express, implied, or apparent authority, or must act according to the attorney's inherent agency power.

For the reasons explained below, we conclude that the sole act of retaining an attorney does not give the attorney the implied or the apparent authority to settle or compromise a claim in an out of court proceeding. Specifically, retention in and of itself neither confers the implied authority to settle a claim, nor is it a manifestation by the client to third parties such that the attorney is clothed with the apparent authority to settle. However, under longstanding Indiana authority, retention does equip an attorney with the inherent power to bind a client to the results of a procedure in court. We hold that for purposes of an attorney's inherent power, a procedure governed by Indiana's Rules for Alternative Dispute Resolution is a procedure "in court" if the parties are expected to appear by representatives with authority to resolve the matter. Accordingly, in the absence of a communication of lack of authority by the attorney, as a matter of law, an attorney has the inherent power to settle a claim when the attorney attends a settlement procedure governed by the ADR rules.

Authority is the power of the agent to affect the legal relations of the principal by acts done in accordance with the principal's manifestations of consent to him. Authority can be express or implied and may be conferred by words or other conduct, including acquiescence. Implied authority can arise from words used, from customs, or from the relations of the parties. The agent is authorized if the agent is reasonable in drawing an inference from the principal's actions that the principal intended to confer authority. It is well settled that an attorney, by virtue of the representation, becomes a powerful agent with a great deal of authority. Retention confers on an attorney the general implied authority to do on behalf of the client all acts in or out of court necessary or incidental to the prosecution or management of the suit or the accomplishment of the purpose for which the attorney was retained. Litigants must necessarily be held bound by the acts of their attorneys in the conduct of a cause in court, in the absence, of course, of fraud. A variant on this theme is that in court the client speaks through the attorney who is deemed the same as the client. The reason behind this rule stems from the setting of an in court proceeding and the unique role of an attorney-agent in that setting. Proceedings in court transpire before a neutral arbiter in a formal and regulated atmosphere, where those present expect legally sanctioned action or resolution of some kind. A rule that did not enable an attorney to bind a client to in court action would impede the efficiency and finality of courtroom proceedings and permit stop and go disruption of the court's calender.

The question remains what constitutes an "in court" proceeding in this age of alternative dispute resolution. We conclude that the same reasons that justify the exception to the general rule for in court proceedings are present in proceedings governed by the ADR rules, in which a rule, an order of the convening authority, or the agreement of the parties provides for authorized representation. An ADR method is a formal proceeding where the parties are assembled in a setting subject to the court's jurisdiction, before a court appointed or otherwise approved official, in a court sanctioned environment, for the express purpose of settling a claim, and with the set expectation that those attending have the authority to do so. These are unlike an unstructured negotiation, where it is reasonable to conclude that the client may not have authorized the settlement and there is no reasonable assumption that the attorney was empowered with the authority to settle. In sum, the rule that an attorney has the inherent power to bind the client to an in court judgment applies to proceedings governed by the ADR rules in which the parties are ordered, required by the rule, or agree to appear through authorized representatives. These proceedings are "in court" for purposes of an attorney's inherent power, irrespective of whether they actually occur inside a courtroom. This rule will not only further the successful practice of mediation and other ADR methods, as effective means of resolving disputes without resort to a full fledged trial, but it also supports Indiana's strong judicial policy in favor of settlement agreements.

What Are Some Examples of Software-Enhanced Negotiation Sites?

Automated blind-bid sites allow parties with cases involving primarily uncontested, economic issues to trade offers and demands conveniently. Some cases, however, present disputes over facts or issues, questions of law, and/or a range of remedy options, both economic and noneconomic, that are not well suited to the automated blind-bid process. These cases are still negotiable online but are better handled in a different forum. Software-enhanced negotiation sites offer parties the opportunity to negotiate complex cases with the same ease of access and technological assistance as automated blind-bid sites offer in less complex matters.

There are fewer web sites offering this service than there are offering blind-bid processes, but three vendors warrant consideration in this chapter. Smartsettle™ (www.smartsettle.com) has developed a software package that takes disputants through a six-step negotiation process aimed at resolving disputes with, according to the site, any "combination of quantitative or qualitative issues." The software, which is provided to users free, is downloaded onto the computers of each party and used locally throughout the process; uploads of user input into the software take place frequently, but at the user's discretion. In addition to the assistance provided by the software, a Smartsettle facilitator works with the parties throughout the process, offering support with the software as well as managing the administrative aspects of the case.

The interactive Smartsettle software with optimization algorithms was developed at Cornell University. It is designed to assist parties, of which there may be any number, throughout each step of the process by comparing input results from all parties. The software seeks common language about the dispute, identifies issues and options upon which there is agreement and guides the parties to solutions that seek to be fair to all the parties. The six Smartsettle negotiation steps are as follows.

- *Prepare for Negotiation*: Parties review and agree to abide by Smartsettle Guidelines for Conduct. They may also examine numerous examples of cases negotiated via Smartsettle posted on the company's website. If they decide to use the process, parties request a case number and engage a facilitator; if a case involves particularly sensitive information, trade secrets perhaps, each party may request its own private facilitator.

- *Qualify Interests*: The facilitator sets up the case online, provides Smartsettle access codes to each party, and assists the parties in using the Smartsettle software to refine their interests and identify the issues requiring resolution; specific settlement demands are not yet made. This step in the process ends when parties agree independently on a "Framework for Agreement," which describes all unresolved issues between them on which they will negotiate.

- *Quantify Satisfaction*: Continuing to use the client software and with the further assistance of the facilitator, bargaining ranges are created with values from each party. The Smartsettle facilitator works independently with each party to elicit their initial, private preferences for settlement. Confidentiality is maintained throughout the process; parties decide what information is shared with the opposing party as well as when, how, and in what form it is shared.

- *Establish Equity*: Parties exchange information either through the web site and facilitator or directly with one another. They may also offer concessions to their initial settlement preferences, again either privately to the facilitator for use in assessing the likelihood of settlement or directly to the other side. Based on party preferences and concessions made by each party, the software assists the parties in creating comprehensive settlement packages for party consideration. "Equity" is achieved when parties accept an identical settlement package as a tentative solution.

- *Maximize Benefits*: The process doesn't end there. The software is designed not simply to achieve agreement, but also to assist the parties in realizing settlement agreements that exceed the minimum acceptable range of options. Party preferences are refined by the parties using the software and with help from the facilitator; during this step parties generate improvements to the tentative solution reached in the preceding step.
- *Secure Commitment*: The "Framework for Agreement" is completed and signed by all parties when a final resolution is reached.

The Smartsettle process allows parties to combine online and face-to-face meetings if they choose to do so or to conduct the entire process using the software and the facilitator. Access to the site is available anytime, day or night. Smartsettle does not impose any fixed time limit for negotiation or fixed limit on the number of proposals that parties can make in the course of negotiation. Parties are in complete control of how long they wish to negotiate and may terminate a case at any time. If they do so, they may export their private settlement information to a file on their own computers for their permanent records. At that point, any information remaining on the Smartsettle site associated with that party is no longer accessible. Negotiations not completed successfully with Smartsettle can continue in some other venue, whether traditional ADR or litigation.

The Smartsettle system is based on a negotiating approach called "preference analysis", by which Smartsettle software assesses how each party can be satisfied. With that knowledge, Smartsettle can offer settlement suggestions that will simultaneously satisfy all parties when they reach an impasse. Because each party has Smartsettle software installed locally, preferences relative to settlement can be elicited and analyzed locally and confidentially. Only after that local analysis is completed does a party communicate with the patented Smartsettle neutral site.

The website is strictly guarded by Smartsettle. The parties' data are protected by password; a party may change any aspect of their confidential information, including password and access codes, at any time. If a settlement is reached, the terms and conditions of the final agreement are known only to the parties themselves. The site is invisible to the user, who sees only the software installed on the local PC, and the physical location of the server is not public knowledge. Further, Smartsettle server functions are contained within a "Virtual Private Network" controlled by ICAN Systems Inc., the license holder of the software, to maximize protection of client confidences. Communication between the server and clients is encrypted using OpenSSL algorithms with a 168-bit triple-DES encryption algorithm. The Smartsettle process can be seen in its entirety through a fascinating model negotiation at the following link: http://www.smartsettle.com/more/cwk2003/content.php?results.html.

Another option for software enhanced negotiating is OnlineResolution.com (http://www.OnlineResolution.com). The site provides a variety of online tools for negotiators that assist in developing a problem-solving agenda, contribute to effective dialogue on the issues, and help identify potential solutions. The OnlineResolution process can also evaluate the likely strengths and weaknesses of any proposed settlement agreement and will even assist in organizing and drafting a final settlement agreement. The OnlineResolution proprietary software enables parties to consider important factual aspects of the dispute, to express thoughts and emotions, and to think clearly and creatively about the best way to solve the problem, as well as how to present desired outcomes to the other side.

The process starts when one party completes the "confidential information form" describing the case. Information contained on the form is initially seen only by the party completing it and an OnlineResolution administrator, who contacts the other party to solicit its participation. If the other party agrees to participate, that party also completes the form. Thereafter, by amending the form, each party may share proposals to settle the case and the information and arguments that support those proposals. OnlineResolution software tracks points of agreement and allows parties who cannot negotiate a resolution to enter into online mediation or arbitration at the same web site.

Another example of software-enhanced negotiation comes from a company called GroupMind Express (http://www.groupmindexpress.com), which has developed an online negotiation package that allows parties to prepare a case for negotiation and, if one wishes, to actually negotiate the matter via its software at its secure web site. Individuals or teams from multiple locations can use the software to prepare for and conduct negotiations, discuss terms and conditions online, edit potential contracts, and finalize agreements. In this sense the software is not only for dispute resolution, but also for the formation and conduct of long-term business relationships.

GroupMind Express offers a secure web site at which parties can manage all their negotiation preparation and execution. The software manages information about participants in a negotiation as well as all discussions conducted to prepare for negotiation. The site is even able to preserve a summary of actual negotiation preparation and bargaining sessions to assist parties in finalizing agreements accurately. The site also offers redlining features and a mechanism that prevents overwriting of new portions of an offer with older versions when multiple users are negotiating by providing a single negotiation-preparation document that is always accessible to all participants. In addition, private discussions with others assisting in preparing or participating in the negotiation are possible. Significantly, access to the online software can be obtained at any time, even among geographically dispersed participants. Lotus QuickPlace (http://www.lotus.com/home.nsf/welcome/quickplace) offers a similar collaborative software platform.

Negotiating online with software assistance has several advantages. First, complex cases can be managed in an environment that avoids personality conflicts and misunderstanding. Second, depending on the software package used, the online process may replace or augment mailed or faxed documents with a single current version of the working document or settlement package, which is constantly improving. Third, like blind-bid models, it may reduce the cost, in both time and money terms, of reaching agreements by streamlining the process of negotiation preparation and actual bargaining and by reducing the administrative tasks associated with complex negotiation. Fourth, and perhaps most significantly, given the sophisticated fashion by which options are created and assessed, the results of the process may be better than anything that can be achieved face-to-face.

Do Asynchronous Discussion Negotiation Sites Provide Another Useful Online Negotiation Option?

In cases in which a negotiator feels unable to present a case well face-to-face but in which contact with the other party is desirable, asynchronous online negotiation may be the best option. Several web sites provide an asynchronous discussion option, including SquareTrade.com (http://www.squaretrade.com), which offers "Direct Negotiation," a process that involves two parties involved in a SquareTrade case in a direct electronic discussion. After the parties have agreed to participate in ODR, they discuss their issues through a password-protected "Case Page" on the SquareTrade web site. SquareTrade cases are ordinarily limited to relatively minor online transaction disputes, so this process is somewhat less feature-rich than some other online services. This initial phase of the service is a completely automated web-based communications tool and is currently free of charge to all users. Using SquareTrade's secure Case Page, the parties try to reach an agreement by communicating directly with each other.

Like other forms of online negotiation, asynchronous discussion allows parties to remain physically distant from one another, whether because they are geographically distant or because they prefer computer over face-to-face communication. It also shares many of the cost and expediency advantages of other online negotiation approaches. It has the capacity, however, to produce agreements that are as rich and nuanced as face-to-face negotiation processes, and perhaps even better.

Are There Other Innovative Approaches or Features Online Negotiators Should Seek?

Online negotiators have numerous vendor options from which all three online negotiation models are available. In assessing those options, they may wish to look for some of the following features on the sites they are considering. There are a variety of timing options available to parties using the automated blind-bid process. Some automated blind-bid sites give parties time limits for each round of negotiations in an effort to expedite settlement responses and preserve a sense of certainty in terms of timing. The parties may have, for example, twenty days to respond in round 1, ten days to respond in rounds 2 and 3, and shorter time periods if the negotiations start close to a trial date. Other blind-bid sites allow parties to make an unlimited number of offers within a set time period. All these sites normally also allow parties to modify the time limits or terminate the negotiation when that is necessary.

The bidding process itself may also be conducted differently from site to site. Some sites require parties to move a given percentage, say 10 percent, toward their adversary with each new settlement bid to encourage good-faith negotiation. Another approach to assuring meaningful participation is to charge user fees by the bid rather than by the case. This approach encourages thoughtful use of each bidding round and discourages outrageous offers meant to artificially inflate settlement amounts. In addition, there are sites that offer a mechanism for withdrawing an offer if it has not yet been reviewed or accepted, should a party have second thoughts about the offer. Finally, users may benefit from sites that utilize a "final bid" feature that notifies the opposing party that their adversary has entered a "settle or walk away" figure.

In addition to differences in timing and bidding approaches, users of online negotiation should consider the importance of the following matters to their cases irrespective of the negotiation model being used:

- Consistent with most live ADR services that seek to avoid the appearance of conflicts of interest, some sites require equal payment from both parties for participation in the process. Sites may also disclaim any economic relationship with large volume users for the same reason.
- A number of sites offer online case management and reporting features that enable users to monitor and measure the results of ADR use for both online and traditional ADR procedures. Detailed reports from these sites outline important aspects of particular cases and summarize overall ADR results.
- At some sites, unsuccessful final offers may be disclosed through an agreement reached at the beginning of the negotiation process. In an effort to assist parties to reach settlement, if the filing party and opposing party agree to the disclosure arrangement, the final offers are disclosed to the parties in an effort to spur settlement at a later date or facilitate the use of other alternative dispute resolution procedures.
- Most sites offer special features that allow parties to check the status of ongoing cases simply by logging into the site. On other sites, parties are provided with case status pages that reflect all significant elements of each case on which a party is using the site to negotiate.

ODR IN THE DIGITAL ERA Global Business Dialogue on Electronic Commerce	Cochaired by the heads of America Online and Time Warner, the Global Business Dialogue on E-Commerce (GBDe) is a coalition of well-recognized, multinational companies that share an interest in the promotion of online commerce and in the prompt, reliable resolution of disputes resulting from e-commerce. GBDe recognizes the unique nature of online commerce and of the disputes it fosters. Jurisdiction is never clear, existing laws are contradictory, and the value of the goods or services at issue is often eclipsed by the cost of resolving the disputes they create. They argue that ODR mechanisms are the most expeditious, least expensive, and, therefore, most attractive option for resolving those disputes from both business and consumer perspectives.

(continued)

The group has as its principal objective the development and adoption of business-friendly, but meaningful, international self-regulatory codes of online conduct for e-commerce companies. In addition, the group supports the creation of private, independent ODR systems for the resolution of consumer complaints about e-commerce transactions and activities. Accordingly, the group addresses recommendations to providers of ODR. Finally, the group regards government regulation of ODR as counter-productive and proposes a "hands-off" approach for government at all levels.

The final draft of the GBDe recommendations, entitled *Alternative Dispute Resolution and e-Confidence Recommendations*, was approved in August 2000. Since that time, GBDe representatives have endeavored to lobby both businesses and governments to adopt all or some of the recommendations. In general, the recommendations urge online companies to offer consumers ODR approaches for the resolution of complaints resulting from online commerce participation. More specifically, e-tailers are urged to try in-house dispute resolution initially but to offer mediation and arbitration options to consumers when in-house options fail, because in-house mechanisms may lack the level of impartiality that consumers seek. The code also addresses government regulation of online dispute resolution by proposing that legislative bodies decline to regulate ODR and defer to the ODR service providers the right of self-regulation through meaningful codes of conduct. The bottom line for the group: building and maintaining consumer confidence in online commerce by addressing the possibility of complaints with methods of resolution that are clear, fair, and prompt. New recommendations, meant to address technological advancements, are posted as approved at the GBDe web site at http://www.gbde.org/gbde2003.html.

How Does One Prepare to Negotiate Online?

One prepares to conduct an online negotiation basically the same way, irrespective of the online or offline model chosen. Thorough preparation is essential to effective negotiation, and there are at least three aspects of good preparation to negotiate. First, one must carefully gather and assess the facts underlying the dispute, because effective negotiators begin the process with a clear understanding of the factual background of the case and a set of well-defined goals and objectives relative to settlement. At this stage negotiators will consider both economic and noneconomic issues.

Second, one must establish a case value and devise specific settlement options consistent with that value. Costs to pursue other avenues for resolution, like arbitration or a trial, should be factored into the analysis of case value as well. Attorney fees are a critical factor in evaluating the cost to settle or adjudicate versus the value of the case.

Third, one must anticipate the offers and strategies likely to be used by the opposing party, including anticipated counteroffers and assertions of fact. One might also consider how a jury or a judge is likely to respond to the case at trial or arbitra-

One approach to making an informed judgment about the settlement value of a case is to develop a decision tree. Decision trees are sophisticated tools for numeric analysis. Although the decision tree can be fairly elaborate, even in a relatively simple matter, the value of this approach can be significant.

Essentially, a decision tree assists a negotiator in evaluating the dollar value of a case by considering the options that will arise at various points in the case, assigning probabilities to the outcomes at those points, and making economic judgments about expected outcomes. Here is a very simple, but illustrative, example of a decision tree used to resolve the following question: how much should one bet on a coin flip after which the correct guess gains $5.00 and an incorrect guess costs $1.00?

How Much Would You Pay to Play?

You win $5.00 if heads comes up but lose $1.00 if tails is the result!

Solution

Two possibilities: heads or tails
Probabilities: 50% for each possibility
Probabilities × possibilities = estimated value for each potential outcome

$$50\% \times \$5.00 = \quad \$2.50$$
$$50\% \times -\$1.00 = -\$0.50$$

Therefore, the right bet is $2.00

tion to fully understand the risks of using venues. It is important to note that one who lacks experience in evaluating and settling disputes may benefit from consultation with an attorney possessing experience in the disputed area.

There are a number of software options for preparing for online negotiation as an alternative to the traditional "pen-and-paper" analysis. We have already discussed  Beachfire's negotiation software. Another program is Negotiator Pro™ (http://www. negotiatorpro. com), which takes a negotiator through a specialized interview to assist in thoroughly understanding the underlying facts of the case and to generate settlement options. The latest international version has several different question formats and lengths; the more complex the case, the more questions one might benefit from answering. Each question has standard responses built into the software to assist the negotiator in preparing, but the software allows for case-specific, user-generated responses as well. A printable summary of the questions and responses is made available to the negotiator for use during the negotiation.

In addition, the package provides more than 700 minitutorials on negotiation theory and practice. Most of the material is excerpted from experts in the field of negotiation and is intended as a resource to support the completion of the questionnaire. In addition, the package includes an extensive hyperlinked glossary. Finally, the software's "small expert system" helps identify personality types of negotiation participants that might effect the negotiation based on input from the negotiator. You may wish to surf the web to sample other helpful online negotiation preparation sites, such as previously mentioned GroupMind Express (http://www.groupmindexpress.com).

What Advantages Can Be Obtained through Online Negotiation?

Perhaps the most significant advantage to online negotiation in all its varieties is that it is available at the convenience of the user, anytime, any day, and from almost any terminal. There are many additional advantages that are also worth discussing. More than any other online process, this one is able, at least under ideal circumstances, to achieve considerable economic savings. The fees for use assessed by the sites are nominal, generally speaking. Indeed, many sites charge less to resolve a case through online negotiation than the fees assessed in most state or federal courts just to file a claim. Furthermore, the process is so simple that the need for legal advice regarding participation in the process is likely to be minimal in most cases. In fact, it is possible to proceed without counsel at all, and even if one uses an attorney, the time spent on the process is so minimal that legal fees are likely to be somewhat reduced relative to other forms of ADR and vastly reduced relative to litigation. On the whole then, substantial money savings are possible.

Time savings are also very likely to be realized in this process. The automated blind-bid process does not require one to explain or justify offers or demands made. Instead, it simply transmits numbers from one party to the other; other processes typically expect abbreviated statements of support for proposals offered. As a result, parties do not spend nearly the time required to prepare for face-to-face processes. Of course actual participation time is also reduced, because it is limited to input sessions at the web site rather than travel to and participation in a live meeting of the parties. Indeed, once one has mastered a particular online system, the time spent entering data can be significantly reduced.

Online negotiation is generally cheaper and faster than litigation; indeed, it may be cheaper and faster than face-to-face forms of ADR. As a result, online negotiation can serve as a sort of case filter for lawyers and business clients by settling cases ripe for early agreement and identifying by failure the cases that will need more significant attention and involvement. As lawyers and insurance professionals manage larger and more complex dockets, this ability to dispose of some cases inexpensively and rapidly, and in doing so to devote greater resources to more complex matters, is a very attractive benefit of online negotiation.

Moreover, by settling appropriate cases early, the risk of unusual or surprising outcomes is limited significantly. Parties have greater control over the outcome of each case because they set the outside boundaries within which the case will settle or make carefully crafted online proposals through software-enhanced or asynchronous sites. Parties may be pleasantly surprised by a blind-bid case settling at an amount lower than expected, but the risk of a judge, jury, or arbitrator deciding a case negatively is eliminated from the process.

Furthermore, the process may be a useful antecedent to face-to-face ADR or litigation because it narrows the settlement range. Parties have the benefit of submitting offers and demands to attempt a quick agreement on terms they deem favorable. Failing agreement online, parties have a sense of the range in which the other party seeks to settle because of the offers or demands that have been made and rejected. In addition, each side can test its top or bottom settlement amount, because if the case does not settle, the other side will not learn what the highest or lowest numbers were.

Online negotiation probably allows parties an environment where error is less likely because parties are not coerced or deceived by more effective or unscrupulous negotiators into a settlement they would not otherwise accept. Parties don't physically see one another, nor do they have an obligation to respond to the other side immediately, so they have time to think, refine and calculate. Furthermore, because the offers are always transmitted via computer, there is a permanent record of the offers and demands and the concomitant certainty that such a record provides. Parties with disabilities may benefit significantly from online negotiation if they need more time to prepare and deliver an offer or demand because virtually all forms of online negotiation provide such time.

In addition to the practical and pecuniary advantages, the process offers intangible benefits as well. Parties who dislike face-to-face negotiating processes are spared engaging in them. Parties need not fear appearing weak by letting the other side know what their settlement value is because demands and offers are private. In fact, because settlement offers and demands are generally kept confidential, users can negotiate without the fear of "benchmarking" their position in the event the case does not settle. This allows both parties to make their "best" offer or demand without the risk of having it used against them at a later point in some other settlement or adjudication process.

Finally, online negotiation has great promise in cases involving parties with different language or cultural backgrounds. Both parties, in effect, have entered a truly neutral place—the Internet—so there is no debate about where a negotiation will take place or whose customs will apply. Arguments supporting offers and demands to settle can be thoughtfully constructed, presented, fully translated, and digested upon receipt and before a reply is made. Moreover, parties translating offers and demands into another language may need more time to prepare at each step of the negotiation, and online processes provide that time without creating the appearance that one negotiator is more prepared or more capable than another.

Quick Clicks: Review the Fine Print   Go to Cybersettle.com and review the "fine print," namely, the *Terms of Use* at this link: www.cybersettle.com/legal/terms.asp; the *Legal Disclosure* at this link: www.cybersettle.com/legal/statement.asp; and the *Privacy Statement* at this link: www.cybersettle.com/legal/privacy.asp. Who is the primary beneficiary of these legal protections, you or the site owner? Are you satisfied that all your important legal rights are addressed? If you could make changes, what would you add or change, from a user perspective, before using the Cybersettle.com service?

What Disadvantages May Be Entailed in Online Negotiation?

Before we consider some of the substantive disadvantages of online negotiation, it is worth reviewing some of the potential technological difficulties users may encounter. Online negotiation processes will obviously function only on computers with Internet access, but it is important to note that interactive processes such as asynchronous discussion function much better on computers with high-speed access, perhaps DSL or cable. Memory, the proper graphics card, and other hardware-oriented matters may also affect one's ability to negotiate online effectively. In addition to Internet access and hardware issues, software compatibility should be considered. Older browsers, for example, may not always support the applications available to online negotiators. Furthermore, because some of the sites providing the service have the capacity to integrate documents, a party's ability to scan and/or fax documents may also play a role in deciding whether one can negotiate online effectively.

Automated blind-bid negotiation is probably better suited to smaller cases that cannot justify the expense of more costly ADR methods because it is a process with several downsides. First, the process is generally suitable for money settlements only; there is little or no room for creativity in the negotiation approach or in the invention of novel or noneconomic settlement options. The negotiator who would profit from approaches that are unconventional is less well served by online blind-bidding sites. Furthermore, blind-bid negotiation diminishes the value of good negotiation skills, so the genuinely effective negotiator will probably still prefer face-to-face processes with inflection, body language, and other nonverbal cues. Finally, online automated blind bidding may encourage premature participation by parties who have not yet fully assessed a case but think they do not have to do so because they will not be required to argue in favor of any offer made online.

All models of online negotiation are impersonal, so the processes do not allow for the same potential long-term relationship building that more traditional forms of ADR permit and, in fact, encourage. Online negotiation, and to an extent all online dispute resolution, depersonalizes problems. Indeed, one of the advantages of virtually all online processes most frequently touted is that they eliminate from the resolution of the dispute the ugly personal confrontations that associate themselves with litigation or even "live" dispute resolution methods. But, users may not feel the same sense of relationship building in online settings that is found in offline ADR processes.

In addition to the fact that online negotiation tends to treat conflict as being distinct from the people involved, there is the related objection that it fails to inculcate effective personal dispute resolution habits in users. The claims adjuster who comes to rely solely on online mechanisms for settlement may never achieve a level of interpersonal competence that would allow tackling more complex problems involving real people seen face-to-face. There is, in short, something unsettling about processes for management of disputes that remove live, personal interaction between people from the dispute resolution equation, although the same criticism could be made of negotiation over the telephone or via the fax machine.

The legal effect of agreements reached via online negotiation is a matter on which the courts have yet to rule directly. Consequently, participation of lawyers in settlements online is probably no less important than offline. It appears that parties who accept the "terms of service" on a web site are bound by that acceptance. We have already discussed one case on web site acceptance terms, and in the case of *Hotmail Corp. v Van$ Money Pie* (47 U.S. Patent Reporter 1020, 1998), the court determined that clicking the "I Accept" button appearing above a site's section on terms and conditions bound the party who clicked that button to an enforceable contract. Furthermore, courts have consistently held that parties who buy and sell over the Internet are bound to the terms of the purchase agreements they reach online. However, the question of whether acceptance of the "terms of use" on an online dispute resolution site binds participants remains an open question, because such a transaction is, arguably, different than a simple purchase agreement.

It is also unclear whether a settlement reached online has the effect of precluding further litigation on the matter; some sites specifically preclude this effect. One could, theoretically, settle a case via negotiation online and still face a lawsuit regarding some aspect of the same matter at a later date. In addition, the law is unclear on the matter of whether an attorney must have a client's permission to settle a case through online negotiation methods, and clients certainly have an interest in knowing if an attorney is using such a mechanism to negotiate settlement.

Finally, questions of confidentiality and information security arise despite the significant efforts made by vendors to protect online information. Virtually all web sites place "cookies" on user's hard drives unless a user's browser software specifically prohibits acceptance of the "cookie." Sophisticated computer users can gain access to "cookies" on other user's machines. Depending on the nature of the "cookie," a third party could gain information about a case simply by reviewing the "cookie;" access to one's case online is also a possibility if the "cookie" contains log-in information for rapid access to a site.

It is also uncertain whether information transmitted over the Internet is private for the purposes of discovery in civil lawsuit. Discovery is the fact-finding component of a civil lawsuit. In that period of pretrial preparation, lawyers are entitled to obtain from one another's clients information that is not protected. It is possible that a court could rule that information transmitted over the Internet is subject to discovery if it has been placed on a third-party server or otherwise left the control of one party. In a significant civil case, this could be a disaster.

Finally, several of the online negotiation sites offer incentives in pricing to insurance carriers and other high-volume users. Doing so may create the appearance of impropriety, if not outright conflicts of interest. Individual users should be cautious of any site that has a substantial, ongoing relationship with a large insurer or other institutional user and to whom discounts for use are provided, because such a relationship could compromise the objectivity of the online vendor.

ODR Bytes

Negotiation, the most common form of alternative dispute resolution both on- and offline, is the process of agreeing on issues requiring resolution, establishing settlement alternatives, and selecting the appropriate option or options for settlement.

In automated blind-bid negotiation models, parties use an online service provider to enter dollar offers of settlement, either all at once or in rounds of traded offers and counteroffers. The case is settled when the offer and demand are within an agreed-upon range.

Software-enhanced negotiation allows parties to enter information into groupware applications that assist them in identifying and refining issues, seeing points of agreement, and generating mutually acceptable settlement options.

Asynchronous communication allows parties to use a web site to communicate with one another through a variety of means to evaluate the case electronically and consider a range of settlement options.

Automated blind-bidding is best suited to cases that involve uncontested facts and that are likely to be settled for money. Software-enhanced and asynchronous-discussion approaches can be used in more complex matters involving disputed facts and legal issues and noneconomic settlement options.

Thorough preparation is essential to effective online negotiation; PC-based resources such as Negotiator Pro may be helpful in preparing to negotiate claims online.

Online negotiation has many potential advantages, including cost and time savings, risk and error reduction, and a variety of intangible, but important, psychological benefits.

Automated blind-bidding has a number of potential disadvantages that render it unsuitable for some cases, including the fact that it is normally a "money-only" approach.

All forms of online negotiation are impersonal and may fail to establish or enhance long-term relationships or to develop parties' conflict resolution and communication skills.

The law related to online dispute resolution is still developing, and issues of enforcement, conflicts of interest, and information privacy remain unresolved.

ODR Bookmarks

Online Negotiation Service Providers

Cybersettle
http://www.cybersettle.com

OnlineResolution
http://www.OnlineResolution.com

Resolutionforum
http://www.resolutionforum.com

Smartsettle
http://www.Smartsettle.com

SquareTrade
http://www.squaretrade.com

Negotiation Software and Preparation Sites

GroupMind Express
http://www.groupmindexpress.com

Lotus QuickPlace
http://www.lotus.com/home.nsf/welcome/quickplace

Negotiator Pro
http://www.negotiatorpro.com

Selected ODR Bibliography

Baumer, David, and J. C. Poindexter. *Cyberlaw & E-Commerce*. Columbus, OH: McGraw-Hill Irwin, 2002.

Eidsmoe, Daniel C. "Online Dispute Resolution." *Alternative Dispute Resolution*. Chicago: Illinois Institute of Continuing Legal Education, 2002.

Epstein, Lynn A. "Alternative Dispute Resolution in the Twenty-first Century: Cyber E-Mail Negotiation vs. Traditional Negotiation: Will Cyber Technology Supplant Traditional Means of Settling Litigation?" *Tulsa L. J.* 36 (2001): 839.

Katsch, Ethan, Janet Rifkin, and Alan Gaitenby. "E-Commerce, E-Disputes, and E-Dispute Resolution: In the Shadow of 'eBay Law.' " *Ohio St. J. on Dispute Resolution* 15 (2000): 705.

Kreindler, Tony. "Multinational Cos. Offer Recommendations for E-Commerce ADR." *ADRWorld.com* (September 13, 2000).

Perritt, Henry H. "Dispute Resolution in Cyberspace: Demand for New Forms of ADR." *Ohio St. J. on Dispute Resolution* 15 (2000): 675.

Rustad, Michael L., and Cyrus Daftary. *E-Business Legal Handbook*. New York: Aspen Law & Business Publishers, 2001.

Thompson, Leigh. *The Heart and Mind of the Negotiator*, 2d ed. Upper Saddle River, NJ: Prentice Hall 2001. Contains a useful, skills-oriented chapter entitled "Negotiating via Information Technology."

Ware, Stephen J., and Sarah R. Cole. "Introduction: ADR in Cyberspace." *Ohio St. J. on Dispute Resolution* 15 (2000): 589.

Online Mediation

Process Introduction and Overview

Mediation is the fastest growing form of business dispute resolution in America today because it represents a meaningful alternative to "win–lose" adjudicative processes such as arbitration and litigation. Disputants seeking fast, relatively inexpensive, and confidential dispute resolution are turning to mediation in a variety of settings, including court-annexed, private, and online. Mediation allows parties to resolve disputes themselves through negotiation and with the help of a neutral party rather than relinquish control of the dispute to a judge, jury, or arbitrator.

Mediation is a private, voluntary negotiation process employing a trained, neutral third party to facilitate a final, contractually binding settlement. Unlike adjudicative processes, which consist of some type of formal evidentiary hearing, mediation employs semiformal negotiation between the parties, generally without use of evidence or witnesses. Mediation is a significantly more formal process than negotiation because it involves the intervention of a third party and is often conducted pursuant to procedural rules agreed to by the parties. Like negotiation, it may be done either through legal representatives or directly with one's adversary. The process is virtually always voluntary in terms of both the decision to participate and the decision to settle. It is also virtually always private, so no court record is created, nor is any party information revealed to the public.

Mediators do not evaluate and decide cases as judges and juries do. However, they are not merely passive referees. The mediator is an active participant who assists parties to refine and understand the issues in a case and to negotiate collaboratively toward solutions that both sides can accept or reject. In addition, mediators assist the disputants in presenting their positions and in generating and evaluating options to resolve the dispute.

The mediation process normally consists of five stages, beginning with a brief, relatively informal mediator opening statement. That statement describes the process and role of the mediator to the parties and confirms the agreement of the parties to participate in the process. Following the mediator opening statement, party opening statements are directed to the mediator. These statements set forth the facts, the issues requiring resolution and the desired outcomes in the case from each party's perspective.

The heart of the mediation process is the facilitated negotiation, which occurs next. During this period the mediator assists the parties in articulating their cases to one another in productive and useful ways. The mediator clarifies and summarizes positions, asks questions calculated to elicit additional information from the parties, and suggests settlement approaches not yet considered by the parties. The mediator may also assist in identifying assets useful for settlement but not previously considered by the parties.

At some point in virtually all mediation conferences, the mediator will hold one or more caucuses with the parties. The caucus is a private meeting taken with each party to allow the parties to address issues not suitable for open-session coverage, such as strengths and weaknesses of a particular aspect of the case. In addition to allowing the mediator to address and be addressed by the parties much more candidly, the caucus can be held to overcome a negotiating impasse, a point at which the parties refuse or are unable to bargain. When the parties have negotiated to a point of agreement, the mediator will assist them with closure by assisting the parties in evaluating, clarifying, and memorializing the agreement they have reached.

What Is Online Mediation?

Online mediation employs new technology to deliver to the parties a process that is based on and very similar to traditional in-person mediation. The process itself and the role of the parties and mediator are changed only insofar as the communication in which they engage is electronic, rather than live. In online mediation, parties negotiate with one another under the auspices of the mediator via email or on specially designed Internet sites that provide virtual "rooms" in which the parties congregate electronically. The mediator still has private communications resembling caucuses with the parties, again via email or in separate "rooms" on an Internet site. And, parties may still reach binding resolutions through the process.

A very helpful chart describing online mediation can be found at the following web page: http://www.squaretrade.com/cnt/jsp/hlp/help_med.jsp;jsessionid=e14ccxvj31?vhostid=tomcat4&stmp=ebay&cntid=e14ccxvj31.

In addition to e-mail and chat technology as vehicles for communication, parties may use interactive forms and surveys to facilitate the delivery of facts and offers to one another in standardized form. Mediators may review and contribute to the creation of the forms or may even be permitted by the parties to edit them, so the contents will be received by the opposing party in as favorable a light as possible. With the rapidly expanding availability of web-based conferencing using digital cameras and microphones, it is even possible to conduct a mediation conference that is the functional equivalent of a live session but involves parties at remote locations. Attorneys or others may represent parties in online mediation if they desire, though disclosure of the fact that a representative is participating is required at most online mediation vendor sites.

Given the similarity between online and live mediation, it is not surprising that purveyors of online mediation have modeled the standards of practice enforced on most web sites after those followed by traditional, in-person mediators. Indeed, online mediation poses precisely the same sorts of ethical issues for both parties and mediators as for traditional mediators. SquareTrade^{SM}, a major provider of online mediation, has an excellent example of a well-crafted set of online mediation ethical standards at its web site (www.squaretrade.com). The standards are generally based on live mediation approaches but are drafted to meet the specific needs of parties mediating online.

SquareTrade Standards of Practice for Online Dispute Resolution

Adherence to the highest ethical standards when conducting alternative dispute resolution (ADR) is critical. Due to the unique circumstances created by providing ADR services online, the SquareTrade Standards of Practice extend beyond traditional ADR standards.

Neutrality and Impartiality: A SquareTrade mediator or arbitrator will only handle disputes in which he or she can remain neutral and impartial. SquareTrade will only engage in contractual relationships that promote and maintain mediator and arbitrator neutrality.

Conflicts of Interest: A SquareTrade mediator or arbitrator will disclose to all parties any and all conflicts of interest, potential or actual, as soon as he or she becomes aware such a conflict may exist.

Confidentiality, Privacy and Security: SquareTrade posts its privacy policy and confidentiality guidelines on its web site; a SquareTrade mediator or arbitrator will maintain all such relevant privacy and confidentiality provisions. SquareTrade deploys state of the art security and data back-up systems so that all data and case records are maintained in accordance with SquareTrade's privacy policy.

Competence and Quality of the Dispute Resolution Process: A SquareTrade mediator or arbitrator will only handle disputes that he or she has the qualifications, experience, and ability to handle. Each mediator or arbitrator will make every effort to provide the highest possible quality service to both parties involved in a given case.

Fair Process: A SquareTrade mediator or arbitrator will encourage both parties to seek information and advice from relevant sources during the course of the dispute resolution process.

Transparency: A SquareTrade mediator or arbitrator will ensure that the online dispute resolution process is transparent to both parties, and will make every effort to ensure that both parties understand the process. The cost of dispute resolution is posted for users before they enter the process.

Technological Competence: A SquareTrade mediator or arbitrator will have the technological competence to conduct the dispute resolution process effectively and efficiently. SquareTrade's technology itself supports SquareTrade's Standards of Practice, and can effectively handle multiple thousands of complaints simultaneously.

Accessibility: SquareTrade's system is accessible using standard systems, browsers and ISPs. The system is up 24 hours a day, 7 days a week and 365 days a year, except during regularly scheduled maintenance downtimes. Users are consistently able to check the status of their cases, and have access to customer support generally within 24 hours, 7 days a week. User inquiries are tracked and archived.

Confidentiality, discussed briefly in the SquareTrade *Standards of Practice*, is a hallmark of genuine mediation. Parties, mediators generally believe, are much more likely to engage in good-faith efforts to resolve their claim, often through negotiations that reveal damaging facts or include concessions of liability or apologies, if they are absolutely sure such statements cannot later be used against them in court or elsewhere. Courts have generally supported this view of mediation and enforced confidentiality agreements that do not violate public policy. WebMediate[SM], a site we will consider in greater depth shortly, has a confidentiality policy that affords users of their service a level of protection that is virtually identical to that offered in traditional mediation, but it has been written for online contexts, which pose some unique privacy challenges.

Neither the WebMediator nor WebMediate (including its agents and employees) may be called to testify or compelled to provide documents or information regarding any WebMediation in any adversary proceeding, judicial forum, or alternative dispute resolution proceeding. All parties agree, by agreeing to be bound by these Rules, to oppose any effort by any person to make WebMediate or any WebMediator a witness in any adversary proceeding, judicial proceeding, or alternative dispute resolution proceeding related to the Matter or the WebMediation.

The parties and their representatives, if any, shall maintain the confidentiality of the WebMediation and may not rely on or introduce as evidence in any adversary proceeding, judicial forum, or alternative dispute resolution proceeding any information or communications within or related to the WebMediation to the same extent provided in [federal] Rule 408 of the Rules of Evidence for United States Courts and Magistrates. The parties may elect to sign an appropriate confidentiality undertaking prior to taking part in the WebMediation.

Courts have also consistently concluded that confidentiality is a central tenet of mediation. The following cases both explain why and explore the boundaries of confidentiality in offline mediation in a fashion that could certainly be extended to online mediation.

KEY CHAPTER CASES

Two Views of Confidentiality in Mediation

Foxgate Homeowners' Association, Inc. v Bramalea California, Inc., 26 Cal. 4th 1; 25 P.3d 1117 (Supreme Court of California, 2001)

Fact Summary: Plaintiff and defendant were involved in a complex lawsuit over construction defects. The case was sent to mediation with an order that confirmed that all privileges applicable to mediation applied; the parties were also ordered to make their best efforts to cooperate in the mediation process. Defendant's attorney made significant efforts to derail the mediation process including arriving late, failing to bring required participants, and insulting the mediator personally; the mediation process was terminated as a result. Plaintiffs requested sanctions against defendant, and a memorandum from the mediator supported that request. The memorandum included information taken from the mediation sessions, including quotations from defendant's attorney. Defendant argued on appeal that the court violated the confidentiality of mediation when the judge considered the report of the mediator in assessing the events and communications that occurred during the mediation in imposing sanctions.

Opinion: The opinion of the court was delivered by BAXTER, J.

. . . [W]e face the intersection between court-ordered mediation, the confidentiality of which is mandated by [California statutory] law and the power of a court to control proceedings before it by imposing sanctions on a party or the party's attorney for statements or conduct during mediation. The Court of Appeal held that the mediator may report to the court a party's failure to comply with an order of the mediator and to participate in good faith in the mediation process. In doing so, the mediator may reveal information necessary to place sanctionable conduct including communications made during mediation.

We conclude that there are no exceptions to the confidentiality of mediation communications. Neither a mediator nor a party may reveal communications made during mediation. We also conclude that, while a party may do so, a mediator may not report to the court about the conduct of participants in a mediation session.

The Court of Appeal concluded that the purpose of mediation confidentiality is to promote mediation as an alternative to judicial proceedings and that confidentiality is essential to mediation. The Court reasoned, however, that it should balance against that policy recognition that, unless the parties and their lawyers participate in good faith in mediation, there is little to protect. Defendants contend that the confidentiality policies are absolute except to the extent that a statutory exception exists. The only such exception they acknowledge is the authority of a mediator to report criminal conduct. They argue that the report of the mediator, which plaintiff submitted to the court with its motion for sanctions and which the court considered, was a form of testimony by a person made incompetent to testify and violated the principle that mediators are to assist parties in reaching their own agreement, but ordinarily may not express an opinion on the merits of the case.

The legislative intent underlying the mediation confidentiality provisions of the Evidence Code is clear. The parties recognize the purpose of confidentiality is to promote "a candid and informal exchange regarding events in the past . . ." This frank exchange is achieved only if the participants know that what is said in the mediation will not be used to their detriment through later court proceedings and other adjudicatory processes.

In the only other reported case arising in California in which a mediator's testimony about events during mediation was compelled and admitted, a federal judge, Wayne Brazil, an expert in mediation law, ruled that the testimony of a mediator could be compelled because the evidence was necessary to establish whether a defaulting party had been competent to enter into a settlement that another party sought to enforce. (*Olam v. Congress Mortgage* Co.) There the plaintiff had waived confidentiality and the defendant had agreed to a limited waiver of confidentiality. Nonetheless, the judge concluded that a weighing process should be used to determine if the parties' interest in compelling the testimony of the mediator outweighed the state's interest in maintaining confidentiality of the mediation. After doing so, the judge concluded that the testimony was the most reliable and probative evidence on the issue, and there was no likely alternative source, the testimony was crucial if the court was to be able to resolve the dispute and was essential to doing justice in the case before him.

We do not agree with the Court of Appeal that the court may fashion an exception for bad faith in mediation because failure to authorize reporting of such conduct during mediation may lead to "an absurd result" or fail to carry out the legislative policy of encouraging mediation. The Legislature has decided that the policy of encouraging mediation by ensuring confidentiality is promoted by avoiding the threat that frank expression of viewpoints by the parties during mediation may subject a participant to a motion for imposition of sanctions by another party or the mediator who might assert that those views constitute a bad faith failure to participate in mediation. Therefore, even were the court free to ignore the plain language of the confidentiality statutes, there is no justification for doing so here.

Olam v Congress Mortgage Company, 68 F.Supp.2d 1110; 1999 U.S. Dist. LEXIS 17538 (United States District Court for the Northern District of California, 1999)

Fact Summary: The parties participated in a lengthy mediation. At the end of the mediation, the parties signed a "Memorandum of Understanding" (MOU) that states that it is "intended as a binding document itself. . . ." Contending that the consent she apparently gave was not legally valid, plaintiff has taken the position that the MOU is not enforceable. She has not complied with its terms. Defendants have filed a motion to enforce the MOU as a binding contract. The plaintiff and the defendants have expressly waived confidentiality protections conferred by the California statutes quoted above. Both the plaintiff and the defendants have indicated, clearly and on advice of counsel, that they want the court to consider evidence about what occurred during the mediation, including testimony directly from the mediator.

Opinion: The opinion of the court was delivered by BRAZIL, J.

The court addresses in this opinion several difficult issues about the relationship between a court-sponsored voluntary mediation and subsequent proceedings whose purpose is to determine whether the parties entered an enforceable agreement at the close of the mediation session. One of the principal issues with which the court wrestles, below, is whether evidence about what occurred during the mediation proceedings, including testimony from the mediator, may be used to help resolve this dispute. California law confers on mediators a privilege that is independent of the privilege conferred on parties to a mediation [which] has the effect of making a mediator the holder of an independent privilege [and] prohibits courts from compelling disclosure of evidence about mediation communications and directs that all such communications "shall remain confidential."

[I]t is important to emphasize one critical and undisputed fact: at the end of the mediation, the parties and their lawyers signed a document, typed clearly by the mediator, which appears on its face to contain the essential terms of an agreement, which expressly states that it "is intended as a binding document itself," and which affirms the parties' agreement that "the court will have continuing jurisdiction over the enforcement of this memorandum of understanding as well as the ultimate settlement agreement and any disputes arising therefrom . . ."

The trial judge is to weigh and comparatively assess (1) the importance of the values and interests that would be harmed if the mediator was compelled to testify (perhaps subject to a sealing or protective order, if appropriate), (2) the magnitude of the harm that compelling the testimony would cause to those values and interests, (3) the importance of the rights or interests that would be jeopardized if the mediator's testimony was not accessible in the specific proceedings in question, and (4) how much the testimony would contribute toward protecting those rights or advancing those interests—an inquiry that includes, among other things, an assessment of whether there are alternative sources of evidence of comparable probative value.

This is not a matter of time and money only. Good mediators are likely to feel violated by being compelled to give evidence that could be used against a party with whom they tried to establish a relationship of trust during a mediation conference. Good mediators are deeply committed to being and remaining neutral and non-judgmental, and to building and preserving relationships with parties. To force them to give evidence that hurts someone from whom they actively solicited trust (during the mediation) rips the fabric of their work and can threaten their sense of the center of their professional integrity. These are not inconsequential matters. Like many other variables in this kind of analysis, however, the magnitude of these risks can vary with the circumstances. Here, for instance, all parties to the mediation want the mediator to testify about things that occurred during the mediation—so ordering the testimony would do less harm to the actual relationships developed than it would in a case where one of the parties to the mediation objected to the use of evidence from the mediator. We acknowledge that the possibility that a mediator might be forced to testify over objection could harm the capacity of mediators in general to create the environment of trust that they feel maximizes the likelihood that constructive communication will occur during the mediation session.

The interests that are likely to be advanced by compelling the mediator to testify in this case are of considerable importance. Moreover, as we shall see, some of those interests parallel and reinforce the objectives the legislature sought to advance by providing for confidentiality in mediation. The first interest we identify is the interest in doing justice. Here is what we mean. For reasons described below, the mediator is positioned in this case to offer what could be crucial, certainly very probative, evidence about the central factual issues in this matter. There is a strong possibility that his testimony will greatly improve the court's ability to determine reliably what the pertinent historical facts actually were. Establishing reliably what the facts were is critical to doing justice. It is the fundamental duty of a public court in our society to do justice—to resolve disputes in accordance with the law when the parties don't. Confidence in our system of justice as a whole, in our government as a whole, turns in no small measure on confidence in the courts' ability to do justice in individual cases. So doing justice in individual cases is an interest of considerable magnitude.

[Justice] is not the only interest that could be advanced by compelling the mediator to testify. According to the defendants' pre-hearing proffers, the mediator's testimony would establish clearly that the mediation process was fair and that the plaintiff's consent to the settlement agreement was legally viable. Thus the mediator's testimony, according to the defendants, would re-assure the community and the court about the integrity of the mediation process that the court sponsored.

That testimony also would provide the court with the evidentiary confidence it needs to enforce the agreement. A publicly announced decision to enforce the settlement would encourage parties who want to try to settle their cases to use the court's mediation program [as well as] encourage parties to take mediations seriously, to understand that they represent real opportunities to reach closure and avoid trial, and to attend carefully to terms of agreements proposed in mediations. In sharp contrast, refusing to compel the mediator to testify might well deprive the court of the evidence it needs to rule reliably on the plaintiff's contentions—and thus might either cause the court to impose an unjust outcome on the plaintiff or disable the court from enforcing the settlement. If parties believed that courts routinely would refuse to compel mediators to testify, and that the absence of evidence from mediators would enhance the viability of a contention that apparent consent to a settlement contract was not legally viable, cynical parties would be encouraged either to try to escape commitments they made during mediations or to use threats of such escapes to try to re-negotiate, after the mediation, more favorable terms—terms that they never would have been able to secure without this artificial and unfair leverage.

In sum, it is clear that refusing even to determine what the mediator's testimony would be, in the circumstances here presented, threatens values of great significance. We conclude that the mediator's testimony was sufficiently likely to make substantial contributions toward achieving the ends described above to justify compelling an exploration, under seal, of what his testimony would be.

Finally, the matter of mediator neutrality is considered essential in any form of mediation. Parties will not, for obvious reasons, employ the services of a mediator in whom they are not absolutely sure they can place their trust. The need to disclaim conflicts of interest is perhaps even greater in online contexts because mediators are not likely to be known personally to the parties and may be residents of different states or localities. Knowing that such a "stranger to the transaction" does not possess any vested interest in the outcome of the dispute is crucial to the parties. Accordingly, most vendors of online mediation services prohibit persons with any financial or personal interest in a matter from mediating the dispute, except with informed and voluntary consent of the parties. Informed consent is always the product of complete disclosure of any interest in a case by the mediator. So, a mediator who holds shares in a company for which he or she has been asked to mediate should advise the parties of that potential conflict. Furthermore, prior to accepting an appointment, prospective mediators are ordinarily required to disclose any circumstances that may create even an appearance of bias.

Which Cases Are Appropriate for Online Mediation?

Virtually all disputes are appropriate for some form of mediation. As a result, the more important question is, Which cases are particularly well suited to the mediation process? The most significant factor supporting the use of mediation for dispute resolution is the presence of an important and potentially on-going business relationship. This is true because mediation is the only process that offers the parties the opportunity to resolve their dispute without disrupting the relationship and in a way that may actually strengthen the relationship for the future. Furthermore, cases involving parties who desire settlement but, after endeavoring to reach one through direct negotiation, have failed are also well suited for mediation. The addition of the third party neutral, trained to move intransigent or incapable parties, may remove impediments to a desirable settlement and avoid resort to an adjudicative process. In addition, when the economics of a case require a rapid resolution to avoid further harm to one or both parties, mediation can provide a forum for a very expeditious settlement. Finally, cases that involve conduct that may not reflect well on an individual or company may also be addressed best through mediation because of its very private nature.

It should be noted that some cases may not be appropriate for mediation or settlement and probably should be adjudicated. For example, cases likely to create an important legal precedent may be better resolved through a legal judgment that clarifies the law for everyone. Given the fact that cyberlaw is an emerging and sometimes unclear area of law, these types of "nonnegotiable" cases may occur more frequently online. It is also widely believed that cases involving serious criminal behavior should not be privately mediated.

Several types of online disputes are especially excellent candidates for mediation. Cases involving parties who desire a settlement but are reluctant or unable to meet with one another directly work well in mediation, for example, cases involving e-commerce partners who live in geographically distant locations from one another. In addition, cases that involve highly confidential or proprietary information are addressed very well in mediation. If, for example, a disputed business arrangement involves trade secrets,

---

ODR IN THE DIGITAL ERA
Getting the Other Party to the Table

Mediation is voluntary, so opponents not willing to give the process a try can thwart parties desiring to participate. One method of assuring participation is the inclusion of a mediation clause in the terms and conditions of use on a web site or the insertion of such a clause in a written contract between the parties. Generally enforceable, such clauses get the parties to the table, so the process can be commenced. The following helpful mediation clause was written by The InternetNeutral[SM]. Note the requirement that the parties endeavor to settle the case themselves via negotiation before starting mediation.

In the event of a dispute related to [any transaction involving this website] (or) [this Contract], the parties shall use the following procedure as a condition precedent to either party pursuing other available remedies:

1. A party who believes a dispute exists (the "disputing party") shall put such dispute in writing to the other party (the "responding party"). Such writing shall clearly, though as briefly as practicable, state the substance and scope of the dispute, the disputing party's position relative thereto, including legal and factual justifications therefor, the remedy sought, and any other pertinent matters.

2. The responding party who receives such a writing shall respond in writing to the disputing party within ten days. Such writing shall clearly, though as briefly as practicable, state the responding party's response to each of the items included in the disputing party's writing and any other pertinent matters.

3. A telephone conference shall be held within ten days between representatives of the parties having decision-making authority regarding the dispute to negotiate in good faith a resolution of the dispute.

4. If, within ten business days after such telephone conference, the parties have not succeeded in negotiating a resolution of the dispute, the parties' representatives shall submit the dispute to the Internet Neutral in accordance with the Internet Neutral Rules (see http://www.internetneutral.com/rules.htm), or if the Internet Mediator is then unable or unwilling to perform due to a conflict of interest, schedule conflict, or otherwise, to a mutually acceptable neutral person, able to utilize the Internet for mediation services similar to the Internet Neutral (the "neutral"). The fees of and authorized expenses incurred by the neutral shall be shared equally by the parties.

5. The parties hereby agree to be bound by the rules and procedures of the Internet Neutral, or those of its replacement neutral, as then-existing.

6. The parties agree to mediate in good faith for a minimum period of ten days from the actual commencement of "online" Internet mediation. If the parties are not successful in resolving the dispute through Internet mediation, as above, then the parties may agree to submit the matter to binding arbitration, or either party may pursue other available remedies upon ten days written notice to the other party specifying its intended course of action.

7. The parties may mutually agree to extend any of the time periods stated herein.

8. The parties agree that the mediation provided for here is a compromise negotiation for purposes of all international, federal, and state rules of evidence. The entire procedure will be confidential. All conduct, statements, promises, offers, views, and opinions, whether oral or written, made in the course of the mediation by any of the parties, their agents, employees, representatives, or other invitees to the mediation and by the neutral, who is the parties' joint agent for purposes of these compromise negotiations, are confidential and shall, in addition and where appropriate, be deemed to be attorney-client privileged. Such conduct, statements, promises, offers, views, and opinions shall not be discoverable or admissible for any purposes, including impeachment, in any litigation or other proceeding involving the parties and shall not be disclosed to anyone not an agent, employee, expert, witness, or representative for any of the parties. However, evidence otherwise discoverable or admissible in a later proceeding is not excluded from discovery or admission as a result of its use in the mediation. If not entirely enforceable, the parties intend that the court enforce this provision to the extent enforceable by such court.

such as proprietary software code or new business plans, parties will probably be attracted to the complete privacy afforded by mediation. Finally, cases in which the dollar value is too low to litigate or arbitrate, as in online auction disagreements, can be quickly and inexpensively resolved in online mediation. Irrespective of case type, new e-commerce sites seeking to establish high levels of customer confidence can benefit from the use of online mediation to achieve fast, mutually agreeable solutions as well.

How Does a Typical Online Mediation Site Work?

WebMediate (www.webmediate.com) is a site that employs dispute resolution and business professionals, attorneys, and "some pretty sharp techies" to deliver online

mediation services. The company mission is to "offer a fair, fast, independent, and inexpensive process for the online resolution of business disputes that combines new web-based technologies with the proven dispute-resolution expertise of world-class Circle of Neutrals." WebMediate styles itself an "E-Commerce Safety Net^{SM} that makes strong (existing) relationships stronger and new . . . relationships possible." WebMediate is an independent provider, not affiliated with any other website or company. As such, impartiality is clear and easily communicated to the parties. WebMediate does not accept investments from insurance companies or other businesses that use WebMediate to resolve disputes; some of the other online mediation services do. They do, however, contract with online e-commerce sites to provide dispute resolution services and may even rely on these sites to assist in bringing parties to the table to mediate.

WebMediate fees are based on the time devoted by the WebMediator to the matter; the fee is divided equally between the parties. WebMediate's services are entirely Internet-based, so no special software or hardware is required. Parties need nothing more than the software and hardware normally used to access the Internet to participate in a WebMediation. Parties with similar capacities may use video conferencing if they choose to do so.

WebMediate provides an online setting in which all communications between the parties and the WebMediator are conducted via WebMediate's secure "resolution forums" and are completely confidential. As with all mediation services, recourse to some other dispute resolution process remains an option for users who do not settle in mediation, and WebMediate offers arbitration in that eventuality. In addition, parties retain the right to go to court should settlement be unsuccessful and agree before mediating that settlement discussions conducted through WebMediate are inadmissible in any subsequent legal proceeding to the same extent as settlement discussions in the offline world. Parties also agree up-front to honor any solution to which they agree.

Unlike live mediation, which is normally a process that takes place over the course of a single conference lasting some number of hours, WebMediation takes as long as the parties choose to participate. Because the parties construct offers and demands in writing and then send them through the mediator, the process has no set duration and may last days or weeks. The company represents that most cases are completed within fourteen days when the parties are "reasonably attentive to the process."

The WebMediate process is a relatively simple affair, conducted through online forms and meeting spaces. It has five steps; here is how the WebMediate site describes each step in the process:

Step One: *New Matter Form.* A matter comes into WebMediation by one party (called the Initiating Party) completing our online New Matter Form and selecting the WebMediation process. The Initiating Party may also select WebArbitration as a backup process if WebMediation is not successful.

Step Two: *Notification of Other Party.* WebMediate notifies the Replying Party that the Matter has been submitted to WebMediation and is ready to be resolved online.

Step Three: *Setting up the WebMediation.* WebMediate appoints a WebMediator from our Circle of Neutrals to assist the parties in discussing the matter, exchanging relevant information, and exploring options for resolution. WebMediate also creates three secure virtual conference rooms for the WebMediation: a Common Resolution Space, in which the parties and the WebMediator can discuss the matter together, and two Private Resolution Spaces for each of the parties to communicate privately with the WebMediator.

Step Four: *The WebMediation.* Within WebMediation, the parties present their respective views, facts, and arguments to each other and to the WebMediator. The parties are also encouraged to engage in private one-on-one communications with the WebMediator that may not be viewed by the other party. The WebMediator's role is to assist the parties in communicating their viewpoints, identifying their respective interests, and generating options for arriving at a mutually acceptable resolution of their dispute. Although the WebMediation can generally be conducted in any manner that suits the parties, certain basic rules apply to this process.

Step Five: *Resolution.* If the parties are able to reach a satisfactory resolution of their matter, the WebMediator will assist the parties, if they choose, in creating a written record of their agreement.

WebMediate offers a staged approach to agreement. Before parties attempt to mediate they may use the WebSettlement option on the site to reach a very rapid conclusion without the intervention of a third-party neutral. WebSettlement is simply a form of online blind-bid negotiation. If the negotiation process fails or if the parties deem the case unlikely to settle in negotiation, they may move the case to WebMediation; WebArbitration, an adjudicative mechanism, can be used in the event the facilitative options do not work. A section on the site for each user called the "My Matters" Page allows users to manage multiple cases simultaneously.

WebMediate provides for a completely electronic version of the mediation process by including careful language regarding electronic signatures in the terms and conditions of use accepted by all users. The policy states specifically:

You acknowledge that the standards of the Electronic Signatures in Global and National Commerce Act (E-Sign Act) apply with regard to your execution of this Agreement as well as to your execution and submission of any and all documents and agreements pertaining to the Services offered by WebMediate and any and all writings, affirmations, affidavits, declarations, or sworn testimony that you submit.

An online mediation environment somewhat different in look and function than the one available at Webmediate.com is available at themediationroom.com (https://www.themediationroom.com/), a British concern. Using software created by theclaimroom.com (https://www.theclaimroom.com/index2.lxp#), this site endeavors to simulate the feel of a live mediation. Unlike the Webmediate.com process, which is largely asynchronous, themediationroom.com creates an electronic setting in which the mediator can bring all parties together simultaneously to negotiate with the mediator's assistance. The technology allows for plenary sessions involving all parties and genuinely private caucuses; instant document uploads to support the process are also available. The environment even allows for the use of experts in either plenary or caucus sessions. Mediation "transcripts," records of the proceeding, are archived, so unsuccessful parties can return to the records to try again later should they wish to do so. Sample cases are available for viewing at http://adr.themediationroom.com.

How Does One Select an Online Mediator?

All online mediation services allow parties to select a mediator from a roster or panel of available neutrals. The WebMediate "Circle of Neutrals" is a good example; view it at (https://www.webmediate.com/cgi/Circle.cgi). Selecting the right neutral for a case is critical, and it stands to reason that the neutral selected should understand and be experienced in the process of mediation. But, experience alone may not be enough.

It is important to note that the mediator does not have the authority to force the parties to settle a case. As a result, the mediator has two critical roles during the mediation process. In choosing a mediator, parties should look for a person capable of acting as an effective facilitator of party communications, able to identify issues, able to state them clearly and in neutral terms, and able to structure a process aimed at resolving them. In addition, the mediator is a resource for the parties, offering settlement options, assessing the options offered by the parties, and perhaps connecting the parties with outside experts to assist in the evaluation and resolution of the case. The most capable mediators are skilled at crafting settlement options that include ideas generated by the parties as well as by the mediator, resulting in a package that advances the interests of all parties.

In addition to procedural expertise, parties often look for a mediator with significant substantive expertise in the area of the dispute, such as product liability or contractual disputes. The mediator with substantive expertise offers the parties the ability to grasp the facts of the case quickly, to understand the points that need resolution efficiently and accurately, and to provide the parties with useful settlement options on the basis of personal experience. In addition, this sort of mediator may have knowledge of the approaches taken by other parties with similar problems and of options available that the parties may not yet have considered. However, mediators with extensive background in a particular kind of case may appear biased toward one side or the other and sometimes appear to be endeavoring to settle the case in a way that is consistent with their own view of the dispute.

The following is the code of conduct to which SquareTrade mediators ascribe:

General Responsibilities

SquareTrade Mediators have a duty to the parties, to the profession, and to themselves. They should be honest and unbiased, act in good faith, be diligent, and not seek to advance their own interests at the expense of their parties'. SquareTrade Mediators must act fairly in dealing with the parties, have no personal interest in the terms of the settlement, show no bias toward individuals and institutions involved in the dispute, and be reasonably available as requested by the parties.

Responsibilities to the Parties

Step One: *Impartiality*. The SquareTrade Mediator must maintain impartiality toward all parties. Impartiality means freedom from favoritism or bias either by word or by action and a commitment to serve all parties as opposed to a single party.

Step Two: *Confidentiality*. Maintaining confidentiality is critical to the dispute resolution process. Confidentiality encourages candor, a full exploration of the issues, and a SquareTrade Mediator's acceptability. The SquareTrade Mediator must follow the terms of SquareTrade's Confidentiality Agreement with users as well as the Mediator's Confidentiality Agreement with SquareTrade.

Step Three: *Conflict of Interest*. The SquareTrade Mediator must refrain from entering or continuing in any dispute if he or she believes or perceives that participation as a SquareTrade Mediator would be a clear conflict of interest and under any circumstances that may reasonably raise a question as to the SquareTrade Mediator's impartiality. The duty to disclose is a continuing obligation throughout the process.

Step Four: *Promptness*. The SquareTrade Mediator shall exert every reasonable effort to expedite the process.

Step Five: *The Mediation or the Resolution and its Consequences*. The dispute resolution process belongs to the parties. The SquareTrade Mediator has no vested interest in the terms of a settlement but must be satisfied that agreements in which he or she has participated will not impugn the integrity of the process.

Use of Multiple Procedures

The use of the recommended resolution procedure by the same SquareTrade Mediator involves additional responsibilities. Because SquareTrade's Dispute Resolution Process involves mediation with the possibility of a recommended resolution, the SquareTrade Mediator must take care to advise the parties that information revealed during mediation will be used to make a recommended resolution if the parties choose that procedure.

Furthermore, parties should choose mediators and mediation vendors that provide a clear set of ethical guidelines that govern the process they deliver. Mediation is not, in general, a regulated field, so private agreements on ethics and conduct are ordinarily the best protection available to parties.

Parties often inquire into the professional affiliations of the mediators they consider as well. Membership in the Association for Conflict Resolution (http://www.acrnet. org/) is desirable evidence of meaningful professional development in mediation practice. Because mediators often have professional credentials, such as law licenses, parties may wish to seek information about a mediator from state bar associations or other regulatory bodies.

Finally, online mediation presents the need for a unique mediator qualification: technological expertise. The mediator is responsible for making the process easy and accessible for the parties. To the extent that parties require assistance with the technological aspects of the process, the mediator is likely to be the individual to whom they turn to obtain it. While web site technical service may help with mundane matters, parties will not want to disclose confidential information to individuals not involved in the case. Accordingly, it makes good sense to obtain mediation services from an online mediator conversant in and facile with the many technologies that make the process work well.

ODR IN THE DIGITAL ERA
Does It Work?

During a two-week period in March 1999, the Online Ombud's Office, a project of the University of Massachusetts Center for Information Technology and Dispute Resolution, conducted a pilot program in conjunction with the online auction site eBay (www.ebay.com). During that two-week period, 225 buyers and sellers found and followed a link placed on the eBay web site offering free resolution of auction-related complaints. The link was associated with the customer service area of the eBay site, although eBay made no special effort to advertise the availability of the service. Nondelivery of goods was the most common complaint; nonpayment, damaged goods, and inability to reach the other party were also sources of complaints. Finally, parties also complained of negative feedback written about them on the eBay site.

The Online Ombud's Office decided to use a very basic online mediation format to attempt to resolve the complaints because they assumed parties would be more likely to accept mediation, which is not a binding process, than arbitration, which does conclude with a binding determination. In addition, they decided that a single mediator, rather a panel, was preferable in order to achieve a high level of consistency among the cases mediated. The mediator used an online version of "shuttle mediation," whereby he managed an e-mail conversation between the parties. The Office declined to use a more sophisticated software package offering greater connection between the parties after they determined that parties were most comfortable with e-mail.

The process conducted looked like this:

1. After a party, usually a buyer, filed a claim on the eBay website, the mediator e-mailed the other party to explain the online mediation process and the Online Ombud's Office project. The e-mail solicited information about the claim and an agreement to participate.
2. If the second party agreed to mediate, both parties were offered an opportunity to provide "narratives" of the problem, stating facts of the dispute and desired outcomes.
3. The mediator used these narratives as well as additional inquiries of both parties via e-mail to refine the issues and suggested outcomes and to seek a way of settling the case that would be satisfactory to both parties.
4. At some point thereafter, parties would reach a point at which one party would be confronted with a decision to agree or withdraw, and the mediator would either facilitate final agreement or a decision that agreement could not be reached in the process.

The Office found a reasonably satisfactory degree of success in resolving the eBay cases through online mediation. Specifically, of the 225 cases submitted, 144 were mediated; in the remainder the second party declined to participate. It is important to note that a substantial number of those who declined to participate declined not because they distrusted the process, but because the complaint resolved itself or because the dispute was not related to an eBay transaction. In the cases in which mediation was attempted, just under half (46 percent) were settled to the satisfaction of the parties.

What Advantages Can Be Obtained through Online Mediation?

The general advantages of the mediation process are obvious. First, it is normally far less costly than adjudicative processes, and it may be done much earlier in a dispute than a trial or arbitration and with considerably less preparation. Second, the process is more time efficient than most evidentiary processes. Mediation requires less preparation from the parties than formal processes and can be accomplished virtually on demand. Third, the process offers a much wider range of settlement options, including long-term structured payments, annuities, and creative noneconomic remedies such as services, public statements of apology, and charitable gifts. Such outcomes are much more likely to continue and even improve an important business relationship. Fourth, the process allows for additional, more formal dispute resolution mechanisms such as arbitration or litigation, so parties are free to strive for a settlement without jeopardizing their positions for a subsequent trial if they are unsuccessful in doing so. Fifth, because parties control the outcome of the case, mediation is without the risk of outright loss associated with trial or arbitration.

There are also a number of advantages that accrue uniquely to online mediation, even relative to live mediation. First, like online negotiation, the communication between the parties is often asynchronous. As a result, parties have an advantage they do not have in live mediation conferences: their ability to thoughtfully craft offers and responses. Live mediation communication is spontaneous and therefore may not as effectively communicate issues or options as a written, asynchronous communications.

Second, the mediator is far less visible in the online world. This offers the advantage of a level of intervention and assistance to the parties not possible in live mediation settings. In all mediation, live and online, the mediator manages and contributes relatively heavily to the discussion. However, in live mediation the extent to which the mediator does so is much more obvious and therefore potentially problematic. Neutrality is harder to maintain, for example. In online mediation, parties can communicate with the mediator without the appearance of bias or coercion, because the other parties are not aware that the communication is taking place. In short, mediators may approve postings or otherwise significantly influence the nature of the discussion far easier and less transparently than in live settings.

Third, the process offers an array of communication methods that exceed those available in live mediation. Online mediation can be done via e-mail, chat, instant messaging, or live web video, based on the preferences and abilities of the parties. Unique caucus formats are possible as well. The timing and format of online mediation allows a mediator to meet for virtual caucuses with the parties simultaneously; in live mediation one party is required to wait through a caucus. A virtual mediator might also caucus with some of the parties and not others and be less concerned in doing so that those with whom a caucus has not been taken will find difficulty with the approach.

Fourth, because online mediation is largely text-based, a very accurate record of the interactions between the parties can be created and archived. Indeed, even where streaming video is used, the complete set of communications can be preserved to create an accurate settlement document or to prove that a settlement was reached in circumstances in which it is appropriate to do so in this fashion. A text-based approach also has the advantage of minimizing the extent to which good and bad speakers can be advantaged or disadvantaged in the process. Emotion is also much more limited in text form, so parties might feel more comfortable communicating with an opponent online in text than live and face-to-face.

Finally, the number and types of available mediators and services increases significantly when geographic separation becomes irrelevant. Parties can find a mediator or a vendor that fits their desired profile perfectly, because they are not constrained by the need to travel or to pay for a mediator to travel to them.

Quick Clicks: Review the Internet Neutral Mediation Agreement   Review the *Internet Neutral Mediation Agreement* at this link: www.internetneutral.com/agreemnt.htm. This is the primary agreement between you, the opposing party, and the mediator. Based on what you know of contract law, is it an enforceable agreement? Even if it is enforceable, is it an adequate device for protecting you in this very sensitive process? Are there ways that you think it could be improved to better address the needs of the parties? The mediator? The web site owner? Are all those sets of rights consistent, or is it necessary to reduce the protections afforded to one in order to enhance the protections afforded to another?

What Disadvantages May Be Entailed in Online Mediation?

The mediation process is not without negative aspects, however. As a private process, it does not afford parties any due process protections because it lacks the detailed procedural and evidentiary rules associated with the trial or arbitration. In addition, settlement offers are contractually binding, so when a mistake is made there is no possibility of appeal. It is certainly possible to argue that an agreement was created under fraud, duress, or some other legal defense, but this is a very different matter than formally appealing a court's judgment or an arbitrator's decision.

Online mediation has some specific shortcomings as well. Reliance on text as opposed to other means of communication results in a loss of the human element to which we referred when critiquing online negotiation. Good negotiators may find their skills minimized in an online, asynchronous setting. Text also does not convey inflection and tone, so participants may not understand the nuances in an offer or statement as well as they might in person: think about how often e-mail messages are misinterpreted. A party may be reluctant to settle in whole or in part for an apology, for example, when they are unable to hear it and gauge the sincerity of the person making it.

In addition, it is likely harder to identify truly capable mediators in the online environment. There is simply no substitute for speaking to a person and measuring the quality of his or her communication and thinking. Although online vendors provide biographies, they do not ordinarily provide means for live interaction with mediators.

It is also possible that the considerable flexibility in communication methods reduces party trust in the process. When a party is not sure when, how, and about what a mediator is communicating with the opposing party, they may be uncomfortable pursuing settlement. The ease with which an online mediator can manipulate and even deceive the parties is much greater than in live settings. Finding a site with a clear, comprehensive, and enforceable code of mediator conduct is, consequently, essential.

Finally, in live mediation it is the practice of most mediators to destroy notes and documents related to a conference to protect confidentiality. The result is that there is nothing left after the mediation for parties, outsiders, or courts to discover. Because there is a very extensive record, on multiple computers, of everything that has transpired in an online mediation, the possibility of a purposeful or negligent disclosure is greatly magnified. In addition, the possibility of a hacker obtaining confidential information is a downside uniquely present in online mediation.

ODR Bytes

Mediation is a private, voluntary process using a trained, neutral third party to facilitate a final, binding settlement consisting of mediator and party opening statements, facilitated negotiation, caucuses, and closure.

Online mediation employs new technology to deliver to the parties a process that is based on and very similar to traditional in-person mediation.

Mediation is well suited to cases involving important and potentially ongoing business relationships in which there is a desire to settle but in which direct negotiation has failed and in which the economics require a rapid resolution to avoid further harm to one or both parties.

Cases involving parties who are reluctant or unable to meet with one another directly and highly confidential or proprietary information in which the dollar value is too low to litigate or arbitrate work particularly well in online mediation.

New e-commerce sites seeking to establish high levels of customer confidence can benefit from the use of online mediation to achieve fast, mutually agreeable solutions as well.

The most desirable mediators possess procedural expertise in facilitation and option creation, substantive expertise in the type of case presented by the parties, and a strong commitment to ethical mediation.

The advantages of mediation include lower costs, better time efficiency, a much wider range of settlement options, more formal dispute resolution mechanisms, such as arbitration or litigation if the process fails, and elimination of the risk of outright loss associated with trial or arbitration.

The advantages of online mediation include asynchronous communication, a mediator who is less visible than in the online world, communication methods that are more diverse than those available in live mediation, a record of the interactions between the parties, and a diverse group of available mediators.

Disadvantages of the mediation process include the absence of due process protections and the possibility of appeal.

The disadvantages of the online mediation process include excessive reliance on text-based communication, the difficulty in identifying capable mediators, the reduction in party trust caused by great flexibility in communication methods and the possibility of a purposeful or negligent disclosure of private information.

ODR Bookmarks

The Claim Room
https://www.theclaimroom.com/index2.lxp#

The Mediation Room
http://adr.themediationroom.com

SquareTrade
www.squaretrade.com

WebMediate
www.webmediate.com/

Selected ODR Bibliography

Center for Information Technology and Dispute Resolution, University of Massachusetts. "Cyberweek 2000 Mediation Simulation Transcript" (2000). http://www.disputes.net/cyberweek2000/tuefeb15.htm.

Center for Information Technology and Dispute Resolution, University of Massachusetts. "Five eBay Mediation Transcripts" (1999). http://www.disputes.net/cyberweek2000/ebay/ebayintro.htm.

Folberg, J., and A. Taylor. *Mediation: A Comprehensive Guide to Resolving Conflicts Without Litigation*. San Francisco: Jossey-Bass, 1984.

Golann, D. *Mediating Legal Disputes: Effective Strategies for Lawyers and Mediators*. New York: Aspen Law & Business, 1996.

Goldberg, S., F. Sander, and N. Rogers. *Dispute Resolution: Negotiation, Mediation, and Other Processes*, 3d ed. New York: Aspen Law & Business, 1999.

Granat, R. "Creating an Environment for Mediating Disputes on the Internet." Paper prepared for NCAIR Conference (1996). http://mantle.sbs.umass.edu/vmag/granat.htm.

Kagel, S., and K. Kelly. "The Anatomy of Mediation: What Makes It Work." *J. Dis. Res.* (1990): 201.

Katsch, E. "The Online Ombud's Office: Adapting Dispute Resolution to Cyberspace." Paper prepared for NCAIR Conference on Online Dispute Resolution (1996). http://mantle.sbs.umass.edu/vmag/katsch.htm.

Katsch, E., J. Rifkin, and A. Gaitenby. "E-Commerce, E-Disputes, and E-Dispute Resolution: In the Shadow of 'eBay Law.'" *Ohio State Journal of Dispute Resolution* 15, no. 3 (2000): 705. http://www.umass.edu/cyber/katsch.pdf.

Lang, M., and A. Taylor. *The Making of a Mediator: Developing Artistry in Practice*. San Francisco: Jossey-Bass, 2000.

MacDuff, I. "Flames on the Wire: Mediating from an Electronic Cottage." *Negotiation J.* 10 (1994): 5.

Melamed, J. "What is Mediation?" (1999). http://mediate.com/articles/whatismediation.cfm.

Moore, C. *The Mediation Process: Practical Strategies for Resolving Conflict*. San Francisco: Jossey-Bass, 1986.

Rogers, N., and C. McEwen. *Mediation: Law, Policy & Practice*. Rochester, NY: Lawyers Co-Operative, 1989.

Online Arbitration

CHAPTER FAQS

What are offline and online arbitration?

Why might one select online arbitration rather than other ODR methods?

How are online technologies utilized in online arbitration?

What are some of the typical duties of an online arbitrator?

What are some examples of online arbitration services?

Do disputing parties need to enter into a written agreement in order to participate in an online arbitration?

Are the decisions of online arbitrators or arbitral panels enforceable in national courts?

What Are Offline and Online Arbitration?

In Chapter 2, we discussed various forms of ADR, including arbitration. Offline arbitration is a private adjudicatory method that tends to be the most formal method of ADR, with strong roots in traditional litigation. Arbitration is an adversarial process in which each party, usually through its attorney, makes a formal presentation of written and oral evidence to one or more neutral decision-makers in a confidential procedure. Arbitration has been widely embraced as a dispute resolution mechanism in a number of business areas, including construction, financial services, credit card, labor and employment, and consumer disputes. The use of arbitration is also quite common in handling international commercial conflicts that may make this process well suited for cross-border e-commerce conflicts.

In domestic U.S. arbitration, the parties follow an abbreviated trial-like process. Before any arbitration can take place, the parties must agree in writing either before a dispute arises (pre-dispute arbitration agreement, or PDAA) or after a dispute has arisen between the parties (submission agreement) to participate in the arbitration process. The arbitration clause or agreement is key to the proceedings because it determines the authority of the arbitrator, the disputes that will be handled through arbitration, the laws that will apply to the arbitration, the place where the arbitration will be convened, and the procedures that will be followed. In some cases, the parties will create their own arbitration process (ad hoc), whereas others will reference the rules of an existing entity, such as the American Arbitration Association or the International Chamber of Commerce, to follow during the arbitration (rules by reference).

Depending upon the parties' agreement, the parties and their representatives may also jointly select the sole arbitrator or members of a three-person arbitration or arbitral panel to decide the case. Some administering agencies will select the arbitrators and allow the parties to strike names of those they do not wish to have serve as their arbitrators. These third party neutrals normally have legal or industry expertise and experience in the disputed field.

Borrowing from standard litigation, the attorneys for the parties engage in some discovery, participate in pre-hearing conferences, and may provide written legal memoranda on case issues to the arbitral panel before the hearing. During the arbitration hearing, the attorneys will make opening statements of their case and the remedies sought, offer both written and oral testimony and evidence, and make closing statements to the arbitral panel. The rules of evidence are relaxed, and the arbitrators encourage parties to make a full presentation of relevant materials for the panel to consider. The hearing may last hours, days, weeks, or months.

The arbitrator or arbitration panel determines the outcome of the dispute. Arbitration awards often indicate merely who won, who lost, and the damages awarded and may not provide written findings of law and fact. Depending on the parties' arbitration agreement, the determination of the arbitrator or arbitral panel may be binding or nonbinding. The parties should agree in advance about what type of award they wish to receive at the end of the process. In instances of binding arbitration, the award is viewed as final, with the grounds for appeal being very limited either by the terms of the arbitration agreement or by applicable law.

International arbitration tends to be somewhat different than U.S. domestic arbitration in two key areas. One major difference is the lack of discovery in international arbitration. In U.S. domestic arbitration, the parties tend to have some opportunity to gather oral testimony and written documents and records from their opponent, although it is much more limited than the discovery process for U.S. litigation. In international arbitration, parties must specifically ask the arbitral panel for the opportunity to undertake some discovery. If the request is granted, the parties are normally much more limited in the information they are allowed to collect. This difference means that parties must gather supportive evidence on their own without being able to ask the other party for information that may be essential to proving their case.

Secondly, the process is primarily written, with little or no opportunity for oral testimony or presentations. The parties have to persuade the arbitrator or arbitral panel to their viewpoint through written statements and documents. If a hearing is actually held, it normally involves the arbitrator or the arbitral panel asking questions of the parties to clarify the written information. It is normally not a chance for parties to employ lengthy oral advocacy or to undertake extensive direct questioning or cross-examination of witnesses.

The fact that international arbitration has successfully handled conflicts using only written materials may bode well for online arbitration because most of the current ODR providers rely heavily on text-based exchanges to review evidence and decide cases. Currently, most ODR service providers allow parties to provide text-based materials through standard e-mail or through software programs that allow parties to post written materials on private listservs or chat rooms.

Broadly defined, online arbitration allows a third party neutral to render a decision for disputing parties using online technologies to support the process. Many online arbitration services also provide sample clauses for online users to insert into their online agreements or web site terms and conditions. Online arbitration borrows some of the general characteristics of offline arbitration. The parties must also enter into a written agreement to use arbitration. The online process is typically confidential, unless otherwise agreed to by the parties. The parties may be involved in selecting the arbitrators, depending on the agreement of the parties and the rules of agreed-upon ODR service provider. Furthermore, counsel may represent the disputing parties, if they wish. The decision of the arbitrator or panel may be binding or nonbinding under the disputants' agreement. For example, ICANN's Uniform Dispute Resolution Policy for dealing with domain name disputes is a nonbinding form of online arbitration, whereas private ODR providers offer both binding and nonbinding online arbitration services.

To help meet the differing demands of online disputants, many ODR service providers provide a menu of ODR options, which may include online negotiation, mediation, and arbitration services. With these varied options to choose from, many ODR service providers are in the position to offer a hybrid process known as med-arb, previously noted in Chapter 2. Med-arb allows parties to use a stepped or phased process, in which the parties are given the chance to negotiate on their own or work with a mediator first. If the disputants are unable to resolve any of the issues raised in the negotiation and/or mediation, then they may ask the mediator to render either a binding or nonbinding opinion on the unresolved issues. Online Resolution, Inc. (http://www.onlineresolution.com), NovaForum (http://www.novaforum.com), and Mediation and Arbitration Services (MARS) (http://www.resolvemydispute.com) are ODR providers that provide med-arb and arbitration services to help deal with online conflicts.

Why Might One Select Online Arbitration Rather Than Other ODR Methods?

The selection of online arbitration should be based on a thoughtful review of an online firm's or online user's conflict resolution needs. As indicated in Chapter 2, arbitration is an adjudicatory mechanism in which an impartial third party, rather than the parties themselves, decides the outcome of a conflict. Online mediation and negotiation are settlement mechanisms that emphasize compromise and the preservation of long-term or ongoing business and personal relationships. In settlement-driven processes, parties play an active role in the process and in determining its ultimate resolution. The parties must decide whether or not they wish to leave the outcome of their dispute in their own hands or those of a third party neutral.

**ODR IN THE DIGITAL ERA
The European Extra-Judicial Network**

Helping Consumers with Cross-Border Conflict Resolution

The continuing commercial development of the Internet has led to the growth in cross-border commercial activity and, therefore, an inevitable rise in cross-border conflicts. Resolving these cross-border conflicts can be particularly challenging for consumers unfamiliar with applicable laws and court procedures in different countries or unable to travel to another country to resolve their complaint. To help deal with concerns about cross-border disputes, the European Commission launched EEJ-Net in October 2001 (http://www.eejnet.org).

The EEJ-Net coordinates consumer conflict resolution through a network of national clearing-houses that work with local, regional, and national consumer organizations that offer a wide range of dispute resolution services. There are also ten European Consumer Centers (called "Euroguichets") operating specifically to help consumers trying to handle transnational conflicts. This pilot project is aimed at improving access to justice for consumers in the European Union (EU) and EU alliance member countries (EEA). Approximately fifteen EU member nations as well as Iceland and Norway participate in EEJ-Net.

EEJ-Net's site serves as the first point of contact for aggrieved EU/EEA consumers. The site is an online clearinghouse of information on and assistance for consumers trying to resolve cross-border disputes with merchants and businesses in other EU countries. Consumers can browse the site to locate ADR entities located in their own country or the home country of the merchant or business that can assist them in their cross-border disputes. Consumers can also file their complaints online through an ADR intake form that will forward their complaint to the proper national clearinghouse. The applicable clearinghouse works with the consumer and updates the consumer on the progress of the complaint and its proposed resolution.

This pilot project will be helpful not only to consumers, but also to other countries considering the development of ADR/ODR programs to address transnational consumer conflicts. For example, in the final report of the American Bar Association Task Force on E-Commerce and Alternative Dispute Resolution, the committee recommended the development of an iADR center. The proposed iADR center may be able to provide educational and informational materials to consumers, merchants and legal professionals trying deal with cross-border disputes. Similar to EEJ-Net, the potential center would offer recommended codes of practice for ODR service providers as well as provide the public with information on ADR/ODR service providers who handle e-commerce disputes.

(continued)

> Lessons learned from EEJ-Net's pilot program may be instrumental in the formulation of the iADR center and other similar ADR/ODR bodies aimed at providing information to consumers about ADR/ODR services and resolving consumer cross-border conflicts in a timely and fair manner.
>
> EEJ-Net *web information courtesy of EEJ-Net. All Rights Reserved.*

Disputing parties may choose online arbitration over online mediation or negotiation for a variety of reasons. Some disputants may be involved in a one-time transaction with strangers and are not concerned with the preservation of business or personal relationships found in settlement-based processes. Others may believe that they are not willing to compromise over a disagreement, so that the use of settlement mechanisms would not be useful to them. Other online parties in conflict may wish to have a third party with relevant expertise and experience to make a quick and cost-effective determination of their rights and obligations rather than take a more active role in fashioning the outcome of their disagreement. Lastly, some parties may not wish to have any further online contact with the other party but may solely prefer to file written materials for a third party to review and decide.

How Are Online Technologies Utilized in Online Arbitration?

Online arbitration streamlines the traditional and somewhat cumbersome process of arbitration by using more simplistic procedures and various online technologies. Online disputants wishing to engage in arbitration often enter their demand for arbitration through a complaint they have filed online, with the defending party replying online, too. The ODR provider may actually offer forms for the parties to complete online to guide the parties and to help speed up the process. Parties may also be limited in the amount of information that they may submit online in recognition of limited server space and to promote concise case presentation.

In online arbitration, the parties are allowed to present their views of the law and facts applicable to the dispute, but the parties must make their case in writing and are normally not afforded the opportunity to make formal presentations of oral testimony and documentary evidence in person, as in offline arbitration. The parties must submit materials in writing online in order to present their case and to try to persuade the arbitrator(s) in written form to accept their view of the conflict. Because the parties and the arbitrator(s) do not meet in person, online arbitration methods utilize different online technologies to facilitate the exchange of information.

Standard e-mail systems appear to be the most common form of online arbitration technology and are currently the basis for domain name arbitration proceedings under the UDRP (discussed in Chapter 2). Some online arbitration programs may augment e-mail with private chat rooms or listservs, as is done in the new Virtual Magistrate arbitration program. Disputing parties and the arbitrator trade documents and other written evidence through e-mail attachments or postings in a private chat room or distributed through a private listserv. Parties may also find it helpful to use scanners whenever possible to distribute relevant materials, such as charts, graphs, or photos, to help support their case. The arbitrator may request additional information or seek clarifications from the parties through e-mail or by posting requests in a private chat room or listserv. The arbitrator's decision may be sent by e-mail to the disputants or posted in a private chat room or on a public web site for review.

Some ODR providers are currently offering more sophisticated groupware, real-time chat rooms, videoconferencing tools, or streaming video over the Web to support online arbitration proceedings. For example, Resolution Forum, Inc., a nonprofit education organization based at the Center for Legal Responsibility at the South Texas College of Law, has developed its own groupware program called the CAN-WIN process (http://www.resolutionforum.com). Online arbitrators drawn from the legal, medical, engineering, real estate, and other business professions administer this system. The CAN-WIN process allows for completely online proceedings using a standard Internet browser. After requesting conferencing services, a case manager assigns each of the online parties a user name/password. Each disputant can log into the conferencing system, which lists all present parties on the screen. The CAN-WIN system allows the online arbitrator or the parties to send a real-time message to the entire group assembled online or to privately communicate through a separate virtual room with their counsel during an online arbitration session. At the end of the arbitration session, the arbitrator may clear the system of all messages and then save a transcript of the proceedings as a permanent record on the center's server. Although the system is completely text-based at present, the Center is planning to adopt a videoconferencing system in the future to accommodate online arbitration proceedings.

What Are Some of the Typical Duties of an Online Arbitrator?

Online arbitrators, like their offline counterparts, are creatures of contract whose authority is determined under the terms and conditions of their online arbitration agreement. Typically, these agreements reference the rules of the administering ODR service provider. To find out what an online arbitrator does, review the terms and conditions of your online arbitration agreement or check out the web site of your ODR service provider for its procedural rules to determine the online arbitrator's responsibilities. An excerpt about the role of an online arbitrator from Online Resolution Inc.'s web site follows.

The Role of an Online Arbitrator

Your Online Arbitrator will:

- Convene the arbitration.
  - Establish and confirm the rules governing the arbitration.
  - Schedule and organize the collection and presentation of evidence (testimony and documents), by direct and cross-examination.
  - Issue rulings on the admissibility of evidence.
  - Obtain agreement on methods and frequency of communication.
  - Determine whether arguments are necessary.
- Establish the basis for the award.
  - Determine what law or other standard (such as principles of equity, good conscience, or fairness) will apply.
  - Decide whether and how the award may be enforced.
- Check and respond to messages in the Resolution Room regularly, on a schedule agreed upon by the parties and the arbitrator.
- Remain unbiased toward all parties.
- Adhere to strict requirements of privacy and confidentiality.
- Abide by the American Arbitration Association Rules for Commercial Arbitration (or such other rules as the parties and the arbitrator may select).

© 2002 *Online Resolution, Inc. All Rights Reserved. Reprinted with Permission.*

What Are Some Examples of Online Arbitration Services?

A number of ODR service providers offer arbitration and med-arb services. Some services, such as the Virtual Magistrate, offer free online arbitration. Others, such as Online Resolution, Inc., charge for their services on an hourly basis or, such as NovaForum, Inc., on a per-party rate based on specific service plans. Under its Fair and Square ADR program, MARS charges a flat fee for claims under $1,000 or 15 percent of the settlement for claims over $1,000. Still other online arbitration services, charge a subscription fee to their member businesses that pays the costs of the process, which is free for consumers. We'll examine the processes of two different online arbitration services, The Virtual Magistrate and NovaForum. The Virtual Magistrate offers arbitration services using a password-protected listserv. NovaForum offers arbitration and med-arb services through its Electronic Courthouse.

The Virtual Magistrate

In 1995, it was a novel and ambitious idea to think of creating a fast, inexpensive, worldwide online arbitration program. This idea was the brainchild of National Conference of Auto-

Use of VMAG web information and logo courtesy of Virtual Magistrate, Chicago-Kent College of Law. All rights reserved.

mated Information Research (NCAIR) and the Cyberspace Law Institute (CLI), and these two organizations worked with AAA and Villanova Law School to establish the first online arbitration program. The initial version of the online arbitration program was geared toward online users faced with conflicts with their online service providers or other users who might have distributed harmful or illegal messages and postings. The project was the first to envision parties filing complaints electronically and the arbitrator/magistrate and the parties exchanging information completely online through e-mail and a password-protected listserv (referred to as the "grist"), which would distribute postings to all the participants. The arbitrator's decision would be posted on the grist for party review.

In its initial incarnation, the Virtual Magistrate also set forth a heady seven-point agenda:

1. Establish the feasibility of using online dispute resolution for disputes that originate online.
2. Provide system operators with informed and neutral judgments on appropriate responses to complaints about allegedly wrongful postings.
3. Provide users and others with rapid, low-cost, and readily accessible remedy for complaints about online postings.
4. Lay the groundwork for a self-sustaining, online dispute resolution system as a feature of contracts between system operators and users and content suppliers (and others concerned about wrongful postings).
5. Help to define the reasonable duties of a system operator confronted with a complaint.
6. Explore the possibility of using the Virtual Magistrate Project to resolve disputes related to computer networks.
7. Develop a formal governing structure for an ongoing Virtual Magistrate operation.

In its original form, the Virtual Magistrate was too far ahead of the public's learning curve, and the online arbitration service foundered. It ultimately attracted only a handful of disputes and rendered only one minor spamming decision, *Tierney and EMail America*, involving one of the program's early advisors. But the project paved the way for other ODR service providers by imagining a completely online arbitration program from the filing of complaints, to private information exchanges between the parties and the arbitrator, to the posting of the final decision.

In 2000, NCAIR and CLI teamed with the Chicago-Kent College of Law to revive the Virtual Magistrate, refocusing its arbitration services to include the burgeoning online consumer conflict environment (http://www.vmag.org). The program has broadened beyond its original dispute areas to include online contract, property, and tort conflicts. The Virtual Magistrate offers free and nonbinding arbitration services for the online community. The new program uses the same basic technological tools of the original program, e-mail and the grist, for communications between the parties and the magistrate.

Once parties agree to arbitrate the claims and to comply with the outcome, an administrator for the program selects an arbitrator with the requisite experience and expertise for the dispute. A copy of the complaint is posted to the grist and parties are directed to post messages to the grist. A private e-mail address for the arbitrator is also given to the disputants, in case private communication with the arbitrator is warranted. The arbitrator conducts the process online and may ask the parties questions, request additional materials from the parties, allow claimants to amend their complaints, and take other online actions that will allow parties to fully present their view of the dispute. The Virtual Magistrate strives to render decisions within seventy-two hours of the disputants' agreement to arbitrate the conflict online. The arbitrator sends the decisions to the parties by e-mail. Unless otherwise ordered by the arbitrator, the Virtual Magistrate's decisions, along with party filings, are made public at the end of the process to guide and inform the online community.

In its 2001 report, *Disputes in Cyberspace* 2001, Consumers International indicated that "[t]he Virtual Magistrate scores high in terms of all key criteria: independence, transparency, affordability, convenience, speed, due process and liberty. The service is especially appealing because it is free to consumers, and because case results are published." The Consumers International report can be found at http://www.consumersinternational.org. Perhaps this time the Virtual Magistrate will catch on with online consumers in need of fast, fair, and cheap conflict resolution services.

NovaForum®, Inc.

This Canadian firm offers parties a stepped or phased process of med-arb as its standard offering to the online community, with options for mediation, arbitration, and early neutral evaluation

NovaForum web information and logo courtesy of NovaForum, Inc. All Rights Reserved.

(http://www.novaforum.com). The parties follow an eight-step process that is patent protected as a "Computerized Litigation and Adjudication Method and System." Each party completes a secure intake form that covers basic party and contact information, a description of the dispute, the type of ODR method being requested, any special language needs, and acceptance of the use of the ODR process. After both parties have completed the intake form, each party must agree to use ODR, to follow NovaForum's Rules of Engagement, and to make the required payment of fees. The case manager then issues each party a user name and password so that each party can log in and begin to work on its case submissions.

The submission form is completed online and allows the disputants to describe the dispute in detail and to make their factual and legal arguments in support of their position. Parties can save their work at the end of their online session and come back to it later for revisions by entering in their user name and password. NovaForum allows each party to circulate its draft submission form through the Secure Client Workroom to their legal counsel or other relevant participants and even the other party, if desired, for comments and input. A party can then submit its case form to NovaForum online but is asked to sign and verify a hard copy of the case submission to ensure its accuracy before moving forward. Disputing parties are allowed one opportunity after their official submission to NovaForum to make amendments or additions to the form.

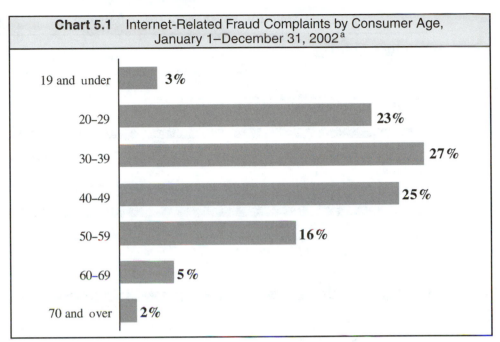

Chart 5.1   Internet-Related Fraud Complaints by Consumer Age, January 1–December 31, 2002[a]

19 and under — 3%
20–29 — 23%
30–39 — 27%
40–49 — 25%
50–59 — 16%
60–69 — 5%
70 and over — 2%

[a]Percentages are based on the total number of Internet-related fraud complaints in which consumers reported their age (62,791); 61% of consumers reported their age.

Chart Prepared by Consumer Sentinel, Bureau of Consumer Protection, U.S. Federal Trade Commission. Used with Permission (http://www.consumer.gov/sentinel/sentinel-trends/page7-pdf; http://www.ftc.gov).

After sending in the final submission, the parties may elect NovaForum's standard med-arb process or other ODR options. The parties may also customize the process further by requesting certain additional translation services in a number of different languages, including English, French, Portuguese, German, Mandarin, Cantonese, Russian, and Polish. Voice conferencing is included in the service, and for additional fees, parties may request video conferencing with the third-party neutral.

NovaForum assists the parties to select an appropriate third-party neutral based on a review of the case and the information provided by the parties in the intake form. The neutral begins to work with the parties within seventy-two hours, based on the availability of the parties for four-hour time blocks per resolution session. The neutral conferences with the parties through a secure online conference room called the ResolutionRoom™, which allows for both synchronous and asynchronous communications. The ResolutionRoom™ also serves as the secure repository for all communications, documents, proposals, and other online exchanges between the parties and the neutral. The neutral will try first to assist the parties in successfully mediating the dispute. If the dispute cannot be resolved through mediation, the neutral can then render a decision that is, by agreement, binding on the parties in a court of competent jurisdiction.

Sample NovaForum Intake Form

Intake Form

This Form is to be completed by parties wishing to undertake a NovaForum Resolution. Completion of this Form does not impose a binding contract.

The NovaForum Intake Form must be completed by both parties to the dispute - the Claimant and the Respondent. On completion of the Intake Forms by both the Claimant and the Respondent, a NovaForum Case Manager will contact you to assess your needs and the parties' commitment to proceeding. Payment will be arranged and a retainer entered into at that time.

Section 1: Description of Parties

○ The Claimant (the party initiating a claim against another party for compensation or other redress) ○ The Respondent (the party responding to the claim by the claimant, who may also be making a counter-claim in response).

Please describe both yourself and the other party below.

• CA. The Claimant is:

○ an Individual (*please complete Section CA*)

○ a Business (*please complete Section CB*)

○ an Organization or Association (*please complete Section CC*)

○ Other [   ] (*please complete Section CC*)

• CB. The Claimant is:

○ female   male
and resides in
○ Canada   ○ Asia   ○ Australia   ○ Europe   ○ USA
   ○ Other [   ]

• CC. The Claimant Corporation is:

○ a Small Business (1-50 employees)

○ a Mid-Sized Business (50-500 employees)

○ a Large Business (500+ employees)

Functions in the following sector:
○ Dot.com   ○ High Tech   ○ Retail   ○ Manufacturing   ○ Services
   ○ Other [   ]

and has it's Corporate Head Office in:
○ Canada   ○ Asia   ○ Australia   ○ Europe   ○ USA

Whether the matter is resolved through mediation or arbitration, the neutral drafts a settlement agreement or decision, which is contained in the Report of the Resolution Professional sent to each party. The report spells out the identity of the parties, a description of the legal and factual elements of the case, a review of the party contentions, and the terms and reasons for the settlement or decision in the case. By contract agreement, the parties agree to abide by the outcomes of the med-arb. NovaForum then creates a digital record of the proceeding for secure archiving and storage.

Do Disputing Parties Need to Enter into a Written Agreement in Order to Participate in an Online Arbitration?

It is a basic tenet of arbitration that the process is a creature of contract. The U.N.'s New York Convention, Federal Arbitration Act, and state arbitration laws help promote arbitration agreements as a desirable alternative to time and expense of standard litigation, but all require that the parties must agree to use the process. To date, there have been no cases that indicate that online arbitration agreements will be treated differently than offline ones, and parties must enter into a written arbitration agreement for online arbitration.

In one recent district court decision, *Parisi v NetLearning, Inc.*, 139 F. Supp. 2d 745 (2001), the court indicated that the UDRP binds only domain name registrants who have entered into the registration agreement to use the UDRP processes. The court stated that "If the parties have agreed to submit a dispute for a decision by a third party, they have agreed to arbitration." The court determined that under the UDRP, only registrants of domain names were required to use the process and not other third-party disputants who have not agreed to the UDRP process. This case clearly supports the notion that parties must enter into an agreement in order to be bound to participate in an online arbitration.

However, that agreement does not need to be a hard-copy contract found in offline arbitration. Courts have upheld online clickwrap licenses for downloaded software as valid agreements even though there is no pen-and-ink signature involved. In addition, with the advent of state and federal electronic signature laws and under proposed revisions to international arbitration standards by the United Nations Commission on International Trade Law (UNCITRAL) Working Group on Arbitration, parties may enter into online agreements through e-mails, electronic data interchange (EDI) (common electronic information exchanges between businesses), or by other electronic or digital messages, such as clicking on verifiable "I Agree" icons after reading the terms and conditions of a web site. Such online agreements would be subject to the same defenses found in all other contract cases, such as fraud, duress, unconscionability, or lack of capacity. In the following case the court must decide whether or not a dispute comes within the terms of an arbitration clause contained in a web site's terms of use.

KEY CHAPTER CASE

Does the Online Dispute Come within the Provisions of the Arbitration Clause in the E-Business's Terms of Use?

Manning v PayPal, Inc., 2001 U.S. Dist. LEXIS 23410 (D. PA 2001)

Fact Summary: The plaintiff, Richard Dey Manning, was a principal and agent for a business owned by his wife that sold goods on the Internet, primarily on auctions conducted on eBay.com. Defendant PayPal Inc. is a business that arranges for the payment of merchandise

(continued)

purchased on the Internet. Buyers and sellers may open accounts with PayPal and provide their credit card numbers and valid bank account information. When a purchaser seeks to pay for goods, he or she does so through PayPal, who holds the money for the seller. The funds are subsequently transferred electronically from PayPal to the seller's previously identified bank account. A dispute arose between plaintiff and defendant over $8.05 in fees allegedly charged by PayPal and $78.68 of plaintiff's funds allegedly being held by PayPal. Plaintiff requested that the money be transferred to his bank account, but the transfer was refused. Defendant still holds and refuses to transfer the funds. Plaintiff has been unsuccessful in his attempts to obtain the money, so he brought this action against PayPal seeking a declaratory judgment and damages. Defendant subsequently filed a motion to dismiss alleging, in part, that the district court lacked jurisdiction because the parties had entered into an arbitration agreement under PayPal's terms of use found on its website.

OPINION: JUDGE JAMES M. MUNLEY

. . . Generally, in cases involving arbitration, the following two questions are presented to the court: A) Did the parties enter into a valid arbitration agreement? and B) Does the dispute between the parties fall within the language of the arbitration agreement? John Hancock Mut. Life Ins. v. Olick, 151 F.3d 132, 137 (3d Cir. 1998). The parties appear not to dispute the fact that they entered into an arbitration agreement. . . . Plaintiff acknowledges that the following paragraph was part of the "Terms of Use" posted on the defendant's website when the dispute arose:

> **Arbitration.** Any controversy or claim arising out of or relating to this Agreement or the provision of Services shall be settled by binding arbitration in accordance with the commercial arbitration rules of the American Arbitration Association. Any such controversy or claim shall be arbitrated on an individual basis, and shall not be consolidated in any arbitration with any claim or controversy of any other party. The arbitration shall be conducted in Palo Alto, California, and judgment on the arbitration award may be entered in any court having jurisdiction thereof. Either you or PayPal may seek an interim or preliminary relief from a court of competent jurisdiction in Palo Alto, California necessary to protect the rights or property of you or PayPal Corp. (or its agents, suppliers, and subcontractors) pending the completion of arbitration. . . .

Accordingly, the question we are faced with becomes whether the dispute between the parties falls within the language of the arbitration agreement. In determining the scope of an arbitration provision, courts examine the language granting authority to the arbitrators and for any language limiting the arbitrator's jurisdiction. . . . The language at issue in the instant case is very broad. By its own terms it states that arbitration is to be applied to any controversy or claim arising out of or relating to the Agreement or the provision of services. . . .

In support of his position that the instant case does not fall within the language of the arbitration agreement, the plaintiff claims that the complaint necessarily refers to the services rendered by the defendant and the Terms of Use, but that does not determine the ultimate question of whether the dispute arises in connection with services rendered by the defendant. We disagree. This whole claim is intertwined with the agreement that the plaintiff and defendant had. Issues include what the defendant was allowed to do pursuant to that agreement and what it was not allowed to do. Considering the broad language used in the agreement and the strong policy favoring arbitration, we find that the dispute certainly falls within the provisions of the arbitration agreement. For this reason, we lack subject matter jurisdiction, and the defendant's motion to dismiss will be granted. . . .

The main dispute regarding arbitration agreements often flows from the timing of the parties' agreement to arbitrate, particularly in online consumer arbitration agreements. Several recent U.S. Supreme Court opinions as well as numerous state and federal court decisions have upheld the use of pre-dispute arbitration agreements (PDAA) in a wide range of disagreements, including disputes involving securities and antitrust violations, employment discrimination, franchise agreements, trademark claims, and consumer goods and service contracts. PDAAs mean that parties give up the right to go to court before a dispute arises between them. Consumer groups have been particularly critical of the use of "take-it-or-leave-it" PDAAs in consumer contracts, contending that such clauses prevent meaningful consumer choice of ADR methods and hamper the benefits of consumer protection laws that are best reviewed and interpreted in the courts. At times, U.S. courts have been willing to strike down PDAAs that were not freely and knowingly entered into by the parties or that involved arbitration programs that did not adequately protect the parties' procedural and substantive rights.

In May 2002, Public Citizen released a report, *The Costs of Arbitration*, that the costs of initiating an offline arbitration are often much greater than the costs of litigation for consumers or employees claiming wrongful discharge. Public Citizen found that arbitration organizations often impose up-front and continuing fees that in a court situation would be absorbed in an attorney's contingent fee arrangement or would be offered for free or at low cost in the public court system (available at http://www.citizen.org). The report indicated that cash-strapped consumers and employees might stop fighting for their rights because of these up-front and continuing costs. These criticisms support the contention that online arbitration can be useful in B2C disagreements only if fees are kept at a low or nominal cost. (See Chapter 7 on ODR system design and Chapter 8 on future trends in ODR.) Despite these concerns, U.S. courts have generally upheld the use of PDAAs unless it can be shown that the arbitration agreement does not comply with fundamental fairness or is found to be oppressive or highly unreasonable.

However, some countries, particularly in the European Union, do not allow consumers to enter into pre-dispute arbitration clauses contained in standard form agreements in e-commerce in an effort to provide greater consumer protection. The burden is on the e-business to prove that the clause was individually negotiated with the consumer. Because individual B2C pre-dispute arbitration agreements are unlikely, global e-tailers may find that they may enter into online arbitration agreements only after a dispute has arisen in order to maximize consumer choice. Although the EU has tended to support the use of settlement-driven mechanisms to resolve online consumer disputes, countries such as Spain and Portugal have used arbitration boards to deal with consumer conflicts in the past.

Online businesses that deal with consumers may wonder how they will deal with these important legal differences. Amazon.com has been able to address these legal differences by inserting different dispute resolution clauses in the terms and conditions of its different national web sites. In recognition of the acceptance of PDAAs in the United States, Amazon.com's web site indicates that any disputes with the e-tailer will be resolved through the use of arbitration. Because PDAAs are frowned upon in the EU, Amazon.com's UK web site contains a dispute resolution clause that allows consumers to bring an action in the courts of the United Kingdom. Online businesses will need to insert different conflict resolution clauses into their web sites until there is greater uniformity in the arena.

Quick Clicks: Examining U.S. and EU Web Sites for PDAAs   Companies that offer products and services in a wide variety of countries need to comply with acceptable approaches to conflict resolution in those markets. Visit a popular web site that offers separate web sites to consumers in different countries. Examine the terms of use of its U.S. site and see if they include a PDAA. Then visit the site of this same online business specifically geared toward the United Kingdom or some other EU member nation. Undertake the same review of its terms of use to determine if they contain a PDAA. Does the online business utilize the same or a different approach to conflict resolution in its U.S. and EU terms of use? Summarize the approach used by the online business in each instance and provide your written report to the instructor for review and/or class discussion.

Are the Decisions of Online Arbitrators or Arbitral Panels Enforceable in National Courts?

One of the challenges of international conflict resolution is enforcement of settlements and decisions. Most online arbitration awards are enforced by party compliance with the terms of their arbitration agreement or perhaps through the withdrawal of a trustmark or seal for noncomplying businesses participating in certification programs. However, if a party does not comply voluntarily under the terms of the agreement or is undeterred by the loss of a seal or trustmark, a party will need to resort to national courts for enforcement. Arbitrators do not possess the authority to enforce their own awards, and if voluntary compliance is not forthcoming from one of the parties, they must rely on the courts for assistance to ensure compliance.

The issue of enforceability depends, in part, upon the type of arbitration process that the parties have agreed to use. If the parties agreed that the outcome was binding with no or little opportunity for appeal, then a court might be quite limited in its ability to review and overturn the outcome. If the parties have consented to a nonbinding form of online arbitration, then a court would not be required to enforce the arbitral outcome. In other instances, such as the UDRP, the online arbitration process envisions the possibility of parallel or subsequent court proceedings, which suggests that its decisions are not binding on courts but may be binding upon ICANN registrars as to the transfer or cancellation of domain names.

The grounds for an appeal of an arbitration award also are based upon whether or not the arbitration decision is a domestic or international one. If the parties are from different states within the United States, then the Federal Arbitration Act (FAA) comes into play in regard to enforcement. The FAA promotes the use of arbitration, and appellate courts are not allowed to reinterpret the factual findings made by the arbitrators. The grounds for appeal are limited primarily to arbitrator fraud, misconduct or corruption, clear lack of due process or fundamental fairness in the arbitration process, and an arbitrator's or panel's actions that exceed its authority under the arbitration agreement. Therefore, if the arbitral decision does not fall into one of these categories, the U.S. courts will typically uphold it.

If the parties are from different countries, then international arbitration issues are applied to the dispute and its outcome. As indicated in Chapter 1, it can be very difficult to enforce a court judgment in the court of another nation. However, it is significantly easier for parties to enforce international arbitration awards than judicial decisions in the national courts of signatory nations due to the existence of the 1958 United Nations Convention on the Recognition and Enforcement of Foreign Arbitral Awards, known as the New York Convention. Well over 100 nations have signed on to the New York Convention, which allows for the reciprocal recognition and enforcement of international arbitration awards between signatory nations. Regional versions of this convention, such as the Panama or Inter-American Convention, sponsored by the Organization of American States (OAS), allows for the enforcement of both domestic and international arbitration awards for signatory nations in the western hemisphere. Decisions under this convention have closely followed those of courts interpreting the New York Convention.

Under the New York Convention, a signatory nation may determine that it will not enforce an arbitral award that violates that nation's laws or public policy or that contravenes the arbitration agreement of the parties. The Convention spells out the following limited grounds that may allow a national court to refuse to recognize and enforce an arbitration award:

1. the lack of due process or fundamental fairness in the arbitration process
2. the improper or illegal composition of the arbitral panel under the parties' agreement to arbitrate or national laws
3. the illegality of the arbitration agreement or illegality of the subject matter of the arbitration under relevant national laws
4. the lack of a final determination or an award for a court to enforce
5. an award exceeding the authority of the arbitrator under the arbitration agreement
6. an arbitral award contravening a well-established public policy in the enforcing country

Similar to the FAA, the grounds for appeal are narrow and do not invite a retrial of the facts of the dispute. If the process and outcomes do not fall into any of the above categories, then the courts of signatory nations should enforce the international arbitration award.

The enforcement of online arbitration awards, both domestically and internationally, has not yet been fully tested in the courts. At this point, online arbitration can expect to be reviewed under the same standards in domestic and cross-border disputes as are currently applied to offline arbitration. At a minimum, any online arbitration process must afford the parties neutral and impartial arbitrators, due process or fundamental fairness in the proceedings, full compliance with the terms and conditions of the arbitration agreement, and outcomes that do not directly contradict national laws and policies.

ODR Bytes

Offline arbitration is an adversarial process in which both parties, usually through their attorneys, make a formal presentation of written and oral evidence to one or more neutral decision-makers in a confidential procedure.

Broadly defined, online arbitration allows a third-party neutral to render a decision for disputing parties using online technologies to support the process and often applying more simplistic procedures.

Med-arb allows parties to use a stepped or phased process in which the parties are given the chance to negotiate on their own or work with a mediator first. If the disputants are unable to resolve any of the issues raised in the negotiation and/or mediation, then they may ask the online mediator to act as an arbitrator and render either a binding or nonbinding opinion on the unresolved issues.

Parties should enter into an arbitration agreement before using online arbitration processes. The United States allows parties to enter into PDAAs in a wide range on disagreements, whereas the EU does not allow the use of PDAAs in B2C disputes.

Disputing parties may choose online arbitration over online mediation or negotiation because they may not be concerned with the preservation of business or personal relationships in one-time transactions with strangers, they are not willing to compromise over a disagreement, they wish to have a third party with relevant expertise and experience to make a quick and cost-effective determination of their rights, or they do not want any further online contact with the other party.

Online arbitrators, like their offline counterparts, are creatures of contract whose authority is determined under the terms and conditions of their online arbitration agreement.

A number of ODR service providers offer arbitration and/or med-arb services, including the Virtual Magistrate, NovaForum, Online Resolution, Inc., and MARS.

The New York Convention allows for the reciprocal recognition and enforcement of international arbitration awards between signatory nations, whereas the Panama or Inter-American Convention allows for the enforcement of both domestic and international arbitration awards for signatory nations in the western hemisphere.

Under the New York Convention, a signatory nation may determine that it will not enforce an arbitral award that violates that nation's laws or public policy or that contravenes the arbitration agreement of the parties.

Online arbitration processes must afford the parties due process, fully comply with the terms and conditions of the arbitration agreement, and not contradict national laws and policies.

ODR Bookmarks

Consumers International
http://www.consumersinternational.org

EEJ-Net
http://www.eejnet.org

Mediation and Arbitration Services (MARS)
http://www.resolvemydispute.com

NovaForum
http://www.novaforum.com

Online Resolution, Inc.
http://www.onlineresolution.com

Public Citizen
http://www.publiccitizen.org

Resolution Forum, Inc.
http://www.resolutionforum.com

Virtual Magistrate
http://www.vmag.org

Selected ODR Bibliography

Consumers International Office for Developed and Transition Economies. "Dispute Resolution in Cyberspace 2001: Update of Online Dispute Resolution for Consumers in Cross-Border Disputes." (November 2001), http://www.consumersinternational.org.

Hill, Richard. "On-Line Arbitration: Issues and Solutions." (December 1998), http://www.umass.edu/dispute/hill.htm.

Ponte, Lucille M. "Boosting Consumer Confidence in E-Business: Recommendations For Establishing Fair and Effective Dispute Resolution Programs For B2C Online Transactions." *Albany L. J. of Sci. & Tech.* 12 (2002): 441.

Ponte, Lucille M. "Broadening Traditional ADR Notions of Disclosure: Special Considerations for Posting Conflict Resolution Policies and Programs on E-Business Web Sites," *Ohio St. J. On Disp. Res.* 17 (2002): 321.

Ponte, Lucille M. "Throwing Bad Money after Bad: Can Online Dispute Resolution (ODR) Really Deliver the Goods for the Unhappy Internet Shopper?" *Tulane J. of Tech. & Intell. Prop.* 55 (2001): 55.

Ponte, Lucille M., and Thomas D. Cavenagh. *Alternative Dispute Resolution in Business.* St. Paul, MN: West Educational Publishing, 1999.

Williams, Jackson. *The Costs of Arbitration.* Public Citizen, 2002.

Online Jury Proceedings

CHAPTER FAQS

What is an online jury proceeding?

Are there online sites providing jury proceedings?

What advantages can be obtained through an online jury proceeding?

What disadvantages may be entailed in an online jury proceeding?

Process Introduction and Overview

To discuss the online jury process, it makes sense to have an understanding of the traditional offline litigation process, so what follows is a whirlwind tour of litigation American style. The civil trial is one in which a neutral fact finder, normally a jury, applies the law to questions of fact to reach a conclusion regarding the claims made by the parties. It is a three-phase process: the pretrial phase of the civil lawsuit involves various practices undertaken to prepare a case for presentation to the judge or jury. The trial is a multi-step proceeding involving the carefully orchestrated staging of evidence by the parties and a decision by the fact finder. The posttrial period involves appeals and efforts by both parties to implement or avoid the judgment reached at trial. (See Chart 6.1.)

The pretrial phase is the lengthiest step in litigation, often requiring years to complete, because it is the phase of litigation least supervised by courts. The initial component of the pretrial stage is case investigation, during which parties, often with the assistance of attorneys, endeavor to understand the dispute by determining the facts and the damages and to evaluate the strength and dollar value of the case. The formal litigation process begins when the plaintiff files a complaint. The complaint is a document that puts parties on notice regarding the nature of the claims and gives a rough estimate of damages. The defendant in turn files an answer. The answer essentially admits or denies the allegations contained in the complaint and lists any defenses. The defendant may also counterclaim, which means sue the plaintiff, or add other defendants, that is, sue parties not listed by the plaintiff but with some relationship to the suit. Discovery, the longest and most complex step prior to trial, is essentially a court-sanctioned investigation of the case through written and oral means.

Pretrial dispositive motions argue that the facts or the law are so clearly favorable to one party that a trial is unnecessary and a judgment should be entered on the pleadings and accompanying materials. In the event the pretrial motions are denied, trial preparation begins. Party witnesses will be prepared, often by rehearsing testimony and participating in mock examinations. Evidentiary and demonstrative exhibits will be created to support and explain the positions taken by the parties.

The trial itself is relatively short compared to the pretrial period, often lasting just days or weeks. The judge makes procedural rulings during the trial and decides which laws apply to the findings of fact made by the jury. The trial begins with jury selection, in which a process known as *voir dire* allows lawyers to exclude certain jurors to eliminate bias or prejudice. Following jury selection, opening statements are made by all counsel; in most jurisdictions these statements are made first by the plaintiff and then by the defendant. These statements tell the jury what it will hear from each of the parties in terms of evidence and law.

Following opening statements, the plaintiff presents a case in chief. In other words, all the plaintiff's evidence is presented to the jury first. Defense counsel is permitted to cross-examine, or test, the testimony of the plaintiff's witnesses during this phase of the trial. The defendant then presents a case in chief as well. The case consists of all of the evidence that tends to show that the defendant is not liable for the injuries suffered by the plaintiff. Defense experts will probably testify, documents rebutting those presented by the plaintiff will be introduced, and the defendant may testify. Plaintiff's counsel may cross-examine defense witnesses.

Closing arguments are, as the name suggests, the opportunity for the lawyers to sum up and interpret the evidence that has been offered to the jury during the trial. Jury deliberations follow the closing arguments. These are conducted in a secluded room, off limits to the judge, lawyers, parties, the press, or the public. The jury receives detailed instructions from the judge, ordinarily prior to beginning deliberations. These instructions guide the jury through the process of assessing the evidence and reaching a decision.

Litigation does not always end with the trial. Indeed, the posttrial period can be very costly and time consuming. The losing party at trial has the opportunity to request that the trial judge set aside the verdict as inconsistent with the evidence. This is permitted in rare circumstances when a judge believes a jury has acted against the overwhelming weight of evidence. The losing party who does not prevail in a motion to set aside the verdict may appeal. On appeal, that party may ask that a panel of higher court judges decide that errors of law were made in the trial such that a new trial or other relief is warranted. No new evidence is introduced at all at the appellate level. Instead, appellate courts hear arguments from counsel that the legal procedure used to reach the verdict was flawed. An appellate court may simply affirm the lower court's judgment, or it may reverse the judgment and remand the case for additional proceedings, perhaps a new trial.

Chart 6.1 Three-Stage Litigation Process			
Pretrial	**Trial**	**Posttrial**	**Considerations**
Plaintiff's complaint	Pretrial motions	Written briefing	Time, cost, risk
Defendant's answer	Opening statements	Oral argument	Settlement possibilities
Discovery	Plaintiff's case	Court deliberations	Remedies: Money only
Dispositive motions	Defendant's case	Decision	Loss of privacy
	Closing arguments	Next level	Loss of relationships
	Jury deliberations		
	Judgment		

What Is an Online Jury Proceeding?

You have seen in previous chapters that online arbitration involves the use of one or more third-party decision makers, normally experts of some kind, to render a binding judgment in a dispute on the basis of evidence submitted by the parties. Although online arbitration and jury processes are both adjudicative, the online jury differs from arbitration in that the process allows peers to judge cases in ways similar to a live courtroom trial. Those few sites offering such a service have endeavored to incorporate most of the steps in the pretrial and trial stages of litigation described previously, but with an online twist: the jury doesn't actually see the parties, nor do they interact with one another to any significant extent.

Online juries remain a relatively rare commodity. We have described a significant growth in the availability and use of online negotiation, mediation, and arbitration, but we offer here only a short introduction to some of the possibilities that may become more prevalent in the future as the speed, bandwidth, and sophistication of Internet users increases—all things necessary for the proliferation of online jury processes. The ODR processes described in the preceding chapters are all possible with fairly basic Internet connections and minimal additional hardware and software. Even arbitration, because it takes place before a single decision-maker, often in an asynchronous format, can be done by parties who do not possess an extensive range of Internet access hardware and software.

Trying a case to an online jury in a fashion that is functionally equivalent to a live jury is a completely different matter. The number of participants and the complexity of the technology required to bring all of them the full range of evidence makes this process far less accessible to most potential users. Moreover, once the evidence has reached the jury, the capacity for deliberation among that body is a necessity—so,

Chart 6.2	Comparison of Jury Proceedings	
	Online	Offline (Courtroom)
Due process protections	No	Yes
Judicial supervision	No	Yes
Formal discovery	Independently, and only if lawsuit is filed	Yes
Motions	No	Yes
Voir dire	Limited	Yes
Witness testimony	Summarized	Live
Binding outcomes	Limited	Yes
Nature of enforcement	By contract	By judgment
Number of jurors	By agreement or by site rule	By court rule
Noneconomic remedies	Yes	No
Right to appeal	No	Yes

judge, jury, and litigants must all have considerable online expertise and fairly high-end technology, including audio/video, scanning, and probably a high-speed Internet connection. Many people lack the technology, so the days of widespread use of the Internet to actually try cases are still in the future. That said, there are services and institutions that make interesting use of the Internet to allow peers to judge peers in ways that are somewhat different than an offline trial.

It is important to note that unlike other ODR processes, the online jury proceeding is not ordinarily intended to be an equivalent process to its offline counterpart. The process is usually fairly abbreviated and its objectives, often advisory rather than binding, are completely different. Indeed, online jury proceedings may be used very effectively to prepare for offline and online negotiation sessions, because they allow parties to establish the value of the case in a fairly objective fashion. Chart 6.2 compares the major characteristics of the two types of jury proceedings.

Are There Online Sites Providing Jury Proceedings?

iCourthouse.com (www.icourthouse.com), owned and operated by Perception Corporation (www.perception.com), overcomes some of the obstacles to peers judging cases by allowing users to post disputes for anyone to judge. The site is essentially a survey site on which litigants submit their cases to the public for judgment on the basis of written statements and fairly basic evidence. Cases are not actually tried in front of specific juries hearing carefully controlled evidence, as they would be in a traditional courtroom.

Instead, parties submit cases via interactive forms that allow for a description of the dispute, visual evidence in the form of scanned documents or pictures, and arguments for particular damages or recoveries. Jurors are simply Internet users who become members of iCourthouse for the purpose of reviewing cases and entering advisory verdicts. Anyone can serve as a juror at any time and on any case at iCourthouse, whether they possess any ability or expertise or not. In fact, anyone can be a party at the site as well, because filing a case at iCourthouse is free; so is serving as a juror. Attorneys can file a case and, for a fee, receive a formal written report certifying official trial results. To achieve a relatively fair result, the iCourthouse rules prohibit the use of proper names or identifying information, such as addresses, in case filings.

iCourthouse members, including parties and jurors, log in to the secure site with a user name and password. At the site, one can choose as many cases as ones wishes to evaluate as a juror as well as review the status of all cases that one is participating in as either a juror or litigant. Links to the plaintiff's and defendant's "Trial Books," the repositories of evidence on iCourthouse, are also provided. Jurors may ask questions of the parties and render verdicts that include explanations for the verdict they have rendered. Screen 6.1 is the initial "My iCourthouse" page that greets users of the site after log-in.

The Trial Books are complete records of a dispute and have internal links to the parties' opening statements, all the evidence submitted by the parties, the parties' closing arguments, and juror questions and party answers in a particular matter. Parties can upload digital files as evidence, including photos, document scans, webpages, e-mails sent and received, and documents in the form of text files. Trial Books also can include legal authorities for jurors by referring to general legal principles, existing jury instructions, and/or state or federal statutes or cases; parties can even enter links to sites containing legal resources for jurors to use themselves. Finally, parties can also type in testimony directly as evidence. Screen 6.2 is a sample opening statement from the site.

A unique aspect of iCourthouse is that it allows jurors to communicate directly with the parties—something not possible in a traditional courtroom. After reviewing the evidence, jurors may enter specific questions about the dispute in the Trial Book; both the question and the answer are permanently preserved in the Trial Book for other jurors to read before rendering a verdict (Screen 6.3).

When a juror has reviewed the case and is prepared to render a verdict, a link on the Trial Book allows a dollar amount and explanation to be entered into the record. Trial Books display all the juror verdicts and comments in a case as well as the median award given by jurors who found in favor of the plaintiff. Each juror has the opportunity to review what others have done in a particular case before entering a verdict himself or herself; this review of the preceding juror's comments is the substitute for live deliberation on iCourthouse. Screen 6.4 is the verdict form used to record dollar amounts and comments in a dispute.

Cases are open until closed by the plaintiff. This ordinarily happens either because the parties agree that there has been a final verdict or because the parties have settled the case. Parties can also leave a case open for juror feedback indefinitely but may agree that only the verdicts given before a specific date and time will count or that only a specific number of the verdicts or verdicts entered during a particular period of

Screen 6.1

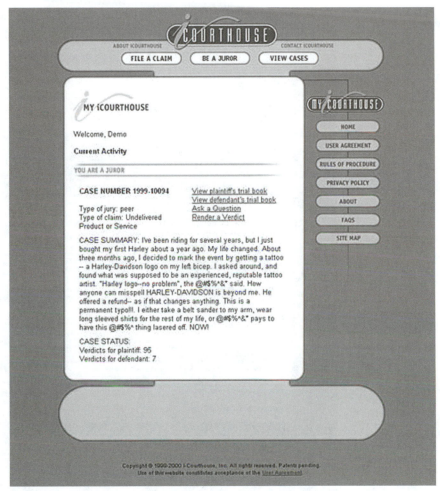

www.icourthouse.com

time will count. Results are enforceable only by agreement between the parties, but the parties can freely agree as to what proportion of the verdicts will constitute a final decision. In fact, parties are free to construct any agreement they wish to on the matter of finality of the verdict; they could take the median verdict, the lowest verdict, or the average verdict from all jurors using established rationale for deciding the case in a certain way, i.e., only those who find some contributory negligence. The verdict summary looks like Screen 6.5.

The iCourthouse service can be extremely valuable to the parties even if they choose not to accept the verdict as binding or to use it to guide them toward settlement in the case. The service offers parties an opportunity to preview the case to a

Screen 6.2

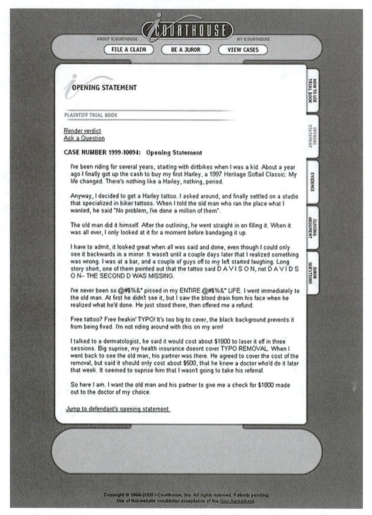

www.icourthouse.com

jury of sorts before trying or arbitrating it in a forum in which the outcome is final and binding. Developing a sense of what real people think the case is worth and why is invaluable to an attorney preparing to present the case. Future versions of iCourthouse.com will allow lawyers to localize their juries to particular geographic regions for a more accurate picture of case worth. In addition, mechanisms for increased and more specific feedback from jurors are planned.

The virtualjury.com site offers an interesting variation on the online jury proceeding. Both iCourthouse.com and Legalvote.com, another similar online jury service, collect case impressions and verdicts, sometimes binding ones, from random, unscreened

Screen 6.3

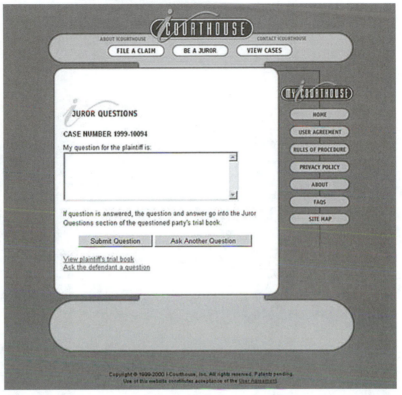

www.icourthouse.com

Internet users who are interested in providing input on a real case. Virtualjury.com screens potential jurors with an intake form that resembles a formal *voir dire* intake form. Potential jurors complete the form, which requires a fairly extensive disclosure of personal biographical information, and are contacted by virtualjury.com if they are selected through "scientific sampling techniques" to participate as a focus-group juror.

Attorneys may purchase a focus-group jury from virtualjury.com on any sort of civil dispute on which a jury could rule. Doing so is an economical way of better understanding how others might see the case—"jury science" on the cheap. When lawyers opt for a virtualjury.com group, a jury of suitable individuals is assembled. If desired, the lawyer may indicate to virtualjury.com what type of people he or she wants for the jury. In a jurisdiction that is heavily populated by a certain ethnic group, for example, a lawyer can request a disproportionate number of that group to achieve a focus group similar to the sort of jury that will likely hear the case in court.

A second departure from the iCourthouse approach is the use of a facilitator. During the live focus-group process, a virtualjury.com moderator facilitates an online

Screen 6.4

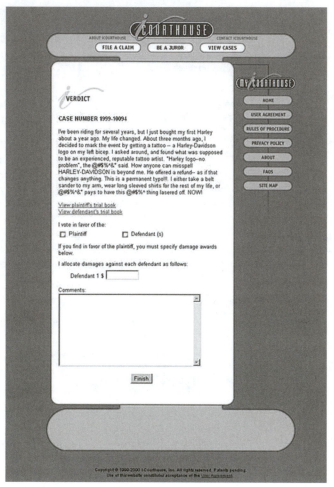

www.icourthouse.com

conversation between the lawyer and all the jurors. The session begins with the attorney providing the jury with a detailed summary of the case. It is also possible to provide the jury with pictures and other visual evidence through the site. Thereafter, the moderator, who has received training and certification in this task from virtualjury.com, manages an online conversation between the jurors and the attorney. The attorney may ask questions of the jury directly or through the moderator, and the moderator may ask questions as well. The questions are not governed by any rules of evidence, but instead are unstructured and open-ended, with a view toward seeing the case as the jury does. Interestingly, the site even permits jurors to interact with one another, so the attorney can observe something akin to live jury deliberation.

Screen 6.5

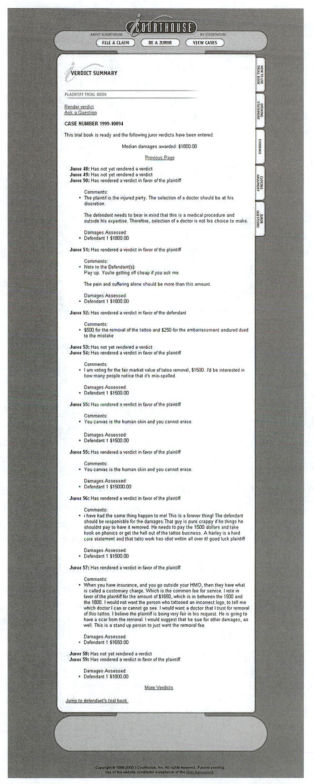

iCOURTHOUSE

ABOUT ICOURTHOUSE   MY ICOURTHOUSE

FILE A CLAIM   BE A JUROR   VIEW CASES

ic **VERDICT SUMMARY**

PLAINTIFF TRIAL BOOK

Render verdict
Ask a Question

CASE NUMBER 1999-10094

This trial book is ready and the following juror verdicts have been entered:

Median damages awarded: $1800.00

Previous Page

Juror 48: Has not yet rendered a verdict
Juror 49: Has not yet rendered a verdict
Juror 50: Has rendered a verdict in favor of the plaintiff

Comments:
- The plaintif is the injured party. The selection of a doctor should be at his discretion.

  The defendent needs to bear in mind that this is a medical procedure and outside his expertise. Therefore, selection of a doctor is not his choice to make.

Damages Assessed:
- Defendant 1 $1800.00

Juror 51: Has rendered a verdict in favor of the plaintiff

Comments:
- Note to the Defendant(s):
  Pay up. You're getting off cheap if you ask me.

  The pain and suffering alone should be more than this amount.

Damages Assessed:
- Defendant 1 $1800.00

Juror 52: Has rendered a verdict in favor of the defendant

Comments:
- $500 for the removal of the tattoo and $250 for the embarrassment endured dued to the mistake

Juror 53: Has not yet rendered a verdict
Juror 54: Has rendered a verdict in favor of the plaintiff

Comments:
- I am voting for the fair market value of tatoo removal, $1500. I'd be interested in how many people notice that it's mis-spelled.

Damages Assessed:
- Defendant 1 $1500.00

Juror 55: Has rendered a verdict in favor of the plaintiff

Comments:
- You canvas is the human skin and you cannot erase.

Damages Assessed:
- Defendant 1 $1500.00

Juror 55: Has rendered a verdict in favor of the plaintiff

Comments:
- You canvas is the human skin and you cannot erase.

Damages Assessed:
- Defendant 1 $15000.00

Juror 56: Has rendered a verdict in favor of the plaintiff

Comments:
- i have had the same thing happen to me! This is a forever thing! The defendant should be responisble for the damages.That guy is pure crappy if he things he shouldn't pay to have it removed. He needs to pay the 1500 dollars and take hook on phonics or get the hell out of the tattoo business. A harley is a hard core statement and that tatto work has idiot writtin all over it! good luck plaintiff

Damages Assessed:
- Defendant 1 $1500.00

Juror 57: Has rendered a verdict in favor of the plaintiff

Comments:
- When you have insurance, and you go outside your HMO, then they have what is called a customary charge. Which is the common fee for service. I vote in favor of the plaintiff for the amount of $1650, which is in between the 1500 and the 1800. I would not want the person who tattooed an incorrect logo, to tell me which doctor I can or cannot go see. I would want a doctor that I trust for removal of this tattoo. I believe the plaintiff is being very fair in his request. He is going to have a scar from the removal. I would suggest that he sue for other damages, as well. This is a stand up person to just want the removal fee.

Damages Assessed:
- Defendant 1 $1650.00

Juror 58: Has not yet rendered a verdict
Juror 59: Has rendered a verdict in favor of the plaintiff

Damages Assessed:
- Defendant 1 $1800.00

More Verdicts

Jump to defendant's trial book

Sidebar tabs: HOW TO USE TRIAL BOOK · OPENING STATEMENT · EVIDENCE · CLOSING ARGUMENT · JUROR QUESTIONS

The object of the exercise is to allow the attorney to learn as much as possible about the factors in the case that appeal to the jury and those that do not. Jurors may be asked to place a dollar value on the case and to provide a rationale for that value. They might also be asked to evaluate the factual or legal claims being made, to consider the evidence an attorney is anticipating using, and to react to language an attorney might employ in an opening statement or closing argument.

The process is nonbinding and ordinarily does not even include the opposing attorney. However, it is a valuable tool in the preparation of a case for trial. Virtualjury.com suggests that the process, which is very similar to the marketing focus group, can be used to do several things:

- forecast jury verdicts
- decide whether to try a case or settle it
- detect potential juror bias
- develop successful trial themes
- design effective visual evidence

The actual process, for which a patent is being sought, looks very similar to a multiparty chatroom. The site offers a very useful demonstration of the process at this link: http://www.virtualjury.com/demo.htm.

ODR IN THE DIGITAL ERA
The Michigan Cybercourt Initiative

Private online dispute resolution is not the only game in town. Even governments understand the efficacy of the Internet for resolution of certain types of disputes; consider Michigan. In an effort to attract high-tech companies and the highly educated and well-compensated employees that they bring with them to the state, a "cybercourt" for cases in which these companies are involved is being developed in that jurisdiction. Eventually, all aspects of select litigation could be conducted online, meaning that lawyers and litigants would never see the inside of a courtroom; instead of hearings in person, arguments and testimony could be presented via teleconference; evidence could be evaluated through streaming video or as digital still images. Better still, normal business hours would not apply to much of the proceeding. The Internet functions all day, every day, so cases could be prepared, presented, and judged day and night and over the weekend.

The cybercourt is the subject of a bill introduced by state representative Marc Shulman with the enthusiastic support of former Michigan Governor John Engler. Both wish to see high-tech businesses join the automotive industry as key elements of the Michigan economy and believe the cybercourt would be a very attractive option for such businesses. Says Engler, a three-term Republican, "at a time when you can go from idea to IPO at warp speed, we need to have a way to get through the court system at a faster rate." "You literally can have companies be formed, have a relatively short life cycle, and go out of business in the time it takes a case to get through court," Engler continues. "I think it will streamline the court process for new-economy businesses, and hopefully that will be something that will lure business to Michigan," adds Democratic former state attorney general, now governor, Jennifer Granholm.

Engler, Shulman, and other supporters envision a court that could adjudicate technology cases valued at $25,000 or more; parties would be required to waive a jury trial and would have to opt into the cybercourt system voluntarily. Although the judge might still hear the case in a courtroomlike space for appearance's sake, witnesses, litigants, and lawyers could participate from their offices. Furthermore, the public could observe online proceedings in cybercourt from any convenient Internet connection point. Indeed, lawyers neither licensed to practice in Michigan nor residents of the state might be permitted to represent clients in Michigan cybercourt. The court would also attempt to emulate the strengths of specialty courts in other states, including the Delaware Chancery Court and the business divisions of courts in New York and North Carolina, all of which are able to expedite the management of litigation effectively.

Some in Michigan and elsewhere have questions and concerns. Some lawyers wonder about the jurisdiction of the court, asking which cases, exactly, it would be empowered to hear and decide. The matter of an appeal is also problematic. Cases tried in cybercourt would present a different record both in substance and in form, from which a reviewing court would be required to make a decision. The expense and sophistication of the equipment required to create and maintain the cybercourt troubles some as well. Finally, preparing judges and attorneys to participate effectively in the system poses considerable challenges—high-tech businesses may know high tech, but without significant training, there is no guarantee that judges and lawyers will. For more information on the Michigan Cybercourt see the following website devoted to the effort: http://www.michigancybercourt.net/.

Michigan is not alone in moving to the web with trial proceedings. Alaska's Superior Court in Anchorage streamed simultaneous court transcription to the web in a closely watched case involving legislative redistricting. The judge in the matter determined that the considerable public interest in the case supported use of the most expeditious distribution of the courtroom proceedings possible. Lacking the technology for a live webcast, the court did the next best thing and streamed the text from the court reporter straight to the public. Look at www.webscriptlive.com to see what the streamed text looks like.

What Advantages Can Be Obtained through an Online Jury Proceeding?

The most compelling strength of online jury processes is actually not in their direct resolution of cases by verdict. It is, instead, their usefulness in preparing parties to settle disputes in a fashion that is objectively defensible—that is consistent with what outsiders think the case is worth. The reality is simply that parties are not often likely to allow a group of strangers who have undergone no scrutiny or examination to decide a case in a binding fashion. However, parties can benefit quite significantly from gathering the wisdom of a broad cross-section of people, all of whom may well represent potential juror profiles in a live trial. It is not by accident that iCourthouse displays prominently for each case the median award of all jurors—the number has great value as a guide to settlement. It is often difficult to set an objective standard for settlement. Try yourself to put a value on the kinds of injuries for which plaintiffs recover: what is one's online reputation worth? What is the value of a collectible that was poorly described or damaged in transit following purchase on an Internet auction site? One can even begin to see how a jury might value physical injuries by entering into evidence a picture of the injury and tracking jury comments on the severity, permanence, and value of the harm. Services such as iCourthouse establish an objective criteria for settlement from which parties can benefit immensely.

A second strength is the potential such sites have for use in pretrial preparation. Lawyers could use such sites to their considerable advantage and at virtually no cost in preparing a case for a traditional trial by reviewing the questions asked of the parties by online jurors. Knowing what decision-makers in a case want to know in order to make a judgment is exceptionally valuable information to the lawyer preparing the case—he or she can prepare a case for the real jury that anticipates juror reactions with greater accuracy and then responds or can modify the case presentation in a fashion most favorable to his or her client.

Furthermore, the opportunity to read the explanations of the jurors for the verdict further educates the attorney preparing a case for a real jury or, as we noted earlier, preparing a case for negotiation on- or offline. If certain parts of the opening statement or closing argument are particularly important to jurors, they can be expanded and delivered more forcefully; arguments that are rejected can be amended or discarded. Evidence that has value in persuading an online jury can be used more prominently in the trial; evidence that was not helpful can be discarded. ICourthouse is, in short, a very effective mechanism for doing jury science that refines a case for the real trial in very cost-effective way.

In addition, in those cases where an online jury makes a binding decision, it is possible to achieve a fast, cost-effective result that can, with appropriate preonline trial preparation, be absolutely binding. Parties can represent themselves with far greater ease than in traditional courtroom settings and can take the case to a verdict sooner than they could if they tried the case in a traditional courtroom. Naturally, parties will benefit from legal counsel, but the parties, not the court, can determine the role of the lawyer, allowing substantial savings in time and money.

Quick Clicks: Look into Professional Jury Science at DecisionQuest.com   Some of the sites we have covered thus far are relatively low-cost jury-sampling options for attorneys preparing cases for trial. The science of jury selection and persuasion is a complex and interesting one. Numerous firms offer jury consultation services to attorneys, and many attorneys use the services in high-visibility cases; the O.J. Simpson defense team, for example, made extensive use of jury consultants in his criminal trial.Check out the range of jury research offerings at *DecisionQuest*, one of the nation's largest firms of this type, at http://www.decisionquest.com/site/trial.htm.

Finally, it is important to note that the American legal system is one in which good lawyering is rewarded instead of good case facts or law. Indeed, cases that lack merit can be won by highly effective lawyering and sufficient resources: good lawyers with lots of money can win bad cases. Online jury proceedings may blunt the effect of good lawyering by keeping the arguments and evidence in text and picture form and eliminating highly emotional or argumentative presentations to the jury by the attorneys trying the case.

Quick Clicks: Render a Verdict at Legalvote.com   Go to Legalvote.com and give your verdict in a case at the link www.legalvote.com/study/ *or* give your damages award in a case at the link www.legalvote.com/worth/. You should have several lawsuit choices at each link from which to choose, so find a case that has interesting facts. Did you have enough case information to make a judgment in the case or were there other facts that you wished you knew? Do you think this site, like virtualjury.com, should know something about you before you respond to a case? Would you submit a case to this site if you were an attorney preparing for trial? If so, what would you hope to gain by doing so? If not, why wouldn't you do so?

What Disadvantages May Be Entailed in an Online Jury Proceeding?

The downsides of this process appear to outweigh the upsides at this point. Indeed, the alternatives—negotiation, mediation and arbitration—offer most of the strengths of online juries, without some of the weaknesses. First, lack of adequate access to high-technology Internet tools deters large numbers of people from trying cases on the web. Whereas one may engage in other ODR processes without lots of extra hardware and software, this process probably requires more than some people possess. This is true even at a site like iCourthouse, at which digital photographic images, scanned documents, and uploaded video are the sorts of evidence jurors review. Moreover, users with better technical skills may fare better on a site like iCourthouse because their cases will look better, even if they are not more meritorious—the talented digital photographer, for example, has a huge advantage over someone who lacks the same skill when he or she can artistically prepare an image and post it for evaluation by jurors.

This leads to a second disadvantage of the online peer jury approach. Although there are very careful standards governing the use of evidence in a real courtroom, the online environment has no such protections. Fraud and deception are not only possible, but they are also likely in the unregulated environment of online juries. In fact, the expert digital photographer who knows how to post an image as evidence may be able to alter the image slightly and post it for jurors, who will take the image at face value.

It is also important to note that online juries are very different than live juries working in courtrooms because there is also very little effort made to assure a representative and fair jury pool. Consider the following case, which explains both the nature of the protection a defendant in an offline courtroom receives in terms of jury selection as well as the process for determining if this right has been violated by the selection of an actual jury.

KEY CHAPTER CASE

Picking the Right Jury

United States v Weaver, 267 F.3d 231, 2001 U.S. App. LEXIS 20723 (United States Court of Appeals for the Third Circuit, 2001)

Fact Summary: Rudolph Weaver appealed his armed robbery conviction on the grounds that the jury pool in the Erie Division of the Western District of Pennsylvania, from which the jury that convicted him was chosen, did not reflect a fair cross section of the community, as required by the Sixth Amendment. The plan approved at the time of the jury selection in Weaver's case, and currently in effect, employs voter registration lists as the exclusive source from which it summons potential jurors for service. Juror names are drawn at random from the voter registration lists of the seven counties in the Erie Division and placed into a master jury wheel. The District Court found no violation of Weaver's constitutional or statutory rights. We will affirm.

OPINION: The opinion of the court was rendered by RENDELL, J.

Weaver challenges his conviction on the grounds that he was denied his right to a jury drawn from a fair cross section of the community as required by the Sixth Amendment's fair cross section. He argues that the pool from which his jury was selected underrepresented African-Americans and Hispanics due to its exclusive reliance on voter registration lists. The Sixth Amendment provides: "In all criminal prosecutions, the accused shall enjoy the right to a . . . . trial by an impartial jury of the State and district wherein the crime shall have been committed . . . ." U.S. Const. Amend. VI.

The American concept of the jury trial contemplates a jury drawn from a fair cross section of the community. It is part of the established tradition in the use of juries as instruments of public justice that the jury be a body truly representative of the community. This requirement of a fair cross section is not without substantial limits—it does not guarantee that juries be of any particular composition. All that is required is that the jury wheels, pools of names, panels, or venires from which juries are drawn must not systematically exclude distinctive groups in the community and thereby fail to be reasonably representative thereof. The objectives of the fair cross section requirement include avoiding the possibility that the composition of the juries would be arbitrarily skewed in such a way as to deny criminal defendants the benefit of the common-sense judgment of the community and avoiding the appearance of unfairness that would result from excluding large groups of individuals, not on the basis of their ability to serve as jurors, but on the basis of some immutable characteristic such as race, gender or ethnic background.

In order to establish a prima facie violation of the fair cross section requirement of the Sixth Amendment, the defendant must demonstrate: (1) the group alleged to be excluded is a "distinctive" group in the community; (2) the representation of this group in jury venires is not "fair and reasonable" in relation to the number of such persons in the community; and (3) the under representation is caused by the "systematic exclusion of the group in the jury selection process." A defendant need not show discriminatory intent.

To prove his claim that the venire underrepresented African-Americans and Hispanics in violation of his constitutional and statutory rights, Weaver introduced the testimony of Dr. Andrew A. Beveridge, who was recognized as an expert in demography. Beveridge compared the number of African-Americans and Hispanics in the adult population of seven counties comprising the Erie Division. Beveridge determined that while census figures indicate that 3.07% of the voting population in Erie is African-American, African-Americans comprised only 1.84% of the 1999 master wheel. He also stated that Hispanics comprised .97% of the population, but only .26% of the wheel.

African-Americans and Hispanics are "distinctive" groups for the purposes of a fair cross-section analysis, [so we move to the second question], whether the representation of the group in the jury venires is fair and reasonable in relation to the number of such persons in the community. This is, at least in part, a mathematical exercise, and must be supported by statistical evidence. Here, Census figures indicate that 3.07% of the voting population in the seven counties comprising the Erie Division is African-American and .97% is Hispanic. The absolute disparity figures—1.23% for African-Americans and .71% for Hispanics—are well below those that have previously been found insufficient to establish unfair and unreasonable representation. Accordingly, the results of this analysis fail to support this element of Weaver's prima facie case.

The defendant [must also] show that the under-representation of the cognizable group is due to systematic exclusion in the jury selection process. The United States Supreme Court held that women were systematically excluded where the under-representation of women on jury lists resulted from their self-exclusion under a state law [gender specific] exemption privilege. However, we found no Sixth Amendment violation where the jury selection process was neutral on its face and was being monitored, and modified, to try to enhance its representative character. Here, the government contends that substantial representation is traceable solely to the exclusive reliance on voter registration lists, and that the underrepresented group has freely excluded itself quite apart from the system itself. In other words, there has been no showing of anything in the system that has discouraged or prevented a group from participating.

Due to Weaver's failure to present sufficient evidence, we will affirm the District Court's denial of Weaver's fair cross section challenge to the jury selection process.

Third, it is unclear what motivates jurors to participate on a site such as iCourthouse, and parties should be wary of the jurors they find at such sites. There is no meaningful filtering process to prevent children, jurors with biases, and jurors lacking sufficient education and preparation from deciding cases. In addition, a relatively sophisticated user could log in under numerous aliases and stack a verdict by voting repeatedly. In fact, nothing significant prevents a party from surreptitiously rendering a verdict in his or her own case. Even when a case is based on the adult judgments of reasonable, intelligent jurors, one wonders how valuable the result is when the jurors who rendered it did it for the sake of entertainment, because they aren't paid to participate on the site.

Quick Clicks: Be a Juror at Virtualjury.com   Register as a juror at Virtualjury.com by following the link www.virtualjury.com/javintro.htm and view the short demonstration of the process at this link: www.virtualjury.com/demo.htm. Now consider the information you provided to secure a spot on the Virtualjury.com roster. What is the purpose of asking questions about ethnicity, religion, spousal occupation, and past participation in a lawsuit? Has enough information been requested to provide litigants with a meaningful profile of you and of others to form an appropriate jury? Why or why not? Are you concerned that there is no verification procedure ensuring the accuracy of the information you entered? Would you be concerned about this if you were a litigant using the service? To what extent would you rely upon the results of a Virtualjury.com focus group to plan your case if you were an attorney representing a real client headed for trial? Now cross your fingers for a real case to come your way!

Fourth, as with other forms of ODR, it is possible that sensitive information will be more widely disseminated than the parties anticipate. Although iCourthouse is not a private site—in fact it is the opposite, offering evidence to anyone who wishes to view it—parties may think, erroneously, that they have some protection against wide distribution of images, facts, or documents posted in their case. Imagine, for example, pictures of a scarring injury posted at iCourthouse for the purpose of reaching a settlement being used to embarrass a plaintiff in another setting entirely.

The public online jury, in short, is probably best for cases with facts that are not private and about which the parties do not disagree. In such cases, the feedback of the jurors who view and rule on the evidence can either lead to a settlement both parties think is similar to what a real, but more expensive, jury would do or end a case with a verdict on terms the parties create themselves.

ODR IN THE DIGITAL ERA Cyber Jurisdiction: A Primer	Offline trial courts must struggle with questions of jurisdiction that online courts can avoid completely, and any law student or lawyer will agree: jurisdiction is one tough area of law. Jurisdiction is simply defined as the power a court possesses to hear a case and render an enforceable verdict, but it is far more difficult in practice to identify which court or courts have jurisdiction. Generally, jurisdiction is found either at the location at which a person or business "lives" or the place where the act that gives rise to a dispute took place. So far, so good, but that is for people and places that exist in flesh and blood and brick and mortar. Where does a web site–only business live? Where does an Internet transaction occur? On the consumer's computer? On a server somewhere else? Where, in short, does a plaintiff file suit to resolve an online complaint? The Internet is without boundary, border, or geographical limitation; it is, therefore, the most difficult source of jurisdictional dilemmas.

A very significant argument in favor of ODR is that jurisdictional questions are no longer relevant—the parties agree to forego the courthouse in favor of the Web. That said, all cases are not appropriate for ODR, and a jurisdictional decision must be made in those cases that are destined for the courthouse. Here is a short checklist for determining jurisdiction in cyberspace, to the extent that rules for doing so are settled:

1. If the parties agreed formally prior to a transaction that a certain court will have jurisdiction, that agreement virtually always binds the parties and establishes jurisdiction. For example, when a party clicks an "I Agree" box following site conditions and terms that describe jurisdiction, the terms are normally binding even if the party did not actually read them.

2. If an implied agreement on jurisdiction can be established, perhaps through the installation of software by a party or the use of a product beyond a certain period of time, the terms of jurisdiction in the implied agreement normally bind the parties. For example, when a consumer purchases a computer with a thirty day return or retain guarantee, the terms of jurisdiction contained in the owner's manual become binding if the consumer does not return the computer within thirty days, even if the consumer never looked at the owner's manual.

3. If the parties did not agree on jurisdiction prior to the transaction, and no implied consent can be found, an interactive web site ordinarily establishes jurisdiction in the state or locale in which the consumer lives and concluded the transaction.

4. Use of a passive web site does not normally result in the creation of jurisdiction over either the user or the site operator.

No rules are without exception, and jurisdiction is a very complicated area of law, but this four-step process should be helpful in considering where to sue or where one can or will be sued. Answering those questions is often critical in determining whether an ODR process is preferable to a conventional lawsuit.

ODR Bytes

The American civil trial is one in which a jury applies the law to questions of fact to reach a conclusion regarding the claims made by the parties in highly orchestrated fashion.

Online juries processes are rare relative to other forms of ODR because the technological requirements for effective participation are significant.

ICourthouse.com, virtualjury.com, and Legalvote.com have all created systems that borrow some procedures from the traditional jury system but provide a unique online process allowing peer jurors drawn from the world of Internet users to rule on cases to assist in settlement or to impose a final judgment.

Online peer juries can be fast, inexpensive ways to render a verdict or can serve the very useful function of assisting to prepare a case for trial in a traditional courtroom by providing insight into how a jury is likely to view and value a case.

Online peer juries cannot deliver due process and may, if the technological abilities of the parties are disparate, work an injustice on the less technologically savvy party.

ODR Bookmarks

iCourthouse
www.i-courthouse.com

Intellicourt
www.intellicourt.com

Legal Vote
www.legalvote.com

Michigan Cybercourt
www.michigancybercourt.com

Virtual Jury
www.virtualjury.com

Web Dispute
www.webdispute.com

Selected ODR Bibliography

Gellman, R. "A Brief History of the Virtual Magistrate Project: The Early Months." (1996), http://mantle.sbs.umass.edu/vmag/GELLMAN.HTM.

Goldsmith, J., and L. Lessig. "Grounding the Virtual Magistrate." Paper prepared for NCAIR Conference on Online Dispute Resolution. (1996), http://mantle.sbs.umass.edu/vmag/groundvm.htm.

Johnson, D., and D. Post. "Law and Borders: The Rise of Law in Cyberspace." *Stanford Law Rev.* 48, 1367. (1996), http://www.cli.org/X0025_LBFIN.html.

Mudd, C. "Cybercourt: A Virtual Resolution of Differences of an Alternative Proposal for Law and Order in Cyberspace." (1995), http://www.mudd.org/professional/articlesclm/cybercourt.htm.

Post, D. "Engineering a Virtual Magistrate System." Paper prepared for NCAIR Conference on Online Dispute Resolution. (1996), http://mantle.sbs.umass.edu/vmag/DGP2.HTM.

Thornburg, E. "Going Private: Technology, Due Process, and Internet Dispute Resolution." U.C. *Davis L. Rev.* 34 (2000): 151.

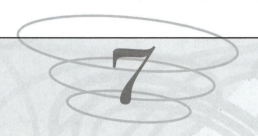

Online Dispute Resolution System Design

CHAPTER FAQS

What main options does an e-business have in the adoption of an ODR process?

What major factors should an e-business consider in the development of its ODR policies and system?

Are there any other special considerations that an e-firm needs to consider in establishing ODR systems for online disputes?

Should an e-business consider employing a third-party ODR service provider?

Are ODR service providers regulated for quality?

Earlier chapters have given a good sense about the nature of disputes that may arise in the online environment and some of the basic limitations of traditional litigation in resolving these disagreements. You should now be aware of some of the main benefits and limitations of ODR processes. Furthermore, you have information about some real world examples of settlement and adjudicatory processes. Now you may be wondering how you might adopt ODR programs that best meet the needs of your e-business. In this chapter, we consider the major issues an e-business should consider in ODR design and implementation.

What Main Options Does an E-Business Have in the Adoption of an ODR Process?

As indicated earlier, the conflict resolution needs of each e-business may be different, and one solution does not fit every situation when dealing with online disagreements. In some instances, an e-business may prefer to use negotiation or mediation to handle disputes in order to maintain ongoing business relationships or to promote good customer satisfaction. Other e-firms, especially those involved with external parties in one-time transactions, may decide that adjudicatory mechanisms will work best for them. This chapter outlines some of the main issues that an e-company may wish to address in deciding which ODR approach will achieve their conflict resolution goals.

In establishing an ODR policy and program, an e-business may wish to decide whether the ODR program will be used to deal with both internal and external conflicts. Some e-businesses may adopt only an external system to resolve conflicts with parties outside of the company, such as customers, vendors, and suppliers. Others may decide to create a comprehensive program that also provides an ODR option for dealing with internal conflicts between internal parties located at a distance from each other. Our primary focus in this text has been on e-commerce, so this chapter discusses external ODR policies and systems.

In e-commerce, an e-business must also determine whether its ODR use will be a requirement of doing business before a dispute arises or as a voluntary option once a dispute has arisen. From a legal perspective, offline businesses and consumers have challenged mandatory pre-dispute ADR clauses in the U.S. courts, which usually have upheld such clauses if they are fair and reasonable. However, the validity of ODR clauses on websites is largely untested in the U.S. courts so it is unclear whether or not such pre-dispute clauses will also find judicial support.

For e-firms that do a great deal of business outside of the United States, it is important to note that pre-dispute clauses in consumer dealings are not favored in other parts of the world, especially the European Union. From a practical perspective, e-businesses must decide if such clauses may make customers wary about doing business with them. Also, if an e-business has a bricks-and-mortar counterpart, it may want to avoid a perception that its offline customers have more conflict resolution choices than its online customers.

Aside from the form of ODR that is selected, the e-business also needs to decide who will administer these ODR services. Some e-businesses with existing ADR programs and policies may decide to reshape these prior policies and programs to create their own in-house ODR programs. However, these e-businesses should recognize that it might take a great deal of time and money to develop and implement ODR systems and the needed ODR software platforms to support their use. For e-businesses with little ADR experience, it may be useful to contract out these services to established, quality, third-party ODR service providers. Later in this chapter, we discuss the potential benefits of outsourcing ODR services to third-party providers.

What Major Factors Should an E-Business Consider in the Development of Its ODR Policies and System?

E-businesses must consider a number of factors in deciding whether or not ODR will be beneficial in resolving their online conflicts and should undertake a thoughtful process in determining the proper use of ODR in handling their online disagreements. Typically, conflict resolution experts recommend the following phases: (1) the initial assessment of common disputes and existing conflict resolution methods; (2) the determination of the appropriate conflict resolution mechanism with applicable company staff; (3) the implementation of the ODR policy and program; and (4) the monitoring and updating of the ODR program after a period of operation. Let's discuss what these different phases may involve.

Chart 7.1 Internet-Related Fraud Complaints by Reported Amount Paid, January 1–December 31, 2002	
Amount Paid	Percentage[a]
$0	21%
$1–25	11%
$26–50	10%
$51–75	6%
$76–100	5%
$101–250	14%
$251–500	11%
$501–1,000	10%
$1,001–5,000	11%
More than $5,000	2%

[a]Percentages are based on the total number of consumers who reported amount paid (94,502); 92% of consumers reported this information.

Chart prepared by Bureau of Consumer Protection, U.S. Federal Trade Commission (http://www. consumer.gov/sentinel/; http://www.ftc.gov). Used with permission.

Initial Assessment of Common Disputes and Existing Conflict Resolution Methods

Before an e-firm can determine the usefulness of an ODR policy and program, the e-firm needs to determine that nature of its online disputes. First, an e-business should review its current and past conflicts to gain an understanding of the nature of its typical disputes. Here are some questions that an e-business may wish to consider in examining the nature of its online conflicts:

- Are the e-firm's disputes centering on disagreements with consumers (B2C), other businesses (B2B), or government authorities (B2G)?
- Do its online disagreements tend to involve strangers in one-time transactions or parties with whom the e-business hopes to maintain long-term commercial relationships?
- Do most of the e-company's disputes arise outside of the borders of its home state and country?
- Do its online conflicts involve complex factual and novel legal issues that may require extensive investigation, discovery, and legal research?
- Do most of the e-firm's disagreements deal with less complicated factual disputes over such issues as the timely delivery and quality of products and services or late payments for goods and services provided?
- Is the e-business concerned about setting legal precedents in its conflicts with others?

- Are there any important cultural, linguistic, and disability differences that may impact the selection and implementation of an appropriate ODR system?

Answering these and other questions in the evaluation of its current and prior conflicts may help an e-business determine the viability and usefulness of an ODR program. For example, if most of an e-company's online disputes involve parties in different states and different countries, then ODR may be a useful tool for handling conflicts and improving commercial relationships without the time and expense of cross-border litigation. On the other hand, if its main conflicts concern problems with suppliers or vendors located in the same state, the e-business may wish to consider the development of an offline ADR program or to continue accessing local courts.

Secondly, an e-business should determine what conflict resolution skills and methods the e-firm is already utilizing. If the e-business already has an internal mediation program to handle employee disputes, that firm may want to review the success of that program. Information from surveys or interviews can help determine the benefits and limitations of the existing mediation program. After gathering this information, the e-business may decide that it can learn from and use this earlier experience to develop a suitable mediation program for resolving online customer or other third party disputes.

If the e-business finds that it does not have any previous conflict resolution experiences outside of standard litigation, it may wish to consult with other e-firms in its field or industry associations to which it belongs to help find out what conflict resolution methods have proved useful. A review of successful ODR programs in one's industry could help an e-business to select and tailor ODR that best meets their dispute resolution needs. An e-business may also enlist the assistance of consultants with ADR/ODR experience who can help them to assess their conflict resolution needs. This option is discussed further later in this chapter.

Determining an Appropriate Conflict Resolution Mechanism

After assessing an e-firm's primary disputes and current conflict resolution methods, an e-business needs to decide what its goals and objective are in developing an ODR program. The e-firm should hold discussions with pertinent staff, such as legal personnel, purchasing managers, or customer service representatives, to obtain their input and to listen to their suggestions about the company's culture and its conflict resolution needs. Gaining input from all levels of the organization can also help in the long term to strengthen the company support for and use of the selected conflict resolution method.

A review of an e-business's goals and objectives plays a major role in the selection of an appropriate ODR method. Different e-companies may have different conflict resolution strategies that will influence the nature of their ODR program. For example, if an e-business is interested mainly in keeping down legal costs and promoting customer satisfaction or vendor relationships, it may select a more informal, settlement-based ODR program involving the use of negotiation and mediation. If an e-firm decides that its disputes are often highly technical, requiring industry expertise, and involve disputes over proprietary rights, then the e-business may wish to select an adjudicatory method of conflict resolution, such as arbitration. In arbitration, the arbitrators possess extensive experience in a given field and can render awards that are normally final and binding. If an e-firm decides that its goals are to maximize its procedural protections, to be able to engage in discovery, and to set legal precedents, then standard litigation, not ODR, may be more appropriate to meet its goals.

In designing its ODR system, an e-business must be certain to create a program that is fundamentally fair in accordance with the constitutional mandates of due process. Adequate notice is required in regard to issues of disclosure and informed consent about the ODR program as well as notice about the claims in dispute and the scheduling of the ODR session. Due process typically requires that the ODR process must provide disputing parties with reasonable access to necessary documents and to the process set forth in the ODR policy. Participants must also be provided an opportunity to be heard during the ODR process in a confidential and impartial setting. If appropriate, parties may be offered the option of third-party representation, such as the assistance of a lawyer or other advocate. Fundamental fairness may also call for reasonableness as to the costs of the process. E-businesses and ODR service providers should also consult the Final Report and Recommended Best Practices for ODR Service Providers of the American Bar Association Task Force on E-Commerce and ADR (ABA Task Force) for further guidance on these issues in the creation and implementation of a fair and effective ODR program (http://www.law.washington.edu/ABA-eADR/documentation/index.html). These recommended best practices are addressed in Chapter 8 and found in Appendix A of this text.

Any e-company that deals primarily with customers, who are individual consumers rather than other businesses, faces some additional responsibilities and challenges. A wide range of consumer protection laws may come into play in disputes with consumers, and e-businesses should be aware of relevant consumer laws that may impact their industry. In the global marketplace of the Web, this patchwork of consumer laws, regulations, and industry standards may be further complicated for e-tailers due to differing international perspectives on consumer protection. Any ODR program should be crafted in a manner that does not violate national laws. In addition, these firms should consider important cultural, linguistic, and disability differences that may impact the selection and implementation of an appropriate ODR system.

Implementing an ODR Policy and Program

Before rolling out a final and comprehensive set of ODR policies and procedures, an e-business may wish to experiment with a pilot ODR program. A small number of disputes can be handled using the specified ODR process. The ODR program can be evaluated in light of the e-firm's stated goals and objectives. The pilot can help to identify any unexpected challenges or areas requiring further improvement before finalizing the program.

The successful adoption of a final ODR system involves the active participation of all levels within an organization. An e-business should inform all its personnel about the program, not just those regularly involved in conflict resolution. The ODR program should be communicated directly to staff through the company e-mail system or posted on the company's internal web site. Hard copy of the ODR policy can also be sent to employees through the internal mail system or posted on central an-nouncement or bulletin boards. The ODR program should also be discussed in any employee handbook and regularly revisited in the e-firm's internal communications network, such as through e-mail updates or an e-firm's newsletter. The ODR policies and programs should be spelled out in clear and easily understood language. Com-mon examples of online conflicts that confront an e-business should be supplied to illustrate both the steps in the process and value of the e-firm's ODR program. If pos-sible, the ODR policy can be introduced in the e-company's orientation session and ODR skills can be taught in applicable company training programs.

An e-business should also think about how it will inform its online customers, ven-dors, suppliers, and other business associates about its new ODR program. As when outlining the program to employees, e-businesses should describe the ODR program in a straightforward and nonlegalistic manner. It is neither good customer service nor ethically sound to throw lots of legalistic jargon about the ODR program at online customers. By providing a clear road map about the nature and use of the ODR pro-gram, online customers will have greater confidence that conflicts with the e-firm will be promptly resolved. Furthermore, the e-company may be able to avoid later legal challenges based upon inadequate disclosure or the lack of informed consent.

Rather than bury the ODR policy in its terms of use, the e-business may wish to in-sert a dispute resolution icon prominently on its web page, similar to distinct links of-ten provided to identify online privacy policies. Most e-commerce stakeholders view up-front disclosure and plain language explanations as important aspects of any fun-damentally fair ODR system. An e-firm may wish to promote its ODR policy as a way to help quickly handle consumer and commercial conflicts as well as to show the e-firm's desire to promote good customer relationships.

It may be helpful to have the separate ODR icon link directly to the e-firm's ODR pol-icy clause or other relevant information about the ODR process. It is also good practice to clearly identify the existence of an ODR policy or program to allow potential cus-tomers to review the ODR policy before making any purchases. In this way, an online buyer or supplier is being put on clear notice about the program and can decide whether or not to continue to interact with the site. The dispute resolution icon can link to a page that explains the ODR policy in simple terms and outlines the main steps involved in the selected ODR process. An e-firm may wish to use the popular FAQ format to help explain the main steps of the ODR program. An FAQ page should include responses to some typical questions regarding the chosen ODR method. An e-business may also find that the use of simple pictures or flowcharts can be effective in explaining the ODR process to a diverse global audience. An e-business should also be sure to translate the ODR policy and program materials into the languages of the online markets they serve. The ABA Task Force recommended that ODR service providers should use ODR systems that respect cultural and linguistic differences between the disputing parties.

To assist those with physical disabilities, the e-business may wish to seek "Bobby" approval for the manner in which it has posted its ODR policy and program on its web site (http://www.cast.org/Bobby/Bobby311.cfm). The creation of the not-for-profit Center for Applied Special Technology (CAST), Bobby is a Web-based tool

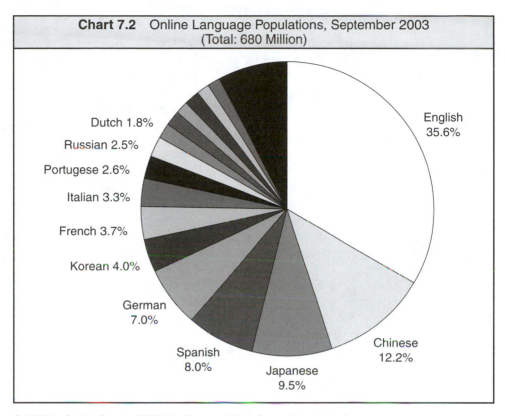

Chart 7.2 Online Language Populations, September 2003 (Total: 680 Million)

English 35.6%

Chinese 12.2%

Japanese 9.5%

Spanish 8.0%

German 7.0%

Korean 4.0%

French 3.7%

Italian 3.3%

Portugese 2.6%

Russian 2.5%

Dutch 1.8%

that helps those developing Web pages to determine if their site needs to be revised to make it easier for the disabled to visit and use. Bobby compliance is considered to be a valuable way to increase access to the Web for the disabled and to adhere to the requirements of the Americans with Disabilities Act. For example, pictorial graphics in both color and black and white that outline the main steps in the ODR process may help the visually impaired to better understand the flow of your ODR program. Complying e-businesses can add the Bobby seal to their site to show their concern and efforts to make their site more accessible to all, regardless of disabilities.

In an effort to help educate consumers and other online businesses about ODR, the e-business may provide useful hypertext links to major ADR/ODR home pages on its web site. A number of web sites already exist that provide balanced and objective descriptions of ADR/ODR processes, such as the Conflict Resolution Information Resource (http://www.crinfo.org), the Shidler Center for Law, Commerce and Technology (http://www.law.washington.edu/lct/), and Online Resolution, Inc. (http://www.onlineresolution.com).

Monitoring an ODR Program

Once the finalized process has been put into practice, an e-business should regularly monitor the ODR program. The e-firm should strive to use the ODR program on a consistent basis so the benefits and limitations of the program can be properly evaluated. Although the benefits of an ODR program may not always be easy to quantify, it is important to undertake regular assessments of the value of the ODR policy.

As part of this monitoring process, an e-business should collect data about the program, including the number of cases handled, the length of time it took to resolve conflicts, the cost of the program, the nature and outcome of the disputes, and overall party satisfaction with the process. An e-business may wish to undertake surveys or request other feedback from company and third-party participants to learn about the advantages and disadvantages of the practical application and party satisfaction with the ODR program. If possible, both external and internal parties can be interviewed in person or over the telephone to generate more lengthy discussions.

Once the data have been collected, the e-firm should review the ODR program in light of its stated goals and objectives in creating the program. For example, if improving customer satisfaction was a major objective, then the e-business may wish to review surveys and other feedback about its ability to handle online conflicts quickly and fairly. If reducing legal fees was a key goal, then the e-firm should analyze whether or not its costs for legal assistance in handling conflicts has been reduced. Although it is not easy to measure the impact of an ODR policy, it is important to try to make consistent use of the ODR process and undertake periodic assessments. Through regular reviews of its ODR program, an e-business can determine areas that need improvement or revision.

Are There Any Other Special Considerations That an E-Firm Needs to Consider in Establishing ODR Systems for Online Disputes?

Many online companies have adopted comprehensive ODR programs to handle conflicts with both consumer and commercial customers. In creating their ODR policies, these firms needed to consider a number of legal and ethical matters in adopting an ODR system. These important issues include concerns regarding the impartiality of ODR neutrals, the confidentiality of the ODR proceedings, and the accessibility of the process. These key issues are also addressed in the ABA Task Force's Final Report and Recommended Best Practices, which are considered in Chapter 8.

Impartiality of ODR Neutrals

It is a well-accepted principle of ADR and ODR practice that any fair conflict resolution system must be impartial. If a firm elects to use ODR methods that involve third-party neutrals, such as online mediation or arbitration, these neutrals must be able to gain party confidence in the objectivity of the process. Claims of bias can result in successful legal challenges of the ODR process and its outcomes in court. An e-business may raise bias issues by using only internal staff to resolve conflicts or selecting third party providers who may have a conflict of interest. If an e-business decides to utilize internal staff as mediators and arbitrators, it risks alienating external parties and provoking litigation grounded in bias. Furthermore, an online company may raise issues of bias when it has some ownership interest or wholly compensates the chosen ODR service providers.

One way to help limit concerns about bias is for e-firms to utilize third-party ODR neutrals of well-respected and independent organizations, such as the Better Business Bureau (http://www.bbb.org), to administer the ODR program. If an e-business decides to utilize a for-profit ODR provider, that provider should maintain an extensive rotating pool of qualified neutrals that are required to make full disclosure of any potential conflicts of interest to avoid unfair advantage. The ODR program should also be set up to allow both the online company and the customer to have equal roles in the selection of an appropriate online neutral. Parties should be given a reasonable opportunity to object to a neutral regardless of whether or not the neutral discloses any potential conflicts of interest. Online neutrals should be able to present evidence of adequate training and experience in handling online disputes as well as being willing to certify their adherence to ethical standards of practice, including impartiality and confidentiality. Following is a key U.S. Supreme Court decision on the importance of impartiality and avoiding even the appearance of bias in ADR proceedings that would also apply to ODR processes.

KEY CHAPTER CASE

Is Even the Mere Appearance of Bias Sufficient to Overturn an Arbitration Award?

Commonwealth Coatings Corp. v Continental Casualty Co., 393 U.S. 145 (1968)

Fact Summary: Commonwealth Coatings Corporation (Commonwealth) was a subcontractor that sued a surety, Continental Casualty Company, to recover money damages for painting work from a prime contractor's bond. The original painting contract included a predispute arbitration agreement (PDAA) that allowed the use of arbitration before a three-person panel for any disputes that arose under the contract. Under the terms of the PDAA, each party chose an arbitrator with the subcontractor and the prime contractor required to mutually agree upon the third neutral, Mr. Capacete, who operated an engineering consulting firm in Puerto Rico. The prime contractor was one of Mr. Capacete's customers and he had regularly provided significant consulting services to the prime contractor over the past four to five years, including consulting efforts on the same projects currently in dispute. However, there had been no business dealings between the prime contractor and Mr. Capacete for about a year before the arbitration. Mr. Capacete failed to disclose his business dealings with the prime contractor, and Commonwealth was unaware of these business contacts before or during the arbitration. After the arbitration hearing, the panel unanimously found for the prime contractor. In the district court, Commonwealth challenged the arbitral award, in part, based on claims of bias. The district court did not vacate the award, and the court of appeals affirmed. The U.S. Supreme Court granted certiorari.

OPINION: MR. JUSTICE BLACK delivered the opinion of the Court.

At issue in this case is the question whether elementary requirements of impartiality taken for granted in every judicial proceeding are suspended when the parties agree to resolve a dispute through arbitration. . . .

In 1925, Congress enacted the United States Arbitration Act, 9 U.S.C. sections 1-14, which sets out a comprehensive plan for arbitration of controversies coming under its terms, and both sides here assume that this Federal Act governs this case. Section 10. . . sets out the conditions upon which awards can be vacated. . . .[and] does authorize vacation of an award where it was "procured by corruption, fraud or undue means" or "[w]here there was evident partiality . . . in the arbitrators." These provisions show a desire of Congress to provide not merely any arbitration but an impartial one. It is true that petitioner does not charge before us that the third arbitrator was actually guilty of fraud or bias in deciding this case, and we have no reason, apart from the undisclosed business relationship, to suspect him of any improper motives. But neither this arbitrator nor the prime contractor gave to petitioner any intimation of the close financial relations that had existed between them for a period of years. . . . It is true that arbitrators cannot sever all their ties with the business world, since they are not expected to get all their income from their work deciding cases, but we should, if anything, be even more scrupulous to safeguard the impartiality of arbitrators than judges, since the former have completely free rein to decide the law as well as the facts and are not subject to appellate review. We can perceive no way in which the effectiveness of the arbitration process will be hampered by the simple requirement that the arbitrators disclose to the parties any dealings that might create an impression of possible bias. . . .

This rule of arbitration. . . rests on the premise that any tribunal permitted by law to try cases and controversies not only must be unbiased but also must avoid even the appearance of bias. We cannot believe that it was the purpose of Congress to authorize litigants to submit their cases and controversies to arbitration boards that might reasonably be thought biased against one litigant and favorable to another.

Reversed.

Confidentiality of the ODR Proceedings

Confidentiality has normally been seen as an integral part of ADR processes. Traditionally, the confidentiality of the proceedings and related notes and documents has been viewed as necessary to promote an open exchange of ideas and to encourage a willingness to compromise among disputants. A number of states protect ADR materials from disclosure under state statute or case law. Many ODR programs and providers agree with this established view and stress the importance of confidentiality in ODR proceedings. These providers may require their neutrals and the parties to agree to strict confidentiality in the ODR proceedings. In addition, the use of encryption, password-protected pages, and other technological security measures can help to protect the confidentiality of the ODR communications and to avoid the attacks of computer hackers.

Although many ODR providers offer secure and confidential ODR services, some e-commerce stakeholders have challenged the concept of confidentiality in ODR processes. Certain consumer advocates have recommended that ODR decisions and statistics should be published so that online shoppers can make informed choices about doing business with online firms. Others have called for ODR disclosures to assist government and law enforcement agencies to take appropriate civil or criminal action against e-tailers involved in fraudulent or deceptive conduct. In its Final Report and Recommended Best Practices, the ABA Task Force suggested that ODR service providers may wish to periodically post or publish statistical reports on their proceedings that respect party confidentiality to aid in the evaluation of these service providers.

Accessibility of the ODR Process

Through technological advancements, remote parties may be able to communicate to help resolve online conflicts using e-mail, chat rooms, listservs, bulletin boards, conferencing software, software-based negotiation and mediation programs, or video-conferencing. Ideally, ODR allows disputants to stay in their home country while consulting offline with local lawyers, translators, and other conflict resolution experts. However, from a realistic perspective, expensive technologies, foreign language translators, legal representatives, and other aids may be too costly and technically complicated for some online disputes, particularly for online consumer disputes, in which dollar values often range from $300 to $3,000. Although technological advancements have made accessing the Web relatively easy, e-firms must still consider accessibility concerns in designing ODR programs. Also certain cost, linguistic, cultural, and disability issues may create challenges to achieving accessibility to ODR systems. It is important to note that the concept of accessibility is intertwined with concerns about fundamental fairness or due process. In ODR programs, accessibility deals primarily with reasonable access to documents relative to the online conflict, to the technological tools needed for ODR communications, and to the ODR program at a reasonable cost in light of the value of the dispute.

To either bring forth or respond to an online conflict, all parties need to have access to essential information regarding the dispute. In designing the process, the e-business needs to consider what information exchange should reasonably take place. In addition, the e-business may need to consider any cultural, linguistic, or disability matters that may impact the exchange of information and online communications. The more complicated the dispute, the more likely the breadth and number of the documents involved. Barring all information exchanges will probably violate due process considerations, whereas allowing for open-ended discovery could negatively impact the time and costs of processing the dispute and may endanger the protection of proprietary records. In consultation with appropriate experts, an e-firm will need to examine fully the nature of their online disputes and then balance the need for information with the ease and speed of the ODR process.

Secondly, any e-business must recognize disparities in technological tools in designing its ODR system. In particular, consumer or small-business customers may have limited technology resources at their disposal. Not all parties may have sufficient access to the Web or other technological tools essential to undertake even a basic exchange of information as well as to communicate online with the other parties and third party neutrals. For example, in providing another party with information about the dispute, an e-business must determine whether or not disputants can open attachments that may be sent or if disputants have suitable software to access the selected ODR software platform. In addition, an e-business cannot assume that all parties have access to technology tools, such as document scanners, that may be needed to send important information online to the e-business.

The European Union has already drafted an initiative that seeks to develop uniform international ODR technical standards that promote interoperability among ODR platforms, known as odrXML (ODR Extensible Markup Language). This proposed initial version of odrXML strives to aid smooth data exchange in cross-border disputes between various ODR systems. The Organization for the Advancement of Structured Information Standards (OASIS) is reviewing odrXML through its LegalXML ODR Technical Committee (http://www.oasis-open.org). OASIS is a nonprofit international consortium that works to develop global e-business standards with corporate and business members in more than one hundred countries. In the ODR field, its goal is to promote open ODR systems that will improve public access to justice using public and private ODR platforms.

Technological assessments may need to be made on a case-by-case basis. The other party's access to technology can be asked about in any online complaint or intake form. In some instances, particularly involving consumer or small business conflicts, the e-business may need to supplement its ODR process with traditional communication methods such as standard mail, faxes, or telephone contact. Once communications are received, the parties may need to utilize translation services if different languages are involved.

Furthermore, the online disputants need access to a process that allows them to present their situation at a reasonable cost. When B2B dealings are involved, cost may not be a major issue, and it may make sense to split the costs equally to ensure efficient use of the ODR process and to avoid claims of bias. However, ODR systems that deal with online consumers or small businesses may need to consider low- or no-cost ODR options, supported by e-businesses, to ensure accessibility. The National Consumers League 2001 Shopping Online Survey recently found that about 69 percent of the responding consumers made online purchases amounting to less than $500, which may make it impractical for many consumers to spend a great deal of money accessing an ODR system (http://www.natlconsumersleague.org). Also, in the European Union, most customers pay for Internet access by the minute, so programs must be set up that allow parties to resolve conflicts online in a fast and efficient manner.

Under these circumstances, the e-business may end up subsidizing all or a portion of the ODR fees through their insurance premiums, membership fees paid to a trustmark organization, or direct payments made to ODR providers as part of the cost of doing business. Some consumer advocates have called for e-businesses to pay all costs associated with an ODR process. However, this approach may lead to concerns about bias and conflicts of interest if only one party is compensating the third-party ODR service provider. Others have suggested that splitting costs may work when an e-firm has selected a low-cost ODR service provider. Another option is for e-businesses to participate in trustmark or seal programs, such as the BBB*Online* (http://www.bbbonline.org), that provide low- or no-cost independent ODR services to its members funded through the pooling of membership fees. Regardless of the alternative selected in B2C disagreements, accessibility calls for costs to be low in light of the often small amounts in controversy.

Should an E-Business Consider Employing a Third-Party ODR Service Provider?

If an e-business is thinking about handling its ODR program in-house, it should realize that it faces many challenges and must address a number of critical issues. First, the company will need to identify or hire staff with appropriate ADR/ODR credentials and experience to implement the ODR policy. An e-firm must be able to provide enough staff and other resources to quickly and fairly resolve a growing number of online conflicts. Second, the e-business must address the nature and extent of appropriate ODR training that will be provided to its current dispute resolution personnel. There are no clear training standards for ODR neutrals, so an e-business would need to do research and develop an appropriate training program or else outsource training to qualified ODR providers. Third, the e-firm must decide what online software platform they will use for their selected ODR method. The platform will need to be easily accessible to and compatible with a broad range of potential disputants. The ODR software must also provide adequate security to protect confidential conflict resolution sessions in the online environment. Lastly, an e-firm will need to address whether it has the capabilities to deal with a myriad of cultural, linguistic, and specialized disability issues. It is important to recognize that developing one's own ODR staff, training program, and software platform to meet the needs of a global marketplace may be very expensive and time consuming for busy e-commerce professionals.

Rather than reinvent the wheel, it may be helpful to seek the assistance of third-party ODR providers for training and software platforms necessary for undertaking internal ODR programs. (See the special boxed section on page 132.) ODR service providers may be either nonprofit or for-profit organizations. In some cases, an e-business may be a member of a professional organization or a participant in a trustmark or seal program that provides dispute resolution services for its member businesses. Furthermore, trustmark organizations and ODR service providers may possess a broad global network of affiliates that may be able to provide ODR services in the language of the disputants in a context that is sensitive to cultural and specialized disability issues.

Are ODR Service Providers Regulated for Quality?

Qualified, independent, and competent neutrals and ODR service providers are key to a successful ODR system. In the offline world, ADR professionals may look to a patchwork of professional ethical guidelines and standards of practice in carrying out their duties. In addition, court decisions and state laws have addressed the importance of confidentiality and impartiality in ADR proceedings. But the field of ODR is just emerging, and no uniform national or international ethical guidelines or standards of practice have been identified and adopted. The ABA Task Force's Recommended Best Practices established model standards of ODR practice, addressing issues of disclosure, security, confidentiality, conflicts of interest, and record retention that may be helpful in evaluation of third-party providers. These best practices, with explanatory commentary, are provided in full in Appendix A. The committee has suggested that in the future these standards might be enforced through self-certification or a recognized trustmark program. Until ODR standards are set and an enforcement body is identified, e-companies must tread carefully in their selection of ODR providers. At a minimum, an e-business should determine if the ODR provider belongs to relevant professional organizations, adheres to current ADR ethical standards, requires specialized ODR training for its neutrals, and complies with the ABA Task Force's Recommended Best Practices. An e-business should probe the ODR service provider's main areas of expertise and request references from the ODR provider from other online companies in its industry whose conflicts the provider has handled. An e-firm may also wish to contact its own industry organizations or government or court referral agencies for information about qualified ODR service providers. As indicated earlier, if an e-business belongs to a seal or trustmark program, it may contact that organization to determine if it also provides ODR services.

ODR IN THE DIGITAL ERA SquareTrade

SQUARE
TRADE

Building Trust in Transactions

A lack of trust, or "e-confidence," is viewed as one of the main obstacles to the continuing growth of the Internet's global marketplace. Both online consumers and business customers are concerned that if a disagreement or problem crops up, they will have no place to turn to resolve their online disputes. A wide range of e-commerce stakeholders recommend the use of fair and independent ODR programs to help alleviate these online concerns and to build customer trust and confidence in e-commerce. But many e-businesses, scrambling to stay competitive in the fast-paced world of the Web, have little time to focus on the challenges of developing and implementing an effective ODR program. That's why a number of well-recognized online firms, such as VeriSign, Inc., PayPal, and eBay, have turned to Square Trade to help deliver fast, effective, and independent online dispute resolution services (http://www.squaretrade.com).

Established in 1999, the San Francisco–based firm views building trust in online relationships as key to the successful development of e-commerce. To help achieve this goal, it has instituted the Square Trade Seal program. E-businesses earning Square Trade's seal of approval must maintain high standards of online business conduct, such as providing fair and accurate descriptions of their products and services, full disclosure of their pricing, refund, and warranty policies, the adoption of an online privacy policy, and the use of secure sites to protect their online transactions. Square Trade considers its seal program to be the first line of defense in preventing online fraud. The e-firm reports that more than three million online customers view its seal of approval on eBay listings every day.

Its seal program is backed up by its patent-pending web-based ODR services. Square Trade offers disputants the opportunity to choose from a menu of ODR services to try to resolve their online conflicts, including direct negotiation, mediation, and arbitration. Under its ODR program, complaining parties can file their concerns and suggest possible remedies by completing a brief, online case form. This information is sent by e-mail to the other party, who is provided with information for responding to the initial concerns. Parties can then communicate directly with each other to try to resolve the dispute using Square Trade's Direct Negotiation tool. The disputants have the option to request the help of a Square Trade mediator to help them handle their conflict online. For some of its seal members, if mediation is unable to resolve the dispute, the parties may request the provision of a Square Trade arbitrator to decide the dispute. The case and its attendant communications are handled confidentially and securely on a password-protected Case Page on Square Trade's website.

This e-company can call upon its global network of more than 250 professional mediators and arbitrators to help resolve both B2B and B2C conflicts. Square Trade provides special training for its neutrals to help them shape their offline mediation and arbitration experience to meet the demands of the online world using state-of-the-art technology. This premier ODR service provider already handles more than 12,000 cases per month. Between its seal program and ODR services, Square Trade makes it clear that building e-confidence in partnership with online firms is its daily business.

Use of Square Trade Web Information and Logo Courtesy of Square Trade. All Rights Reserved.

Quick Clicks: Determining ADR/ODR Processes under Trustmark or Seal Programs   Search the Web for an e-business that sports a trustmark or seal of approval on its home page. Determine what, if any, form of ADR/ODR that the trustmark or seal program uses to resolve conflicts between online customers and the e-business that bears its seal. Draft a summary of the trustmark's dispute resolution program and determine if it posts statistical reports or actual decisions rendered under its program. Bring this information with you to class for class discussion or instructor review.

ODR Bytes

An e-business must assess the nature of its online disputes in order to determine if ODR will be a useful and viable option.

A review of the conflict resolution methods and skills currently in use by its staff can aid in the establishment of an ODR program.

Determining an e-firm's goals and objectives in creating an ODR system may help to identify which ODR method will work best to meet its conflict resolution needs.

A wide range of consumer protection laws may come into play in disputes with consumers, and e-businesses should be aware of relevant consumer laws that may impact their industry and their ODR system.

Important cultural, linguistic, and disability differences that may impact the selection and implementation of an appropriate ODR system should be addressed in the design of an ODR program.

In designing an ODR system, an e-business must be certain to create a program that is fundamentally fair in accordance with the constitutional mandates of due process.

The e-business should inform its staff, online customers, vendors, suppliers, and other business associates about its new ODR program in clear and straightforward terms.

A separate and prominent ODR icon that is linked to the ODR policy, ODR resources, and an ODR page of frequently asked questions will help to inform potential customers about the e-firm's ODR system, promote good customer relations, and avoid legal challenges to the ODR program based on lack of informed consent or lack of disclosure.

It is important for an e-business to make consistent use of its ODR process and to undertake periodic assessments. Through regular use and reviews of its ODR program, an e-business can determine areas that need improvement or revision.

An e-company should adequately address issues of the impartiality of ODR neutrals, the confidentiality of the ODR proceedings, and the accessibility of the process, when designing and implementing its ODR program.

To save time and money, it may be useful for e-businesses to consult with or outsource their ODR program to third party profit or not-for-profit ODR service providers.

ODR service providers are not currently regulated for quality, so e-firms should make informed decisions about selecting them based on a review of the ODR firm's membership in ODR professional organizations, adherence to ethical standards of practice and the ABA Task Force's Recommended Best Practices, specialized training for online disputes, references in your industry, and participation in respected seal or trustmark programs.

ODR Bookmarks

American Bar Association's Task Force on E-Commerce and Alternative Dispute Resolution
http://www.law.washington.edu/ABA-eADR

BBBOnline
http://www.bbbonline.org

Better Business Bureau (BBB)
http://www.bbb.org

Bobby/CAST
http://www.cast.org/Bobby/Bobby311.cfm

Center for Law, Commerce and Technology
http://www.law.washington.edu

Conflict Resolution Information Resource
http://www.crinfo.org

Consumer Sentinel Network, Bureau of Consumer Protection, U.S. Federal Trade Commission
http://www.consumer.gov/sentinel/

Global Reach
http://www.glreach.com

National Consumers League
http://www.natlconsumersleague.org

Online Resolution, Inc.
http://www.onlineresolution.com

Organization for the Advancement of Structured Information Standards (OASIS)
http://www.oasis-open.org

Square Trade
http://www.squaretrade.com

Selected ODR Bibliography

"Addressing Disputes in Electronic Commerce." Final Report and Recommendations of ABA Task Force on E-Commerce and ADR. http://www.law.washington.edu/ABA-eADR/documentation/index.html.

"Building ADR into the Corporate Law Department—ADR Systems Design." CPR Institute for Dispute Resolution. http://www.cpradr.org.

Cavenagh, Thomas D. *Business Dispute Resolution: Best Practices in System Design and Case Management.* Mason, OH: South-Western College Publishing, 1999.

Constantino, Cathy A. and Christina Sickles Merchant. *Designing Conflict Management Systems—A Guide to Creating Productive and Healthy Organizations.* San Francisco: Jossey-Bass, Inc., 1996. Excerpted in Trachte-Huber, E. Wendy, and Stephen K. Huber. *Alternative Dispute Resolution, Strategies for Law and Business.* Cincinnati, OH: Anderson Publishing, 1996.

Ponte, Lucille M. "Boosting Consumer Confidence In E-Business: Recommendations For Establishing Fair and Effective Dispute Resolution Programs For B2C Online Transactions." *Albany L. J. of Sci. & Tech.* 12 (2002): 441.

Ponte, Lucille M. "Broadening Traditional ADR Notions of Disclosure: Special Considerations for Posting Conflict Resolution Policies and Programs on E-Business Web Sites." *Ohio St. J. On Disp. Res.* 17 (2002): 321.

"Recommended Best Practices for Online Dispute Resolution Service Providers." ABA Task Force on E-Commerce and ADR. http://www.law.washington.edu/ABA-eADR/documentation/index.html.

Trachte-Huber, E. Wendy "ADR System Design: The Pre-Litigation Option." *The Attorney as Consultant* (1993). Excerpted in Trachte-Huber, E. Wendy, and Stephen K. Huber. *Alternative Dispute Resolution, Strategies for Law and Business.* Cincinnati, OH: Anderson Publishing, 1996.

8

The Future of ODR

CHAPTER FAQS

How might ODR be regulated in the future?

Are the courts playing a role in the ODR field?

Are there any model codes of conduct for handling online disputes?

What major issues must be resolved to strengthen ODR use?

How might e-business play a role in educating the public about ODR?

What further experimentation in ODR technologies can be expected?

As you have seen from reading this book, ODR is a newly emerging field that holds great promise in the resolution of both online and offline conflicts. There is broad-based support from a variety of e-commerce stakeholders for the development and implementation of ODR programs that provide fast, fair, transparent, and relatively inexpensive conflict resolution options. Clearly, as with any nascent field, ODR faces a number of future challenges. In this chapter, we will consider some of the main issues and future trends on the ODR horizon.

How Might ODR Be Regulated in the Future?

At the present time, there is no clear, uniform government regulation of the ODR field. The ABA Task Force's Recommended Best Practices provide some general guidance, primarily on disclosure issues to ODR service providers in the United States. Many ODR providers are also looking to a handful of existing laws and professional ethics codes dealing with offline ADR to help guide their conduct. However, this patchwork of Recommended Best Practices and ADR laws and guidelines does not address the legal duties and ethical responsibilities of ODR service providers in the global environment of the Web. In addition, an enforcement mechanism to ensure compliance with internationally agreed-upon standards of practice is needed to boost customer confidence in online transactions and to help promote quality ODR services on the Web. There is a wide divergence in views on the future regulation of ODR, including greater government regulation, expanded efforts at co-regulation, greater use of trustmark programs, and the new development of international governing bodies. Which trend in ODR regulation will prevail depends largely upon which overall approach is applied to regulating the Internet in general. Let's consider some of these different perspectives.

In the early, heady days of cyberspace, many idealists in the online community viewed the Internet as a separate world that should develop its own standards and customs without national government intervention. A number of commentators wrote about the new freedoms of an online community unencumbered by national laws or government regulation. However, in recent years, national governments have sought to extend their traditional sovereignty and national laws to the Internet, addressing issues such as gambling, taxation, privacy, child protection, pornography, money laundering, and terrorism. Many Web experts anticipate that government entities will continue to seek greater control over regulation of the Internet in an effort to uphold their national laws and priorities. If national laws become the main regulatory vehicle for ODR services, then ODR providers and participants located within the same country will be the primary beneficiaries. If the service provider and the parties come from different nations, a reliance on national laws will only further complicate the use of ODR because parties will have to identify on their own or through costly court processes which national regulatory scheme applies to their selected ODR process and service provider.

Obviously, efforts to preserve national sovereignty and laws collide with the desire to develop uniformity on the Web, to simplify business obligations, and to improve the ease of commercial transactions for all parties. Some Web commentators have suggested that the concerns of government bodies can be better addressed through a scheme of co-regulation. Under this concept, national governments working together internationally would draw up broad ODR policies while national entities made up of consumer, professional, and industry stakeholders determine the specifics for obtaining the stated international ODR goals. In some respects this approach is similar to the handing down of an EU directive that sets out uniform standards that EU members must meet but that may allow member nations to further tailor the directive to meet their cultural, social, and legal concerns. Another view of co-regulation allows nongovernmental stakeholders to develop acceptable standards of practice that government agencies enforce on a national or local basis. Either of these co-regulation models could be applied to ODR to help develop international practice policies and training principles for ODR providers that could be further tailored or enforced on a national basis.

The self-regulatory approach has two main views: (1) a market-driven view of Internet regulation that perceives the Internet as a collection of individual electronic markets; or (2) a self-certifying perspective that suggests that ODR service providers should endorse their own compliance with ODR practice standards. In the first instance, each private marketplace determines its participants' rights and obligations under its terms of use. If these obligations are violated, then the private market will protect its parties through the establishment of private dispute resolution structures. Private market owners will compete with one another to provide the most reliable business partners with the best conflict resolution methods in order to attract business or consumer customers to that marketplace. For example, eBay is a private marketplace, and it sets forth its ground rules in its terms of use. Those wishing to buy or sell on eBay must comply with its terms and conditions, with eBay collaborating with Square Trade for the provision of ODR services.

The second approach is one that is currently proposed in the ABA Task Force's Final Report and Recommended Best Practices. The Task Force indicates that ODR service providers should voluntarily apply the Recommended Best Practices and should self-certify their good-faith compliance with these standards. However, there is no enforcing or certifying body to insure that an ODR service provider has acted properly and truly complied with these best practices.

Under the self-regulatory viewpoint, little uniform guidance would be provided to potential parties seeking ODR services, which would lead to public confusion about ODR standards, because each market would set its own quality standards for ODR providers or each provider would determine their own level of compliance. To help provide more uniform ODR standards of practice and quality, the development of a self-regulatory international ODR trustmark or seal program may be needed. Under such a proposed program, an ODR trustmark or seal entity would certify that an ODR service provider meets agreed-upon international standards of proper ethical conduct and that it provides quality ODR services. Standards could be determined through input from ODR service providers, e-commerce businesses, consumer groups, and governmental agencies. To guide potential ODR participants, an international trustmark or seal would be displayed on the web sites of complying ODR firms. The removal or lack of an ODR trustmark seal on a provider's web site would signify the failure of the ODR provider to meet acceptable international standards of business and ethical ODR practice. Through the use of an international ODR certification agency, ODR participants would have a central clearinghouse of information on ODR processes as well as a common location to bring complaints against or gain feedback about ODR service providers.

Consistent with the development of an international trustmark program, the BBBOnline, the Federation of European Direct Marketing (FEDMA) (http://www.fedma.org/), and Eurochambres, the Association of European Chambers of Commerce and Industry (http://www.eurochambres.be), announced in 2001 that they would collaborate on the creation of an international trustmark for online businesses. Under this self-regulatory initiative, online businesses seeking the international trustmark would agree to uphold an international code of commercial conduct, which would include defined and acceptable dispute resolution methods. This effort symbolizes the determination of these organizations to provide compatible best e-business practices and conflict resolution options for European Union and North American online consumers.

Are the Courts Playing a Role in the ODR Field?

With issues of jurisdiction over online disputes (Chapter 1) and the enforcement of ODR awards and outcomes still uncertain, there are few major ODR precedents. To date, the courts have not played a major role in the arena of ODR. Courts have been involved primarily in reviewing trademark and other intellectual property disputes,

Promoting Trust and Confidence on the Internet

Since 1912, the Better Business Bureau (BBB) (http//:www.bbb.org) has been working to encourage ethical commercial practices, to provide business and consumer resources and education, and to help resolve disagreements between member businesses and consumers. Serving more than twenty-four million consumers and businesses in the United States, Canada, and Puerto Rico, the BBB has extended its mission to the World Wide Web with its development of the BBB*Online* (http//:www.bbbonline.org).

With many consumers and businesses confused or concerned about undertaking commercial transactions on the Internet, the BBB*Online* seeks to provide them with confidence in their online dealings through its BBB*Online* Reliability and Privacy Seals. Under these programs, on-line businesses must comply with the BBB*Online's* standards in order to gain the organization's trustmarks on their web site. To earn the Reliability Seal, the participating e-business must be a member of their local BBB and meet applicable truth-in-advertising requirements and good customer service guidelines.

Under the Privacy Seal, a certified e-firm must comply with its stated privacy policy and meet the BBB*Online's* requirements for the proper handling of customers' personal information. The privacy program also offers a separate seal for programs that comply with their obligations regarding children's privacy rights.

Under both seal programs, aggrieved consumers can file complaints online about member e-companies. In addition, the BBB*Online* offers dispute resolution services, such as conciliation, mediation, and arbitration, to help resolve disputes between member online businesses and consumers. These dispute resolution services are funded primarily through member firms' dues.

To help guide online businesses, the BBB*Online* has developed a Code of Online Business Practices. Following is an excerpt from that Code dealing with the responsibilities of online firms to provide good customer service and satisfaction, in part through affordable and effective dispute resolution mechanisms.

Excerpt—Code of Online Business Practices Final Version

Principle IV: Customer Satisfaction
Online merchants should seek to ensure their customers are satisfied by honoring their representations, answering questions, and resolving customer complaints and disputes in a timely and responsive manner.

(continued)

A. *Honor Representations*: Online merchants should comply with all commitments, representations, and other promises made to a customer.

B. *Answer Questions*: Online merchants should provide an easy-to-find and understandable notice of how customers can successfully and meaningfully contact the business to get answers to their questions. Online merchants should promptly and substantively respond to the customer's commercially reasonable questions.

C. *Resolve Customer Complaints and Disputes*: Online merchants should seek to resolve customer complaints and disputes in a fair, timely, and effective manner.

  1. Online merchants should provide an easy-to-find and understandable notice of how a customer can successfully and meaningfully contact the business to expeditiously resolve complaints and disputes related to a transaction.

  2. Online merchants shall have an effective and easy-to-use internal mechanism for addressing complaints and correcting errors. Examples include fair exchange policies, return policies, etc.

  3. In the event the customer's complaint cannot be resolved, online merchants shall also offer a fair method for resolving differences with regard to a transaction by offering either an unconditional money-back guarantee or third-party dispute resolution.

     - If an online merchant offers third-party dispute resolution, it should use a trusted third party that offers impartial, accessible, and timely arbitration that is free to consumers or at a charge to consumers that is not disproportionate to the value of goods or services involved in the dispute.

     - Online merchants should provide customers with easy-to-find and understandable contact information for such third parties, including a link (or similar technology) to any third-party sites used for such means.

which may also be at issue in separate ICANN e-mail arbitrations concerning domain name disputes. In some instances, the transfer or cancellation of domain names has been upheld, whereas in others the courts have questioned or refused to defer to ICANN proceedings because the Uniform Dispute Resolution Policy (UDRP) allows for parallel court proceedings. In the following case, the court determines that it has the discretion to view ICANN decisions as nonbinding because the UDRP permits disputing parties to seek resolution of their domain name quarrels in national courts.

KEY CHAPTER CASE

Does a National Court Have to Defer to an ICANN Domain Name Action under the UDRP?

Weber-Stephen Products Co. v Armitage Hardware and Building Supply, Inc., 2000 U.S. Dist. LEXIS 6335 (N.D. IL 2000)

Fact Summary: Defendant Armitage Hardware (Armitage) registered several domain names allegedly containing registered trademarks and service marks of plaintiff Weber-Stephen Products Company (Weber) intentionally and in bad faith. Weber brought an administrative proceeding before the World Intellectual Property Organization (WIPO) in accordance with the Uniform Domain Name Dispute Resolution Policy (UDRP) of the Internet Corporation for Assigned Names and Numbers (ICANN Policy) seeking the transfer to Weber or cancellation of these Armitage domain names. The following day, Weber also filed suit in this district court, alleging "cyberpiracy" as well as other claims, such as trademark infringement. Weber also claimed that it expected a decision from the panel within forty-five to fifty days from the filing of its ICANN complaint. Armitage's made a motion to declare the WIPO proceeding nonbinding and to stay this cyberpiracy case until the completion of the WIPO administrative action. If the court alternatively found the WIPO proceeding to be binding, then Armitage argued that the court should decide whether or not Armitage must participate in the WIPO process.

OPINION: MARVIN E. ASPEN, CHIEF JUDGE.

No federal court has yet considered the legal effect of a WIPO proceeding. However, the ICANN Policy and its accompanying rules do contemplate the possibility of parallel proceedings in federal court. First, the Policy provides that ICANN will cancel or transfer domain name registrations upon "our receipt of an order from a court . . . of competent jurisdiction, requiring such action; *and/or* . . . our receipt of a decision of an Administrative Panel requiring such action in any administrative proceeding . . . conducted under this Policy." ICANN Policy at P 3. Also, the procedural rules governing the Policy provide that if legal proceedings are initiated prior to or during an administrative proceeding with regard to a domain name dispute that is the subject of the administrative complaint, the panel has the discretion to decide whether to suspend or terminate the administrative proceeding or whether to proceed and make a decision. Uniform Domain Name Dispute Resolution Rules, at P 18. [footnote omitted] And the language of the Policy suggests that the administrative panels' decisions are not intended to be binding on federal courts. . . . [footnote omitted]

Furthermore, Armitage's counsel sent an e-mail inquiry to <domain.disputes@wipo.int>, and the response from the WIPO Arbitration and Mediation Center said that the administrative panel's determination would be binding on the registrar of the domain name, but that "this decision is not binding upon a court, and a court may give appropriate weight to the Administrative Panel's decision." Albeit a vague and rather unhelpful interpretation, Weber does not take issue with this WIPO statement.

We conclude that this Court is not bound by the outcome of the ICANN administrative proceedings. But at this time we decline to determine the precise standard by which we would review the panel's decision, and what degree of deference (if any) we would give

(*continued*)

that decision. Neither the ICANN Policy nor its governing rules dictate to courts what weight should be given to a panel's decision, and the WIPO e-mail message stating that "a court may give appropriate weight to the Administrative Panel's decision" confirms the breadth of our discretion.

Because both parties to this case have adequate avenues of recourse should they be unhappy with the administrative panel's imminent decision, we find no need to stay the pending ICANN administrative action. Instead, we hereby stay this case pending the outcome of those proceedings. It is so ordered.

However, the courts may play a role in ODR development as they tap into online technologies in order to update and reform current judicial processes and associated ADR court programs. For example, in December 2001, the state of Michigan borrowed from the ODR field when it passed a pioneering state law that establishes the creation of a pilot Cyber Court. The Cyber Court pilot plans to apply new electronic and online technologies to judicial processes and to attract technology-based firms to its virtual courtrooms. Although private virtual courts, such as iCourthouse (http://www.icourthouse.com), already exist, the Michigan Cyber Court would be the first state-sponsored court dedicated to offering virtual proceedings. Under the recently enacted law, the proposed Cyber Court would be designed to permit all court hearings and sessions to be conducted electronically using video, audio, and Internet conferencing, with sessions possibly broadcast over the Internet. Funded in 2003, the purpose of the Michigan Cyber Court is to handle commercial disputes between businesses and their customers, competitors, owners, and associates. The virtual courtroom will be particularly helpful in disputes in which parties or witnesses may be located outside of Michigan. The law also calls for the state to promote the application of those new technologies in the ADR field, which could eventually provide a great public boost to all ODR service providers. Michigan court and legal professionals are working on establishing the rules of procedure for these virtual courtrooms. A legislative oversight committee will monitor the Cyber Court pilot program and determine any further changes needed to improve the virtual court experience. To find out the latest developments on the Michigan Cyber Court, visit its web site at http://www.michigancybercourt.net.

Are There Any Model Codes of Conduct for Handling Online Disputes?

At the start of 2001, the American Arbitration Association (AAA) announced the first eCommerce Dispute Management Protocol offering basic principles for resolving B2B conflicts (http://www.adr.org). The protocol calls for online businesses to offer a fundamentally fair dispute resolution process that emphasizes continued business relationships, clear identification of dispute prevention and resolution methods, the development of a variety of conflict resolution options, and the utilization of technology to enhance the resolution of B2B disputes. In light of its B2B protocol, the AAA has also developed Supplementary Procedures for Online Arbitration to aid the use of arbitration over the Internet, a new panel of B2B e-commerce neutrals, and a Dispute Risk Management (DRM) Portal for the online filing of B2B complaints.

American Arbitration Association (http//:www.adr.org)
eCommerce Dispute Management Protocol:
Principles for Managing Business-to-Business Relationships

Global commerce is entering a rare time in history—a time in which business is conducted at unprecedented speed and traditional business practices are being reevaluated. Today, businesses have an extraordinary opportunity to shape the way they conduct themselves in this new world of eCommerce, and they are doing it with foresight and deliberation.

Recognizing the importance of maintaining valued business relationships, forward-thinking companies are incorporating sound dispute management principles in all aspects of their relationships to avoid traditional costly and time-consuming methods of resolving disputes. In the global marketplace, businesses acknowledge the value of fostering an environment in which controversies are anticipated, minimized and resolved in a fair, timely and final manner. By adopting the principles set forth in the eCommerce Dispute Management Protocol, companies can resolve disputes and get back to business.

Fairness

We believe that all businesses are entitled to a fundamentally fair dispute management process that includes access to neutral dispute resolution providers.

Continuity of Business

We believe it is important to isolate disputes and resolve them with minimal disruption to other transactions.

Clear Dispute Management Policies

We believe it is important to clearly identify and support the mechanisms for the prevention and resolution of disputes.

Range of Options

We encourage the use of a variety of cost-effective methods to resolve disputes at the earliest possible stage.

Commitment to Technology

We support the use of appropriate technology to aid the swift and economical management of disputes.

The AAA's protocol was followed by the ABA Task Force's Final Report and Recommended Best Practices for ODR Service Providers released at the end of 2002. These Recommended Best Practices focused primarily on proper disclosures about an ODR service provider's conflicts of interest, credentials and training, funding sources, security measures, and privacy and confidentiality features. The Recommended Best Practices also suggest that e-businesses have disclosure duties in regard to the existence of any predispute ADR/ODR provisions, the type of ODR mechanism that e-business employs, and the nature of any contractual relationships with service providers raising potential conflicts of interest issues. In addition, the ABA Task Force called for the development of an informational clearinghouse, an *iADR Center*, to help better educate online businesses and the general public about ODR processes, best practices, and service providers. The ABA Task Force's Recommended Best Practices are intended to apply to ODR services for both B2B and B2C disputes and are provided in full in Appendix A. The Recommended Best Practices also touch upon some of the main ethical obligations of ODR neutrals. Greater detail on the ethical obligations of neutrals can be drawn from existing ethical codes applied to offline ADR, such as the Model Standards of Conduct for Mediators (http://www.adr.org), the Code of Ethics for Arbitrators in Commercial Disputes (http://www.adr.org), and the Society of Professionals in Dispute Resolution (SPIDR) Ethical Standards of Professional Responsibility (http://www.acresolution.org).

A number of e-commerce industry and public interest organizations have drafted related best-practice recommendations or suggested codes of conduct to help guide online businesses in their dealings with consumer and commercial customers. It may be also helpful to surf the web sites of other organizations such as the BBB*Online* (http://www.bbbonline.org), the Organisation for Economic Co-operation (OECD) (http://www.oecd.org), and the Global Business Dialogue on Electronic Commerce (GBDe) (http://www.gbde.org) to learn more about suggested codes of business conduct for online firms. (See "ODR in the Digital Era.") Although not specifically aimed at ODR service providers, these organizations recommend that online businesses should provide fast, impartial, affordable, and effective dispute resolution mechanisms, particularly when handling B2C disputes, using either internal staff or third-party providers. For example, the GBDE, a private-sector e-commerce policy group that includes companies such as DaimlerChrysler AG, Walt Disney Company, IBM, AOL/ Time Warner, and Bertelsmann AG, has put together extensive recommendations on the creation and implementation of effective dispute resolution programs for B2C conflicts, which can be found on its web site. Also, helpful information on fundamentally fair ODR programs can be gleaned from the National Consumer Disputes Advisory Committee's Consumer Due Process Protocol, which provides detailed model procedures for properly handling consumer dispute resolution programs in the offline world (http://www.adr.org/education/education/consumer_protocol.html). Lastly, the efforts to create an international trustmark that incorporates appropriate conflict resolution mechanisms may help provide future international standards for ODR.

What Major Issues Must Be Resolved to Strengthen ODR Use?

Online disputes will continue to grow as online transactions proliferate on the Web. As with any new field, there are a number of issues that need to be ironed out to help ensure that online disputes are resolved in a fair, effective, and timely manner using up-to-date technologies. In order for ODR to meet effectively the needs and goals of the online community, the following main concerns require further research, practice and clarification: (1) the adoption of recognized and enforceable international or cross-border quality standards for ODR service providers; (2) the examination of and revisions to current ADR ethical codes for their applicability to ODR; (3) the determination of appropriate enforcement mechanisms for

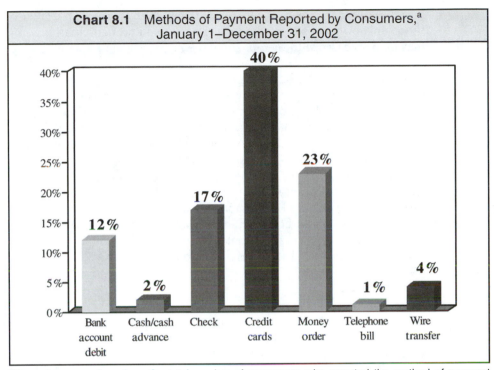

Chart 8.1 Methods of Payment Reported by Consumers,[a] January 1–December 31, 2002

[a]Percentages are based on the total number of consumers who reported the method of payment (39,496); 39% of consumers reported this information.

Chart Prepared by Consumer Sentinel, Bureau of Consumer Protection, U.S. Federal Trade Commission. Used with Permission (http://www.consumer.gov/sentinel/sentinel-trends/page7.pdf; http://www.ftc.gov).

ODR outcomes; and (4) the further education of online businesses and the public about ODR processes.

Adopting Uniform, Enforceable Quality Standards

At the current time, there are a number of model codes of conduct for online businesses to help them carry out their commercial practices in an ethical and legal manner. Trustmark and seal programs help consumers to identify those businesses that meet important business quality standards. Despite the recent efforts of the ABA Task Force, there are no uniform and enforceable international standards of practice for ODR service providers. Any person or business can offer ODR services because there are no clear definitions and no mandated requirements about what makes one an ODR service provider. Although the ABA Task Force's Recommended Best Practices are useful guidelines, online businesses and consumers still have little guidance about which ODR service provider will offer them fair, affordable, and effective ODR services. As a direct result of the lack of uniform and enforceable international standards, there is no guarantee that online disputants will receive quality services from ODR service providers. Online parties may shy away from ODR use because of these unknowns, or those who take the gamble and participate in ODR processes may be displeased with the quality of their services and reluctant to use ODR again in the future.

To help remedy this situation and to promote public confidence in ODR services, efforts need to be undertaken by all e-commerce stakeholders to determine appropriate international or cross-border ODR quality standards in such areas as the training of neutrals, language fluency, technological expertise, fair-practice procedures, truth in advertising, online security, and data retention. Furthermore, proper governmental or self-regulatory professional bodies need to enforce these agreed-upon standards through ODR licensing, certification, or seal programs. The efforts of the ABA Task Force to develop an *iADR Center* or the international seal initiative of the BBB*Online*, FEDMA, and Eurochambres may provide good starting points for achieving enforceable, cross-border standards of excellence for ODR service providers. Without enforceable, international quality standards, online parties will lack confidence in the value of ODR processes and outcomes.

Revising Ethical Codes of Practice

Adherence to ethical codes of practice plays an important role in addressing quality and upholding professionalism in many different fields. There are a number of different ADR codes of conduct that apply to ADR neutrals in the offline world. These codes were adopted with the underlying assumption that all parties would be in the same room, speak the same language, and share the same cultural norms and social values. None of these ethical codes were drafted with the online world in mind and do not specifically address ODR.

Certain ethical issues, such as avoiding conflicts of interest and maintaining objectivity, would easily translate from the offline world to dispute resolution in the online world. However, some traditional ADR principles may need to be reexamined and revised when applied to ODR. For example, it is well recognized that confidentiality is a key component of most ADR proceedings, protecting information exchanged in documents and discussions from being disclosed to third parties. Traditionally, confidentiality is viewed as essential in ADR processes in order to aid the parties in an open and frank exchange of information and ideas. Yet, in the online world, the anonymity of the Web may be abused to defraud parties and to avoid responsibility for poor business practices. It may be useful to disclose information on ODR proceedings and outcomes in order to make the public aware of an online firm's unprofessional or fraudulent business conduct. In addition, by limiting confidentiality in ODR processes, government law enforcement and regulatory agencies may receive the necessary data to act against unscrupulous e-businesses. As regards the conduct of ODR service providers, the ABA Task Force suggested that at a minimum that ODR service providers should post periodic statistical reports on their activities for public review. Therefore, a full review of current ADR or offline ethics codes and their underlying assumptions may be required. Revisions to existing codes may be needed in order to create a new model for ethical ODR practice in the online environment.

Improving Enforcement of ODR Outcomes

Generally, dispute resolution experts believe that disputants are more likely to comply with outcomes that are not imposed upon them by third parties, such as courts. In the use of ODR, it is assumed that the voluntary nature of the process and the ability of the parties to play a role in deciding the outcome of their dispute—or at least to select the final decision-maker—will increase the likelihood of compliance with the resolution of the dispute. In addition, arbitration awards are normally much easier to enforce than court awards due to existing international treaties. But the failure or unwillingness of some parties to comply with the results of ODR processes cannot be ignored and may still present a problem in certain instances. The benefits of the ODR process will be lost if parties must resort to the courts in order to enforce an ODR result. As discussed in Chapters 1 and 2, courts may also be reluctant or lack the authority to enforce ODR awards and outcomes.

If ODR is going to inspire confidence in disputants, policy makers will need to address how such ODR outcomes can be enforced. Under self-regulatory international trustmark initiatives, such as the one between BBB*Online*, FEDMA, and Eurochambres, an e-business may lose its certification due to its failure to comply with the results of an agreed-upon ODR process. Although this approach may help in many cases to ensure compliance, it will not deal with all noncomplying parties. In some cases, a noncomplying online business may not be participating in any voluntary certification programs and therefore would have no concern about losing its seal approval. On the other hand, private parties may be the ones not living up to their ODR outcomes, and they would be beyond the reach of certification programs.

Aside from the loss of a trustmark, other ODR commentators have suggested that parties should be required to post a bond or escrow funds prior to the start of the ODR process to help ensure later compliance. Another option involves the adoption of an international agreement similar to the New York Convention to enforce ODR outcomes in the national courts of signatory nations to help make enforcement easier and faster against noncompliant parties. Furthermore, others have suggested that parties that fail to live up to ODR outcomes should lose some aspect of Web citizenship, such as loss of Web access privileges or domain name use, until they comply with their ODR outcomes. Lastly, some experts have recommended the use of positive financial or professional incentives to parties that comply fully and rapidly with ODR outcomes. Clearly, any decision on the best way to enforce ODR results in the global marketplace of the Web will require international collaboration and the input of e-commerce stakeholders from government, industry, public-interest groups, and the general public.

Increasing Public Awareness

Disputants are more likely to gravitate toward processes with which they are familiar, such as traditional litigation. Although litigation may be a well-recognized method for handling conflicts, its value in the international marketplace of the Internet is dubious. Issues of time, cost, distance, choice of law, jurisdiction, and enforcement make litigation a poor choice for dealing with many online disputes.

E-commerce policymakers realize that the fast, fair, and efficient resolution of online disputes is key to the growth and continued success of online commercial transactions. In this text, we have tried to highlight a wide range of ODR options as well as the main benefits of ODR mechanisms. Although the nature and goals of ODR processes may be well known to many in the ODR field, the concept is still a recent phenomenon that is unfamiliar to a majority of e-commerce professionals and the general public. Public education about ODR methods, advantages, and disadvantages is essential in order for parties to willingly make the ODR choice. Both the public and private sectors must undertake efforts to increase e-business and public awareness about ODR.

Professional e-commerce organizations, trustmark bodies, government and judicial authorities, and public-interest groups can sponsor public information campaigns on ODR using both traditional offline and new online methods. Both in the offline and online worlds, these policy groups can offer educational programs or host public forums for e-business and the general public. Public-service advertising can also be placed in traditional print publications or broadcast media to get the word out on ODR. In addition, online technologies can be utilized to promote ODR options through such mechanisms as online videos, chat rooms, bulletin board services, banner ads, or resource links on home pages to ODR materials. The academic community can also play a role by introducing ODR concepts into applicable business, law, and technology courses. Furthermore, e-businesses can participate in the ODR educational effort (discussed next). By creatively using a multipronged approach, greater public awareness of and appreciation for the value of ODR can be achieved.

How Might E-Business Play a Role in Educating the Public about ODR?

With the myriad of obstacles associated with traditional litigation in dealing with online disputes, it is in the best interests of any online company to participate in educating its online commercial and consumer customers about ODR. E-business can play a central role in educating the public about ODR because online businesses are the primary customer interface on the Web. By working with other e-commerce stakeholders on the ODR educational effort, an e-business shows its commitment to responsible online business conduct and reaps the benefits of the speed and efficiency of ODR processes for its customers and itself. The ABA Task Force's Recommended Best Practices noted that e-businesses should help to increase public understanding of ODR processes.

Companies transacting business online can provide key information to their customers about the ODR processes they employ to resolve their online disagreements. As indicated in Chapter 7, online firms using ODR should clearly and fully disclose this fact to avoid later misunderstandings or legal challenges. On their home page, e-firms can include a separate ODR icon, similar to those found for privacy or terms of use, to highlight their ODR clause or policies to visitors. The ODR program should be spelled out in easily understood terms and in the languages of the markets that the e-business serves. The ODR icon could also link online customers to a brief overview of ODR processes. Alternatively, the e-business could link customers to an ODR resource page with links to other independent sites that offer balanced explanations of ODR processes, benefits, and limitations. The web content on an e-business site may also include FAQs dealing with ODR or public-service banner advertising on ODR issues or events. Through these various efforts, e-business can participate in a positive way to improve public understanding of the importance of ODR in the resolution of online disputes.

What Further Experimentation in ODR Technologies Can Be Expected?

Clearly, there is already a broad range of technological channels for communicating in ODR processes. ODR service providers are utilizing e-mail, automated, and interactive software platforms, secure chat rooms, bulletin boards and listservs, and video and web conferencing to handle both online and offline disputes. But the acceptance of ODR lies in taking technologies beyond merely speeding up the ODR process to replicating more closely the face-to-face experience that may be key to resolving many disagreements. Greater interactivity in ODR software programs and more cost-effective and rapid video and web conferencing need to be developed in the coming years to help parties gain greater access to ODR technologies and to mimic the human elements of an in-person meeting. Further investigation into intelligent systems that help guide online disputants throughout the process is an important next step. The continuing work of OASIS on odrXML will aid in the exchange of information between diverse ODR platforms (http://www.oasis-open.org).

Despite overall agreement that there needs to be greater experimentation in order to better address human factors that are often essential to successful conflict resolution, it is uncertain who will fund these costly developments. Some commentators suggest that because government authorities fund court systems, they should also provide financial support for the development and operation of ODR systems. Others contend that the private-sector, for-profit ODR service providers or online businesses who benefit from increased online commercial activities and the lower costs associated with ODR should foot the bill for such innovations. Certainly, a private and public sector partnership between all e-commerce stakeholders would help to provide appropriate funding for ODR experimentation, development, and operation. This collaborative effort could translate into greatly improved and more accessible ODR options that would help to promote customer confidence in online commercial transactions, boost online sales and associated tax revenues, and avoid a flood of new litigation into already overburdened courts.

Quick Clicks: Reviewing ODR Service Provider Sites for Compliance with ABA Task Force's Recommended Best Practices   Select an ODR service provider and visit that provider's web site. Review the site and see if it meets the disclosure requirements set out in the ABA Task Force's Recommended Best Practices. Write down the instances in which the site complies with the Recommended Best Practices and the instances in which the provider does not meet those standards. Provide this information at your next class meeting for class discussion or instructor review.

ODR Bytes

There is a wide divergence in views on the future regulation of ODR, including greater government regulation, expanded efforts at co-regulation, greater use of trustmark programs, and the creation of international governing bodies.

Various groups have recommended the use of self-regulatory trustmarks and efforts are underway to create an international trustmark for online businesses. Under proposed international trustmark initiatives, participating online businesses agree to uphold an international code of commercial conduct, which would include defined and acceptable dispute resolution methods.

The courts have not been deeply involved in the development of ODR with few major ODR precedents at the present time. However, the courts may play a role in ODR development as they seek to use Internet technologies to update and reform current judicial processes and associated ADR court programs, as found in the Michigan Cyber Court pilot program.

A number of e-commerce industry, professional, and public-interest organizations have drafted best practice codes of conduct to help guide online businesses in their dealings with consumer and commercial customers that include recommendations for fast, fair, and effective dispute resolution programs.

The ABA Task Force's Recommended Best Practices offer guidance to ODR service providers on key disclosures. Details on ethical obligations can be drawn from existing ethical codes for offline ADR processes.

A full review of current ADR/offline ethics codes and their underlying assumptions is required in order to make revisions to existing codes to help create a new model for ethical ODR practice in the online environment.

Public trust in ODR use will be strengthened through the development of international and enforceable ODR quality standards that deal specifically with the training of neutrals, language fluency, technological expertise, fair-practice procedures, truth in advertising, online security, and data retention, as well as the designation of regulatory bodies to enforce such standards.

In the future, international collaboration and the input of e-commerce stakeholders in government, industry, and the general public will be required to determine the best way to enforce ODR results in the global marketplace of the Web.

Both the public and private sectors must undertake efforts to increase e-business and public awareness about ODR by sponsoring public-information campaigns on ODR using both traditional offline and new online methods.

Through full disclosure, ODR icons, FAQs, hypertext links, and public-service banner ads, e-businesses can play a central role in educating the public about ODR, show their commitment to responsible online business conduct, and reap the benefits of the speed and efficiency of ODR processes for its customers and the industry.

Greater interactivity in ODR software programs, more cost-effective and rapid video and web conferencing, and experimentation with intelligent ODR systems need to be developed in the coming years to help parties gain access to ODR technologies that help to mimic the human elements of a face-to-face meeting.

A private and public sector partnership between all e-commerce stakeholders would help to provide needed funding for ODR experimentation, development, and operation.

Improved ODR technologies could translate into faster, more user-friendly and interactive ODR options that will boost customer confidence in online commercial transactions, increase online sales and tax revenues, and avoid a flood of new litigation into already overburdened courts.

ODR Bookmarks

ABA Task Force on E-Commerce and ADR
http://www.law.washington.edu/ABA-eADR

American Arbitration Association, eCommerce Dispute Management Protocol
http://www.adr.org

BBBOnline
http://www.bbbonline.org

Better Business Bureau (BBB)
http://www.bbb.org

Code of Ethics for Arbitrators in Commercial Disputes
http://www.adr.org

Consumer Due Process Protocol
http://www.adr.org

Ethical Standards of Professional Responsibility
http://www.acresolution.org

Eurochambres, the Association of European Chambers of Commerce and Industry
http://www.eurochambres.be

Federation of European Direct Marketing (FEDMA)
http://www.fedma.org/

Global Business Dialogue on Electronic Commerce (GBDe)
http://www.consumerconfidence.gbde.org

iCourthouse
http//:www.icourthouse.com

Michigan Cyber Court
http://www.michigancybercourt.net.

Model Standards of Conduct for Mediators
http://www.adr.org

Organisation for Economic Co-operation (OECD)
http://www.oecd.org

Organization for the Advancement of Structured Information Standards (OASIS)
http://www.oasis-open.org

Selected ODR Bibliography

"Addressing Disputes in Electronic Commerce." Final Report and Recommendations of ABA Task Force on E-Commerce and ADR. http://www.law.washington.edu/ABA-eADR/ documentation/index.html.

Bordone, Robert C. "Electronic Online Dispute Resolution: A Systems Approach—Potential, Problems, and a Proposal." *Harv. Negotiation L. Rev.* 3 (Spring, 1998): 175.

Katsh, E., J. Rifkin, and A. Gaitenby. "E-Commerce, E-Disputes, and E-Dispute Resolution: In the Shadow of 'eBay Law.'" *Ohio St. J. On Disp. Res.* 15 (Summer 2000): 705.

Lide, E. Casey. "ADR and Cyberspace: The Role of Alternative Dispute Resolution in Online Commerce, Intellectual Property and Defamation." *Ohio St. J. on Disp. Resol.* 12 (1996): 193.

Menthe, Darrel. "Jurisdiction in Cyberspace: A Theory of International Spaces." *Mich. Telecomm. Tech. L. Rev.* 4 (1998): 69.

Perritt, Henry H., Jr. "Dispute Resolution in Cyberspace: Demand for New Forms of ADR." *Ohio St. J. On Disp. Res.* 15 (Summer 2000): 675.

Ponte, Lucille M. "Boosting Consumer Confidence in E-Business: Recommendations for Establishing Fair and Effective Dispute Resolution Programs for B2C Online Transactions." *Albany L. J. of Sci. & Tech.* 12 (2002): 441.

Ponte, Lucille M. "Broadening Traditional ADR Notions of Disclosure: Special Considerations for Posting Conflict Resolution Policies and Programs on E-Business Web Sites." *Ohio St. J. On Disp. Res.* 17 (2002): 321.

Puurunen, Tapio. "The Legislative Jurisdiction of States over Transactions in International Electronic Commerce." *J. Marshall J. Computer & Info. L.* 18 (LEXIS-NEXIS Academic Universe—Document) (2000): 689.

"Recommended Best Practices for Online Dispute Resolution Service Providers." ABA Task Force on E-Commerce and ADR. http://www.law.washington.edu/ABA-eADR/documentation/index.html.

"Trend Said to Be Away From 'Hands-Off' Internet Regulation by World's Legal Officials." *Electronic Commerce & Law* 6 (BNA Nov. 14, 2001): 1150.

APPENDIX A

American Bar Association Task Force on E-Commerce and ADR-Recommended Best Practices for Online Dispute Resolution Service Providers[*]

I. SCOPE AND APPROACH

A. Scope

These Recommended Best Practices are intended to assist:

- Organizations that provide online dispute resolution (ODR) services (ODR Providers), concerning disputes that occur online or disputes that lend themselves to being resolved online;
- Individuals who serve as neutrals for ODR Providers;
- Customers of those services, whether personal consumers or businesses; and
- Online merchants or marketplaces.

The term "online" refers to the use of the Internet or related communications technologies (such as email, videoconferencing, or interaction via a website or chatroom) as the primary method of communication during a transaction or related dispute resolution proceeding.

Actions that are taken by ODR Providers consistent with these Recommended Best Practices may (a) take the form of codes of conduct, codes of practice, best practices statements, protocols and similar statements; (b) be reflected in the operation of their websites and in material posted on their websites; or both. The exact form is secondary. The primary points are that the ODR Provider's service is clearly and comprehensively presented to the consumer in a manner that is consistent with the Recommended Best Practices and in fact operates in the manner presented.

[*]The materials contained herein represent the opinions of the authors and editors and should not be construed to be those of the American Bar Association, the Section of Business Law, the Section of Dispute Resolution, the Section of International Law and Practice, the Litigation Section, or the Section of Intellectual Property Law unless adopted pursuant to the bylaws of the Association. Nothing contained herein is to be considered as the rendering of legal advice for specific cases and readers are responsible for obtaining advice from their own legal counsel. These materials and any forms and agreements herein are intended for educational and informational purposes only.

These Recommended Best Practices are not intended for traditional, face-to-face dispute resolution services, though the basic principles may apply in both online and offline environments.

These Recommended Best Practices contain many principles that are applicable in both B2B and B2C disputes. However, they particularly are intended to enable personal consumers to make intelligent choices concerning ODR providers, to help give them confidence in the efficacy of ODR and therefore in B2C commerce generally, and to encourage consumers to use ODR as a means of obtaining resolution of their complaints.

These Recommended Best Practices are also not primarily directed to the codes of conduct, best practices statements, and similar protocols of online merchants or marketplaces (although they may find the Recommended Best Practices useful). Other private and governmental entities have proposed merchant guidelines and best practices for consumer protection in the context of electronic commerce, and this Task Force does not purport to duplicate their efforts. However, with respect to ODR, the Task Force does believe that it is important for online merchants and marketplaces to disclose: (1) the existence of pre-dispute ADR/ODR clauses; (2) the nature of the online merchant's dispute resolution process, including customer service and use of formal ADR/ODR processes; (3) any contractual relationships with ADR/ODR Providers; and (4) information to educate their customers about ADR/ODR methods.

B. Approach

It is not the primary goal of these Recommended Best Practices to set minimum substantive standards. The approach taken by Recommended Best Practices is based mainly on the use of disclosure and addresses both the adequacy of the means whereby the disclosure is given and the subject matter of the disclosures. It is recognized, however, that the fact of comprehensively listing and organizing the topics for disclosure has some effect in setting substantive standards. It is also acknowledged that, when individual ODR Providers come to the act of formulating disclosures that are readily available publicly and easily compared with those of other ODR Providers, a natural effect of a disclosure-based system is to press ODR Providers in the direction of setting strong substantive standards. These effects are intended. In addition, a "Commentary" area follows each of the Sections of these Recommended Best Practices and those Commentaries indicate, among other things, substantive standards that are encouraged. Hence, as a practical matter, the approach in these Recommended Best Practices is unavoidably a mixed system of recommended disclosures and substantive practice standards.

Nevertheless, the intention is to rely mainly on disclosure. There are several reasons for this disclosure-based approach:

1. The ODR community as a whole is quite new and has not generated a sufficient database of information on which to base confidently extensive substantive standards particularly applicable to ODR.

2. Different ODR Providers focus on different markets (service, product, merchant type, geography, etc.) and a single set of substantive standards may not be appropriate in all cases.

3. The ODR community lacks a clear business model or models for sustained profitable operations and appears to be evolving so as to develop such models. Premature standard setting may retard that evolution.

4. From the point of view of the Bar, a consumer's decision to use an ODR Provider (or to make an online purchase taking into account of availability of an ODR mechanism) is a contract decision. A central issue in any contract decision between a vendor (the merchant or the ODR Provider or both) and a vendee (the consumer) is whether the vendee has sufficient information on which to make an informed and intelligent choice. The Bar is not a consumer protection regulatory agency. Its proper concern is more with the fairness of the various processes involved than with the appropriateness of the substance, as might be more the proper concern of a regulatory agency.

5. Disclosure has an important enforcement consequence in that, under US law, if a business fails to adhere to the public disclosures that it makes concerning its services, it may, under many circumstances, be engaged in an unfair or deceptive act or practice in or affecting commerce under Section 5 of the Federal Trade Commission Act (15 U.S.C. §§ 41-58, as amended). This is also the case under the consumer protection laws of many states and non-US jurisdictions.

II. TRANSPARENCY AND ADEQUATE MEANS OF PROVIDING INFORMATION AND DISCLOSURE

A. All information and disclosures, regardless of form, should be accurately and completely stated, should be presented as clearly and simply as the substance permits, and should present the most important points in an appropriately conspicuous manner.

B. All information and disclosures presented electronically should employ identifiable and accessible formats.

C. All information and disclosures on the websites of ODR Providers not related to individual cases should be printable and able to be downloaded electronically.

D. If the ODR Provider handles a substantial number of B2C disputes, regular periodic statistical reports should be published online that permit a meaningful evaluation of the proceedings and that respect the confidentiality of the participants and the individual proceedings.

E. With respect to other disputes, particularly those resolved by arbitration, participants should be encouraged to allow the decisions to be published with any confidential or propriety information deleted.

Commentary: ODR Providers are encouraged to use tables, charts, graphs and similar formats that facilitate analysis and comparisons by consumers. These summary reports should include, e.g., (a) number of cases received, resolved, and pending; (b) the number of cases resolved in favor of the business; (c) the number of cases resolved in favor of the consumer; (d) average length of time the proceeding was pending; and (e) average costs, if any, to consumers.

It is understood that ODR Providers' existing case management systems may not be capable of generating detailed statistical data, and that it may be costly to develop such systems. This Recommendation therefore is prospective in nature, and recognizes the financial and practical concerns involved. It is recommended that until new systems are developed, ODR Providers publish reports that, at a minimum, relate (1) the number of total cases; (2) the number of cases resolved in favor of the business; and (3) the number of cases resolved in favor of the consumer.

With respect to Section II D, an annual report is suggested as a minimum. However, quarterly or semi-annual reports followed by a consolidated annual report are encouraged.

III. MINIMUM BASIC DISCLOSURES

ODR Providers should disclose the following minimum level of information:

A. Contact and organizational information. This includes:
   1. A mailing address, including physical location, not just a post office box number;
   2. E-mail address; and
   3. Jurisdiction of incorporation or registration to do business.
B. Terms and conditions and disclaimers.
C. Explanation of services/ADR processes provided:
   1. Description of the types of services/processes provided (e.g., mediation, arbitration, early neutral evaluation, blind bidding);
   2. Published rules of procedure for all services/processes provided;
   3. Nature of the outcome of each service/process and its legal consequences (e.g., whether binding or non-binding on each party), and an explanation of further possible avenues of action (e.g., appeal); and
   4. If the ODR Provider or an individual neutral is engaged in legal services such as client counseling and advocacy, or is affiliated with a law firm or other organization that provides such services, identify the methods employed to separate neutral services and legal services to avoid conflicts of interest.
D. Affirmation that the ODR proceeding will meet basic standards of due process, including (1) adequate notice to the parties; (2) an opportunity for the parties to be heard; (3) the right to be represented or to consult legal counsel at any stage of the proceeding; and (4) in an arbitration, an objective decision based on the information of record.
E. Any prerequisites for accessing the service, such as membership, or geographic location such as residency in a particular country or state.
F. Any minimum value for the dispute to be submitted to the ODR provider for resolution.

Commentary: This Section is intended to set forth the basic minimum level of information without which it would be difficult for a consumer to make a reasonable decision to participate in the service offered by the ODR Provider. Each of the remaining Sections is intended to present the additional information that

ODR Providers should, in the view of the Task Force, make available as a matter of best practice.

Among the intended principal effects of the procedures that are disclosed are the following: All disputants should be given a reasonable and fair opportunity to be heard. The ODR proceedings should be perceived as treating all parties at least as equitably and fairly as a formal government administrative or legal procedure. Published rules of procedure should clearly ensure that all parties' rights are protected. There should be no unreasonable barriers to access, including unreasonable costs, geographic, linguistic or other barriers. In this regard, ODR Providers should look to existing offline protocols for guidance (e.g., AAA Consumer Due Process Protocol, ABA Managed Care Protocol, or industry associations, etc.) With respect to Section III A, the listed contact and organizational information is often lacking either entirely or partially, on ODR Provider websites. This puts the consumer in the unacceptable position of not knowing exactly who the party is with which the consumer is contracting.

IV. USE OF TECHNOLOGY AND THE ONLINE ENVIRONMENT FOR DISPUTE RESOLUTION
ODR Providers should disclose:
A. Specific Disclosures Regarding Current Technology
   1. Systems requirements (hardware and software) for using the ODR Provider's service
   2. Any limitations on accessibility to ODR systems, such as hours of operation or specific methods of access.
   3. If they employ systems that accommodate the disputants' differences in language and culture and, if so, what these are and how they function.
   4. Any specific electronic techniques offered to enhance the efficacy of ODR and, if so, what these are and how they function.
   5. If they provide techniques for accessibility to persons with disabilities or with low levels of literacy, and, if so, what these are and how they function.
   6. If they employ security to ensure the identity of the participants and to preserve confidentiality and privacy of the participants and, if so, what they are and how they function.
   7. If they have back up and arrangements for alternative emergency access.
B. Specific Disclosures Regarding Training in Use of Online Systems ODR Providers should disclose:
   1. If they educate potential participants in online procedures to help assure access to all users, and if so, by what means (such as through provision of instructions, tutorials, help files, and support personnel via email or telephone.)
   2. If they provide training in the use of the ODR system to neutrals
   3. If they provide training in adapting the neutrals' skills to the online environment (such as training to help overcome the challenges of communicating without face-to-face meetings.)

Commentary: Section IV addresses the current technological practices of the ODR Provider. However, ODR Providers are encouraged to disclose their policies and plans for encouraging and incorporating new technological advances into their ODR processes.

The technological area is one in which context sensitive help files and tutorial can be the most effective mean of providing meaningful information and disclosure to consumers. The use of such techniques is encouraged.

V. COSTS AND FUNDING

ODR Providers should disclose:

A. All costs of the process, what portion of the cost each party will bear, and the terms of payment.

B. In B2C disputes, if there is no cost to the consumer, or if the costs are subsidized, the source of the funding.

C. In B2B disputes, if the costs will not be borne equally by the parties, explain the distribution.

Commentary: Costs of an ODR process should not be so high as to foreclose the opportunity to resolve a dispute; cost should be commensurate with the value of the dispute, while taking into account the need to avoid frivolous claims. Investment in and costs of operating the ODR service, as well as a reasonable profit, also should be considered in setting the costs of the dispute.

VI. IMPARTIALITY

ODR Providers must disclose all matters that might raise a reasonable question about the impartiality of the ODR Provider or its neutral(s). Specifically ODR Providers should disclose the following:

A. Relationship to others concerning providing ODR services

　1. If the ODR Provider provides ODR services under a contractual relationship with other organizations, such as merchants, trade associations, etc.

　2. If the ODR Provider provides any referral compensation (referral fees, rebates, commissions, etc.), and if so:

　　a. to whom it is paid, and

　　b. the amount of the compensation or the basis for calculating the amount of the compensation.

　3. An ODR Provider shall take reasonable steps to cause its Neutrals to disclose whether the Neutral or a person closely affiliated with the Neutral (e.g., spouse, relative, or business partner, etc.) has any conflicts of interest, including but not limited to:

　　a. Any direct personal, business, professional or financial relationship with a party or its representative;

　　b. Any direct or indirect interest in the subject matter or outcome of the dispute, including contingent fee arrangements; and

　　c. Any personal knowledge that the ODR Provider or Neutral has of facts relevant to the dispute.

B. Selection process of neutrals
1. How individuals are selected to become part of the panel of neutrals eligible to handle disputes.
2. How a particular neutral is selected to handle a particular dispute.
3. The process by which neutrals are required to certify that they have no conflicts of interest and have disclosed all matters that reasonably might affect impartiality with respect to a particular dispute.
4. Procedures for disqualification of a neutral for cause.
C. Ethical standards for neutrals
1. Identify and/or link to the ethical rules by which the neutrals are bound.

Commentary: Impartiality of ODR Providers: This section suggests that an ODR Provider should disclose the existence of contractual relationships to provide ODR services on a continuing or repetitive basis to or involving a particular organization. For example, if a merchant contracted with and pays an ODR Provider to arbitrate disputes between the merchant and its customers, that relationship should be disclosed so customers are aware of it. This Recommended Best Practice does not suggest that an ODR Provider must disclose every party to whom it previously has provided ODR services, training programs, etc., which would be overly burdensome and perhaps contrary to the confidential nature of ADR. Further, this Recommended Best Practice is intended to be prospective if for financial and practical concerns it is not possible to capture and disclose information about existing contractual relationships. ODR Providers should use their best efforts to apply this Recommended Best Practice retrospectively, where feasible.

Impartiality of Neutrals: This section affirms as a substantive standard that all neutrals must act impartially and must disclose any conflicts of interest. It is understood that even if an ODR Provider has a contractual relationship to provide ODR services on a continuing or repetitive basis to a particular organization, the neutrals assigned to individual disputes arising under this contractual relationship will be bound by the same substantive standard to act impartially and disclose any conflicts of interest. If the neutrals are bound by a published set of ethical rules, ODR Providers are encouraged to post the full text of such rules, or at a minimum include a link to a page where the full text is posted. If the parties wish to know more about the selection process of a neutral in general or for a particular matter, that information should be available.

VII. CONFIDENTIALITY, PRIVACY AND INFORMATION SECURITY
ODR Providers should be prohibited from disclosing any personally identifiable information without the party's affirmative consent. ODR Providers should disclose:
A. Confidentiality Policies Concerning Information About Participants Provided to the ODR Provider
1. Their general privacy policies.
2. If they are members of any Privacy Seal or Privacy Trustmark program(s) and if so, provide a link to the program.

3. If customer information may be released by the ODR provider, and the circumstances under which that information may be released.
4. If any ODR proceedings being conducted by the neutrals are monitored by the ODR Provider, and under what circumstances.
5. If the ODR Provider reviews customer information as part of a quality control process, and who conducts the review.
6. If the ODR Provider's website uses technological means to identify the participant and/or track the participant's online behavior (e.g., session cookies, persistent cookies, web-bugs, clear gifs, and the like), and whether the ODR Providers provides an opt-out opportunity.

B. Confidentiality Concerning Specific Proceedings
1. The scope of confidentiality accorded to the ODR proceedings, including mediated settlement agreements and arbitration decisions, and the basis for protection from disclosure.
2. If arbitration decisions will be published, the manner and location of publication, and any limitations on accessibility (e.g., subscriber-only access).
3. If aggregate data without personally identifying information will be released.

C. Confidentiality Concerning Both Participants and Proceedings
1. Records retention/disposition policy, particularly concerning retention of information concerning individual participants, as well as records related to specific proceedings.
2. What forms of security for all online processes, particularly from theft or disclosure of information provided by participants and information or documents related to specific proceedings.
3. What kinds of security mechanisms have been put in place to safeguard participant information.

Commentary: ODR users frequently question the privacy commitments of ODR Providers prior to engaging in the ODR process. ODR Providers are encouraged to identify the laws, regulations, standards and/or guidelines regarding privacy (data protection) and information security applicable to them or to which they voluntarily adhere. Examples of such standards or guidelines are those of TRUSTe and BBBOnline. Examples of privacy (data protection) laws are the Gramm-Leach-Bliley Act in the United States, the Personal Information Protection and Electronic Documents Act (PIPEDA) in Canada, and the laws of the various Member States of the European Union resulting from the transposition into national law of Directive 95/46/EC of the European Parliament and of the Council of 24 October 1995 on the protection of individuals with regard to the processing of personal data. ODR Providers should consider that (1) privacy laws often contain information security requirements; (2) privacy and information security requirements may also stem from consumer protection and telecommunications laws; and (3) strong requirements in these areas may derive from sub-national laws, such as state or provincial laws.

With respect to Section VII C, ODR Providers are encouraged to state specifically whether they employ SSL or SET protocols, a Virtual Private Network, or other means to protect data in transmission, whether they employ a fire-wall and anti-virus software, and what back-up practices and other technological and non-technological means of providing information security they employ.

VIII. QUALIFICATIONS AND RESPONSIBILITIES OF NEUTRALS
    A. Responsibilities
    Neutrals shall:
        1. Disclose all conflicts of interest and act with impartiality and independence;
        2. Adhere to applicable ethical guidelines of their jurisdiction and any other guidelines specified by the ODR Provider;
        3. Act promptly and manage the dispute effectively; and
        4. Maintain communication with the parties.
    B. Qualifications
    ODR Providers should disclose:
        1. The minimum qualifications required for inclusion on the ODR Provider's panel of neutrals, such as education level, lawyer/non-lawyer, prior ADR experience and the like.
        2. The qualifications (including ADR training, degrees or certificates, level of experience, and areas of expertise) of individual neutrals.
        3. If the ODR Provider provides additional training for neutrals, and the type of training provided.
        4. If they require that their neutrals have had training specifically with respect to use of the online medium (and how it differs from traditional face-to-face ADR) and the technology used by that ODR Provider.
Commentary: With respect to Section VIII A, possible sources of disclosure standards regarding conflicts of interest are the American Bar Association, the American Arbitration Association, the CPR/Georgetown Legal Ethics Commission, the Association for Conflict Resolution (ACR (formerly SPIDR, AFM and CREnet)), and the International Bar Association Ethics for International Arbitrators.

IX. ACCOUNTABILITY FOR ODR PROVIDERS AND NEUTRALS
    ODR Providers should disclose:
    A. Accountability for Neutrals
        1. What steps they take to require neutrals to fulfill their responsibilities promptly, maintain communication with the parties, and comply with the stated ethical guidelines.
        2. If they provide a process to allow participants to file complaints for neutrals' failure to comply with the above requirements.
        3. If they provide an appeals process for arbitral decisions rendered by the neutrals.
    B. Accountability for ODR Providers
        1. If they comply with published guidelines, such as the guidelines of relevant trustmarks, and the full text of (or link to) of any such guidelines or trustmark requirements.

2. If they provide a process for participants to file complaints concerning the ODR services rendered, both with the ODR Provider itself, and with any relevant external organizations (such as trustmark providers).
3. If compiled, provide the percent of cases in which the parties are satisfied with the process.

Commentary: ODR Providers should display all relevant trustmarks.

X. ENFORCEMENT

ODR Providers should disclose:

A. If they provide any assistance in enforcing any agreement, award or decision reached or rendered through an ODR process.
B. Whether they cooperate with law enforcement officials so instances of fraud can be detected and prosecuted.

Commentary: With respect to X.A., some ODR Providers may determine that enforcement is best left to the parties and courts. Other ODR Providers may determine that it is in their best interest to have their awards enforced, and therefore may choose to provide assistance in a manner that does not affect the ODR Provider's neutrality. For example, at the request of the prevailing party, an ODR Provider may provide certified copies of awards and other documents for use in seeking enforcement before a national court. Further, some ODR Providers may agree to send a reminder letter to a party that has not complied voluntarily with an award. But if an ODR Provider renders assistance, the type and extent of that assistance should be disclosed, and any related costs.

As part of their periodic disclosure ODR Providers are encouraged to provide statistical information regarding the experience participants have had in enforcing prior decisions rendered by the ODR Provider.

XI. JURISDICTION AND CHOICE OF LAW

ODR Providers should disclose the jurisdiction where complaints against the ODR Provider can be brought, and any relevant jurisdictional limitations.

Index